The Bullying Antidote

Superpower Your Kids for Life

Dr. Louise Hart

and

Kristen Caven

Hazelden
Center City, Minnesota 55012
hazelden.org

Library of Congress Cataloging-in-Publication Data
Hart, Louise.
    The bullying antidote : superpower your kids for life / Dr. Louise Hart
    and Kristen Caven.
        pages cm
    Includes bibliographical references.
    ISBN 978-1-61649-417-9 (softcover)
    1. Aggressiveness in children—Prevention.   2. Bullying—Prevention.
3. Parenting.   I. Caven, Kristen, 1964–   II. Title.
    BF723.A35H37 2013
    649'.6—dc23

                                                            2013016432

Editor's note
The names, details, and circumstances may have been changed to protect the
privacy of those mentioned in this publication.
    This publication is not intended as a substitute for the advice of health
care professionals.
    Alcoholics Anonymous is a registered trademark of Alcoholics Anony-
mous World Services, Inc.

16 15 14 13   1 2 3 4 5 6

Cover design: Theresa Jaeger Gedig
Interior design and typesetting by Kinne Design and BookMobile
Developmental editor: Peter Schletty
Production editor: April Ebb

To loving parents everywhere;
from you flows the power to create
a bully-free world.

I think the most important question

facing humanity is,

"Is the universe a friendly place?"

— ALBERT EINSTEIN

Contents

Acknowledgments

This book is not just the creation of two authors; like every solution to social problems, it reflects the efforts of a community—many communities—to whom we offer our gratitude.

First of all, Hazelden is much more than a publisher. Its support centers and publications have helped many generations to become stronger, more caring, and more capable people. We are so grateful for being asked to join the Hazelden community and make this contribution. Thank you to the whole team, specifically Peter, April, Theresa, Kinne Design, Jill, Jody, and the marketing geniuses who came up with the wonderful title that spurred us to define *Zorgos*.

Secondly, to the community of dedicated experts, researchers, and teachers whose evidence-based work we wove together in this book. The thousands of hours we spent on this book reflect the millions of hours of hard work on the part of the people and organizations whose ideas we've shared.

And last but not least, to our community of friends, family, and school networks who not only gave us the support and encouragement we needed for the long journey, but who shared their stories, successes, and frustrations; sent us links and ideas; and shared their personal insights and experiences. Their care and attention helped give us the perspective we needed to build our "unified field theory of bullying."

Indeed, there was magic in the entire process, with just the right ideas emerging at just the right time; we honor the universal flow of intelligence that guided us in writing this book.

Louise's notes:

Full gratitude to my daughter, Kristen Caven, who became a full partner in every stage of this exciting process—brainstorming, researching, outlining, writing, rewriting (and rewriting, and rewriting), and editing —which was more of a dance than a struggle. Many of the stories reflected the experience and wisdom she gained raising my grandson. I'm also grateful for the support of my young grandgirls who would often ask me, "How's the book going, Grandma Lulu?"

Kristen's notes:

My mother has inspired me all my life by pursuing her passion for humanity's well-being. It's been an honor to work with her and an enjoyable challenge to keep up with her remarkable, associative mind that is always searching for solutions. I am also deeply grateful to my friends and family members who have taught me so much, especially my son, Donald, who brings *Zorgos* to life. And I speak for us both when I say none of this would have been possible without the love and contributions of my life partner, Dave.

Connecting the Dots:
From Bullying to Breakthrough

No one wants to raise a bully, and no one wants his or her child to be bullied. But bullying is happening anyway—more pervasively, more indiscriminately, and in some cases more violently than ever before. For example, according to a National Institutes of Health survey:

- About 282,000 students are reportedly attacked in high schools each month.
- Over half of all students have witnessed a bullying crime taking place while at school.
- A reported 15 percent of all students who don't show up for school attribute their absence to fear of being bullied while at school.
- About one in ten students drops out or changes schools because of repeated bullying.
- One out of every twenty students has seen a student with a gun at school.
- The leading cause of death among children under the age of fourteen is suicide.
- Every thirty minutes, a teenager attempts suicide due to bullying.
- One in three teens has experienced cyber threats online.[1]

Clearly, the consequences of bullying are no longer limited to black eyes and stomachaches.

This book sets out to take a deep and cross-disciplinary look at the causes and effects of bullying, in search of a cure. The sad truth that we found is that many common and widespread societal factors, including parenting practices, contribute to the bullying epidemic. Bullying and other risky behaviors have deep roots in history, compounded by changes that have affected families over the last two generations. Parents and corporations with the best of intentions have nonetheless ushered in some enormous negative consequences.

Yet just looking at these realities with clear vision is a step toward healing the problem. One study we reference in depth has revealed the connection between adverse childhood experiences (ACEs) and later-in-life diseases, both mental and physical. Having this information gives us the motivation to protect our kids' childhoods—and helps us find solutions for a national health crisis.

We are excited to report that there is a great deal of good news as we approach the tipping point. Kids and parents everywhere are standing up and saying, "That's enough!" Principals and community leaders are taking new approaches that give would-be bullies options other than bullying. Bullying is even being confronted on national and governmental levels. And many ingrained cultural practices are finally being called what they really are: bullying.

While it's important to label bullying behavior when we see it, it's equally important not to label a child as a "bully" or "victim." Although we occasionally use those labels to describe general roles or identify the two parties involved, it's important to see both the child who bullies and the child who is bullied as whole persons—with needs, desires, strengths, and weaknesses, all of which contribute to who they are as a person. It is important to see that no child is beyond help. Therefore, we choose to use the words *bullying dynamic* in this book, defining the issue as a power structure problem that can be changed with awareness, knowledge, and skills.

This book is for any parent of a child who has bullied or who has been bullied, including parents who have experienced bullying themselves. This book is for all parents, wannabe parents, and grandparents; for married, single, and divorced parents; for child-care providers and educators; for policy makers and school board members; and for everyone else involved in the lives of children. Our focus on prevention is especially helpful for parents of younger children.

Part 1 takes a wide-angle look at "where we're at." The first chapter explores the welfare of children and their problems, many of which relate to bullying. The second examines the enormous cultural shifts that exacerbate these problems, and the third digs into and exposes the roots of bullying found in widespread parenting practices.

Part 2 focuses on understanding, interrupting, and preventing bullying. Recognizing the deep wellspring of power that parents have to change the bullying dynamic, we then transition to a positive focus and envision a bully-free world.

Part 3 focuses on how a positive approach to parenting and healthy emotional development can prevent antisocial behaviors.

As you read, you will find information that loops around and repeats concerning such concepts as empathy, communication, care, positivity, optimism, human rights, warm family environments, upstanders, mindsets, spirals, patterns, power, emotions, and positive child development.

By the time you finish, you will have a big-picture understanding of bullying, and you will be empowered to prevent it in your home and community. Because you will be in possession of a secret power . . .

The Bullying Antidote: *Zorgos*

Bullying is a power dynamic where one person exerts control over another physically, emotionally, or socially. Bullying can be persistent —a focused and repeated pattern—or it can be a single, traumatic event. In the bullying dynamic, one person always loses.

There is no pill, no quick fix for the enormous problem of bullying. But there are thousands of solutions . . . and we'd like you to have access to them all.

There is a superpower with which we'd like to endow your child, and all children. This power enables them to repel bullies and transform their relationships; it allows them to get what they need without resorting to bullying.

By possessing this superpower, children will

- use their hearts and minds for the greater good
- refuse to put up with bad treatment from peers or from strangers
- recognize bullying and stop it before it starts
- trust themselves and inspire others
- become models to others with their upstanding qualities
- uplift those around them to think and act in positive ways

This superpower doesn't just prevent bullying; it is, in fact, the antidote to bullying. This superpower is both a challenge to and a balm for the culture of negativity that has been passed down through generations. An antidote restores health, happiness, and balance, so life can go on.

What is this superpower? Is it friendship? Is it problem solving? Is it understanding? Yes, it is all of these things. It is also empathy, compassion, connection, kindness, and respect. It is safety, self-esteem, and human rights. It is relationship, assertiveness, peace, wholeness, and foresight. It is resiliency.

But to make this huge superpower concept easier to remember, we're just going to call it *Zorgos*.

People who have *Zorgos* are bigger than bullying. You know people like this. You know people who are great leaders, who are peace-makers, who are insightful and kind. They are powerful individuals! People with *Zorgos* are mentally healthy and emotionally intelligent. They keep their balance, and they believe in themselves.

Zorgos has a lot of moving parts, but at its heart it is a very simple idea. Every chapter in this book is full of information and insight, much of it backed up by studies and brain science. We will show and teach you what works. It's not easy building *Zorgos,* but once you get the idea, you will be amazed at how it empowers everyone around you. This book is about how you can superpower your kids for a better life. And just in case you are wondering, *Zorgos* is Esperanto for "I will take care."

Where We're At

The solution of adult problems tomorrow depends on the way we raise our children today. There is no greater insight into the future than recognizing, when we save our children, we save ourselves.

— MARGARET MEAD

The first part of this book provides a "big picture" look at twenty-first-century families in America, along with an overview of the social realities that affect the experiences and quality of life in today's families. Just as it's hard to see the forest when strolling among the trees, or to notice the elements that make up the air we breathe, it is also difficult to grasp the fact that we live in a changing cultural atmosphere.

The first three chapters are somewhat difficult to read, and they were difficult to write. We didn't like having to report bad news. But before focusing on solutions, it's important to have an honest assessment in order to evaluate the pressures and challenges parents and kids face today.

The first three chapters are about seeing clearly.

Parenting calls us to see things in a new way. The profound love we feel for our children can startle us at first, and it shows us both how incredibly powerful and how alarmingly vulnerable we are. If our vision were perfect, we would see everything clearly, with perfect *foresight, hindsight, insight,* and *oversight.*

Foresight

In most cases, the path of parenting begins optimistically, with a vision for the unborn baby's bright future. This vision is the most important first step a young parent can make. Foresight is a powerful force that inspires us to set goals, make plans, and discipline ourselves to accomplish great things. Yet we can never actually know the future; and new parents may not know how to get on the right road to make their dream come true.

Hindsight

We all know the common saying "Hindsight is twenty-twenty." After we've made mistakes, we can look and see how they happened and learn from them; our regrets can awaken greater wisdom. Hindsight is a wonderful tool that we all use automatically when we become parents. We look in the rearview mirror at the good and bad of our own childhood to help shape our vision for the future.

Insight

Insight gives us the ability to turn hindsight into foresight. In psychology, insight is

- an understanding of relationships that sheds light on or helps solve a problem

- the recognition of sources of emotional difficulty

- an understanding of the motivational forces behind one's actions, thoughts, or behavior

Insight is self-knowledge. It is something that we hope our children develop, and it is something that bullies don't necessarily have. Unfortunately, it is also a trait many parents don't have.

Oversight

Put all of these ways of seeing together, and you get the big picture: oversight. No single person can have complete oversight of the vast cultural issue of bullying; this problem needs to be solved on the societal level. But parents can have some degree of oversight of their own family. This is why we want every parent to become an expert on how to raise resilient, confident children. Although it can be a difficult process, when we take a hard look at what happens in normal, everyday families, we can shine a spotlight on solutions.

. . .

1
. . . .

"And How Are the Children?"

"And how are the children?" "All the children are well."

— MASAI GREETING AND RESPONSE

Within the mighty Masai tribe of Africa, a traditional greeting often passes between the warriors: "Kasserian Ingera." It means, "And how are the children?"

This greeting acknowledges the cultural value the Masai have for their children's well-being. Even those with no children will give the traditional answer: "All the children are well."

Anthropologist Margaret Mead observed that "the highest measure of a civilization lies in how it cares for its children." If the well-being of our children is, as Mead observed, an accurate judgment of our society, then we need tools to measure how our children are faring. In this section, we present several studies that do just that.

In the United States, we seem to treat our kids well. We have schools, public parks, playgrounds, and vast industries of toys and games to entertain children. We also provide a basic level of health care access for them through government programs. Many children have access to Disney movies, new clothes, travel opportunities, and theme parks.

A large number of benefits came from earlier generations; kindergarten, recess, child labor laws, health education, and the juvenile justice system were fought for by the PTA a century ago. But the challenges of the twenty-first century are daunting. There are troubling trends to contend with, from alcohol and drug abuse to school shootings.

We need to find ways to battle the culture of conflict and share in the protection of our children. Above all, we need to imagine a better future for them.

At the Bottom of the "Well"

A 2007 United Nations Children's Fund (UNICEF) report found that the United States and the United Kingdom are the worst nations in the industrialized world in which to be a child. Of twenty-one countries, the United States landed near the bottom of the list at number twenty, with the United Kingdom at twenty-one.[1]

Six dimensions of children's well-being were assessed: material well-being, health and safety, educational well-being, family and peer relationships, behaviors and risks, and subjective well-being. This global study also measured other factors such as poverty, deprivation, relationships with family and peers, happiness, and risky behavior. The report assessed whether children feel loved, cherished, and supported within their families and communities, and whether these families and communities are supported by public policy and resources.

The UNICEF report found that American and British youth are more likely to smoke, drink alcohol, use drugs, fight and bully, and be sexually active than youngsters in other industrialized countries. The nations that take the best care of their children, the study noted, are the Netherlands and the Scandinavian countries.

Here's the bullying connection: The countries at the top of the list have been working on bullying issues since the 1970s. For example, the world's foremost bullying prevention program was conceived in Scandinavia by Swedish professor Dan Olweus, at the University of Bergen in Norway. His intervention work has played a key role in the remarkable paradigm shift that has been occurring in many countries, and his work will be discussed in this book. Olweus initiated a mind-shift about how we look at bullying—a new idea that is spreading far and wide: *Bullying is NOT a natural part of growing up, but is a pressing social and public health issue that must be taken seriously and changed.*

At the Top of the List

There is one list the United States is at the top of. According to the International Centre for Prison Studies, the United States incarcerates more people than any other nation, far ahead of populous China.[2] More than one in every hundred adults is in jail or prison. A report compiled by the Pew Center's Public Safety Performance Project found that the incarceration numbers are especially startling for certain groups. One out of thirty men between the ages of twenty and thirty-four is in prison. In the black community, that number is one out of nine. There is a racial disparity for women too; in the late-thirties age group, one out of about 350 is in jail, but for black women, that number is one out of one hundred.[3] Although each prisoner has his or her own story, there are things we know about crime and prison culture.

Although our court system is somewhat functional in upholding rights, many court movies and TV programs convey examples of bullying in the criminal justice system. Even "the good guys" are guilty of it, with many examples of racial profiling and poor treatment of prisoners. The now famous Stanford Prison Experiment had students take turns being prisoners and guards for two weeks; the stress of the situation turned all the guards, even though they were good people, into sadistic bullies.[4]

Here's the bullying connection: Bullying is a disregard of rights, which is generally how society defines crime. Those who have a criminal conviction by age twenty-four had probably been identified as a bully by the age of eight.[5] And those who are locked up had probably been bullied in childhood. Mistreated and abused children are on a path toward crime and prison.

Maltreated to Death

Over the past ten years, the number of children in the United States believed to have been killed in their own homes is four times greater than the number of U.S. soldiers killed in Iraq and Afghanistan. Of the 20,000 deaths due to child neglect and abuse, nearly half were children younger than one year old, and 75 percent were under four years of age.[6]

Here's the bullying connection: Parents can be the worst kinds of bullies. Under stress, adults can become violent when they don't know a better way to resolve an issue. For all the children who are killed, many more are abused, and only a portion of them is served by child protective services. Mistreatment by parents is especially damaging because kids are being hurt by the very people who should be protecting them! Parenting can be the most stressful job in the world, and those who harm their children live in a world of regret. All parents need to have supportive resources and learn ways to manage stress effectively and safely so that they can avoid hurting their children unintentionally. As we will see in the next few chapters, victims of child abuse are more likely to become bullies later on.

Victims of Alcohol and Drug Use

According to the National Association for Children of Alcoholics, "Almost one in five American adults (18%) lived with an alcoholic while growing up."[7] Families with substance abuse problems have more negative interactions and higher levels of conflict than families without these problems. Because alcohol lowers inhibition and impedes judgment and restraint, children in these families are more likely to be abused and to witness family violence. They are more at risk for disruptive behavioral problems and more likely to become alcoholics as adults. Simply put, alcoholism can destroy families.

People use substances innocently without intending to become abusers; however, here are some statistics from the National Association for Children of Alcoholics:

- Approximately three of four (71.6 percent) child welfare professionals cite substance abuse as the top cause for the dramatic rise in child maltreatment since 1986.

- Most welfare professionals (79.6 percent) report that substance abuse causes or contributes to at least half of all cases of child maltreatment.

- 39.7 percent of welfare professionals say substance abuse is a factor in more than 75 percent of the child maltreatment cases.[8]

Alcohol and drug abuse also prevent parents from supporting their children in school, which has a ripple effect on society. Children who see their parents using drugs and alcohol, or who have easy access to these substances at home, are more likely to use them. Television is full of images of people drinking now that Federal Communications Commission rules have been relaxed. Alcohol is accessible in many homes, as are prescription medications. Many adolescents think prescription medications are safer than illegal drugs, but abusing prescription drugs can also lead to addiction, overdose, and death.

Here's the bullying connection: People don't start using drugs with the intent of becoming a bully or an abuser. But addictive substances are dangerous for some of the same reasons they are enjoyable: they tend to relax our inhibitions and let us do things we normally wouldn't do. Furthermore, they affect our ideas of what is right and what is wrong. Certain substances can turn good people into monsters.

Shot at School

Twenty or thirty years ago, news of a shooting at a school would have shocked the nation. Today, gun rampages are more frequent in many environments, from workplaces to military bases to beauty parlors. The shootings that still shock us the most, however, are in schools—colleges, high schools, even elementary and preschools.

Here's the bullying connection: Most mass shooters have a reason they do what they do, beyond the fact that they can get their hands on a gun. Many of these mass murderers see themselves as being victims: of politics, of failed relationships, of bullying.

Jessie Klein, author of *The Bully Society,* makes the argument that school shootings are the consequences of a society that promotes aggressive and competitive behavior. Kids learn that bullying is an everyday reality where sensitivity, kindness, and respect do not always prevail. Klein compiled incidents of school shootings since 1979 that include shooters' reasons for doing what they did. A great percentage of the shooters complained about threats to their masculinity.[9]

This tradition of revenge for perceived insults and threats—which we see all over America, and, indeed, all over the world—unofficially states that a slight to any member of the group must be avenged. This is the cultural mechanism of machismo, or the "culture of honor," that makes it culturally okay, in the perpetrator's mind, to open fire at a funeral, drive through a neighborhood while shooting out a window, or throw acid in someone's face.

Raped by "Friends"

Every two minutes, someone in the United States is sexually assaulted, and 97 percent of rapists never spend a day in jail.[10] About 85 to 90 percent of sexual assaults reported by college women are perpetrated by someone known to the victim; about half occur on a date.[11] The term *date rape*, which describes this phenomenon, was coined in the late 1990s.

Here's the bullying connection: Rape is bullying of a sexual nature. In many war-torn parts of the world, rape is used as a weapon, and it is the worst form of bullying. During times of heightened aggression, rape (of both men and women) can become a ritualized and normalized part of a culture. And when women who are raped are forced to bear the blame—and the children—of these crimes, the scars of hatred and violence are dragged through generations.

Doing Poorly

During difficult economic times, it is hard not to see housing foreclosures and budget cuts to schools as forms of economic bullying. According to the 2011 U.S. Census, almost 22 percent of children under the age of eighteen lived in poverty, which is up from 16 percent ten years earlier.[12] Although being "poor in pocket" does not necessarily mean being "poor in spirit," the world is full of stories about how the constant stress of not having enough money can push parents over the edge. Overwhelmed with their own needs and losses, parents lose the ability to protect and care for their kids as well as they'd like, and neglect and abuse can follow.

Here's the bullying connection: Bullying goes hand in hand with inequality, and economic inequality creates powerlessness. Schoolchildren who are perceived as poor or lower status endure social, economic, and educational exclusion. This treatment is worsened by careless or ritualized bullying, harassment, and discrimination.

Paying the Price of Privilege

Money, however, does not protect children from trouble. Teenagers from well-to-do families are currently experiencing epidemic rates of anxiety disorders, depression, and substance abuse—higher than any other socioeconomic group of young people in this country.

In *The Price of Privilege*, Madeline Levine documents the havoc wrought on children from affluent families in our materialistic, super-competitive society. Overinvolved parents, she asserts, are creating a generation of kids with a poorly developed sense of self. County drug surveys have shown that access to drugs and high-risk situations is easier among the wealthy. "Raising children has come to look more and more like a business endeavor and less and less like an endeavor of the heart," Levine says. "We are overly concerned with 'the bottom line,' with how our children 'do' rather than with who our children 'are.'"[13]

Here's the bullying connection: As mentioned, bullying goes hand in hand with inequality. A sense of entitlement leads to disrespect and abuse of power, and when social status is everything, someone always gets hurt. Children who are guided by material status rather than personal character are especially vulnerable to the bullying dynamic, which is alive and well and often not discussed in the most exclusive prep schools, fraternities, and colleges.

Lost in a Culture of Excess

Materialism is an equal opportunity crisis. Cradle-to-grave media marketing targets everyone at every level of society, even toddlers and babies. Between the ages of two and eleven, a time of intense brain development, children see more than 25,000 advertisements a year on TV alone.[14] Children are being taught to nag their parents until they get what they want. Parental authority is constantly usurped. When exhausted parents give in, traditional values are challenged, weakened, and undermined. "Overindulgence doesn't just drain your bank account; it can cripple your children's chances of becoming healthy, happy adults," says David Walsh, Ph.D., author of *Selling Out America's Children.*[15]

Too much stuff, too much entertainment, too much freedom, and too many choices characterize our generation of children. Exploited by marketers concerned with gain and profits, children are being shaped by forces that don't care what shape they are in.

Here's the bullying connection: Regrettably, a cycle of overindulgence undermines important aspects of human development: for example, self-restraint, self-discipline, responsibility, and participation in family life, including chores. Bullying comes naturally to children without these qualities. Bullies do not have self-restraint, and victims react impulsively.

Dangerously Different

Bullying of minorities has always been a problem in America, where the newest wave of immigrants is traditionally welcomed with insults, suspicion, and discrimination. Racism and bullying go hand in hand.

Bullying of those with different gender orientations, however, is such a severe problem there's a word for it: *gay-bashing.* Not only is there widespread permissiveness for name-calling ("faggot" is the most common epithet on playgrounds), there are many religious organizations who view being lesbian, gay, bisexual, or transgender (LGBT) as a sin, and some even condone hate speech and physical harm.

Bullying becomes discrimination when it is widely accepted. Before the women's rights movement in the 1960s, derogatory jokes about women were normal and considered "funny," just as it is alarmingly common for today's kids and teens to disparage "gayness." Current anti-bullying legislation that calls for tolerance has even been challenged by some groups who wish to remove language about LGBT bullying.

Here's the bullying connection: Child expert Michele Borba says, "After students confirm to me that bullying is indeed a 'big' problem, I ask: 'who do bullies choose for their victims? Is there a specific trait they look for?' The number one word I hear: 'Different.'" Bullies often target a victim based on race, ethnicity, age, religion, disability, beliefs, gender, appearance, behavior, or sexual orientation. Today's American youth are displaying intolerant actions at alarming rates—and at younger and younger ages. The FBI tells us most hate crimes are committed by youth younger than nineteen.[16]

Part of the 25 Percent

One in four U.S. adults experiences mental illness at some point, although researchers believe that the actual number is higher since mental illness is often undiagnosed or not talked about. And of those who suffer, only half receive treatment.

Although there are now more mental health professionals treating people than ever before, the depression rate is ten times higher than it was fifty years ago. Meanwhile, according to the Centers for Disease Control and Prevention, as of 2007, parents reported that approximately 9.5 percent or 5.4 million children ages four to seventeen have been diagnosed with attention-deficit/hyperactivity disorder (AD/HD).[17]

It is no surprise that anxiety plays a large role in both depression and AD/HD. According to a 1999 report from the Surgeon General, 13 percent of children ages nine to seventeen suffer from anxiety disorders.[18] It is also no surprise that anxiety seems normal in this day and age, with fear fueling violence and violence fueling fear.

Here's the bullying connection: Some of the worst bullies are victims of mental illness who have experienced major and/or unresolved trauma in their lives. Certain mental illnesses can cause people to be aggressive or engage in bullying behavior. Other illnesses can result from bullying, such as anxiety disorders, depression, and eating disorders.

Sharing the Responsibility

As we follow the threads of bullying into every level of our society, we find that "the children . . . are *not* so well." We can hope to keep our children from all these dangers, but no one is 100 percent safe from bullying and violence. We cannot control every aspect of our children's environments—home, school, and community—nor can we control the multitude of social and technological influences upon them. There are good reasons to be worried about the well-being of our children, and there are many questions to be asked: *How are we, as a people, teaching kids to be violent? How can we, as parents, change the terrible patterns of history? How do we stop enabling bullying? Where, exactly, is the national conscience?*

History shows us that when children and families have the legal protections, safety nets, and support that they need, the forces of bullying can be turned around. We must have hope and keep trying. It does no good to blame parents or schools or the government or corporations. As a society, we *all* share responsibility for how we raise our kids, and for creating a culture where bullying is not acceptable.

Many institutions play a part in our low international standing when it comes to raising healthy children: family structures, neighborhoods, churches, school systems, the economy, medical and mental health systems, the prison system, advertisers, pharmaceutical companies, and every branch and business of the military-industrial complex. In combination, these institutions help create the web of disrespect and bullying, along with other dysfunctions of American society such as drug use, violence and crime, and various addictions.

But this is primarily a book to support parents, who have the greatest influence of all on the cultural patterns and ideas (good or bad) that are passed on to the next generation.

Battle the Culture of Conflict

A common complaint expressed in a study of middle-class parents was their sense of being overwhelmed by the culture. "Parents see themselves in a struggle for the hearts and minds of their own children," says Barbara Dafoe Whitehead of the National Marriage Project.[19] There is so much more to say *no* to than ever before. Parents have to spend a lot of time doing battle with the culture—like getting kids to eat fruit and drink water rather than eat junk food and drink soda. Today's moms and dads are expected to raise their children in opposition to the dominant cultural messages. And they are judged harshly for letting their children have too much, watch too much, or even experience too much. We live in a time of abundant choices, and the limits must come from within.

This book will help you create your own guidelines for becoming a counter-culture parent who raises strong, assertive, self-directed, and self-regulated children who will hold their own in the face of overwhelming cultural forces.

The Masai saying "All the children are well" means that life is good, that society has not forgotten its reason for being, its proper functions and responsibilities. It means that the daily struggles for existence do not preclude proper attention to the society's children.

Consider one of Albert Einstein's most delightful quotes: "Imagination is everything. It is the preview of life's coming attractions."

So imagine . . . what kind of world do you want your children to grow up in? Imagine that peace and safety prevail, and that our cultural priorities of protecting the young and the powerless are in place. One person can make a difference by seeing things differently; together we can make a difference by supporting each other and by living differently.

. . .

2

••••

Enormous Changes in Society

All change is not growth, as all movement is not forward.

— ELLEN GLASGOW

Imagine a town where there are no suicides, no alcoholism, no drug addiction, very little crime, and no one is on welfare. Imagine a town where people don't die from heart disease, but simply of old age. If you've read *Outliers* by Malcolm Gladwell, you know this town is real. When Roseto, Pennsylvania, was studied for the unusually high quality of health in its inhabitants, researchers were surprised when they couldn't find any dietary or genetic differences between them and people in surrounding areas.

Researchers were also surprised to see the social norms in Roseto. Three generations typically live together in a household. People sit on their porches and talk to each other. Everyone is friendly and supportive of one another. There are no strangers in this town—and there never have been. That's because the original settlers came from a town in Italy of the same name. They moved to America in small groups and duplicated their village, right down to the stonework and rosemary bushes. They brought their relationships with them, along with their customs, their governing principles, and their protective social structure.

We can use the Italian Roseto and the Pennsylvania Roseto as starting points to compare the Old and New Worlds. When we find a slice of the Old World set down in the New World, we can see the enormous changes we've made to our social structures as we've embraced the modern world in our quest for progress.

Culture for any group of people is the product of their history. Yet throughout history, children have often been stripped of their heritage, their language, and their identity in the process of acculturation; Native Americans and African slaves are all-too-familiar American examples. *Acculturation* is a series of occurrences in which members of one cultural group adopt the beliefs and behaviors of another group. In the "melting pot" of America, children of immigrants have all experienced the positive and negative effects of acculturation.

Culture shock is defined as the psychic distress an individual experiences when exposed to a culture that is vastly different from his or her own. The individual is unable to make sense of the behavior of others or to predict it, resulting in profound disorientation. In a nation of immigrants and a world of refugees, culture shock is something that has affected most families outside of Roseto. Roseto residents, who brought the complexities of their culture with them when they moved, were spared culture shock because they did not lose the traditions that connected them and gave their lives meaning.

Culture fatigue is a similar concept that refers to a complex set of reactions related to culture shock. "Culture fatigue is the physical and emotional exhaustion that almost invariably results from the infinite series of minute adjustments required for long-term survival in an alien culture," wrote anthropologist David L. Szanton.[1]

Anyone trying to maintain a website over the span of a decade has felt this. In an attempt to keep up with the latest communication trends, we are bewildered by the frantic pace of technological changes: hyperlinks, animation, contact forms, blogs, interactivity, social media . . . nothing is ever quite enough.

In 1970, Alvin Toffler's book *Future Shock* was an international best seller. He defined *future shock* as a certain psychological state of individuals and whole societies resulting from "too much change in too short a period of time." He explained how "with future shock you stay in one place, but your own culture changes so rapidly that it has the same disorienting effect as going to another culture."[2]

Every modern parent must feel this about his or her children, who have so much more than the parent ever did, and who have such different realms to navigate. Parents often don't understand this new world, or know how to help their children understand it.

Younger parents might assume that what they are experiencing is "normal" and that things have always been as they are now. They may not realize that the American way of "going it alone" has caused a gradual erosion in the way people—including kids—relate to one another. An hour spent watching the daily news or browsing Internet commentary proves that common courtesy is no longer common, but rudeness and disrespect are. Bullying and violence are widespread and present at every level of the society our children are being raised in.

This chapter discusses a few of the enormous changes in this "New New World" that have opened the doors to mainstream bullying.

Busier and Busier

Over the last forty years, how—and with whom—children spend their time has changed considerably. Young children spend more time with kids their own age, and more time in childcare with adults other than their parents. Older children are more involved in outside activities, and parents work more hours away from home. Although parents technically spend more time with their children than they used to (often driving them places and taking them shopping), there are also greater distractions, and everyone's attention is pulled in more directions.

Parents feel stressed for many reasons:

- Two incomes are typically needed to make ends meet. Often both parents are employed far from home and constantly feel "crunched" by time.

- Stretched and stressed out, parents tend to come up short on "down time" for relaxation, play, and just being with their family.

- They may work at home and have to juggle their attention between children and work.

- They feel under-supported and alone in neighborhoods and school communities.
- Grandparents and other caring relatives live far away; parents may not have good relationships with grandparents and in-laws; or relatives themselves may pose a time burden.
- Families are smaller, many with a single parent.
- Parents don't feel safe letting their kids play outside or run around in the neighborhood.
- People have lost the habit of face-to-face neighborliness, and this breakdown of social connections leads to social isolation.
- Texting is the preferred method of communication for teens, with phone calling a close second. Social activities are not focused on socializing but on an activity.
- Community members feel little or no responsibility to correct or guide youngsters; many feel hostile toward or fearful of children.
- Even though TV is an integral part of their lives, many adults are at odds with what kids learn from the TV.
- People are never satisfied and always seem to want more; there never seems to be enough.
- The cycle of compulsive consumerism dominates family life. To compensate for their long working hours, parents amass goods for their children, even though the children might prefer to spend time with their parents.
- Peer pressure drives the insatiable desire to have the next hot toy, outfit, or electronic device.
- The world has become more abrasive. Previously unacceptable language and behaviors have become acceptable—and are broadcast into homes around the globe at all hours.

As our lives have become busier and busier, we have had to work harder to maintain the traditional face-to-face, intimate family interactions that are necessary to teach respect and manners, deepen trust, instill values, and model emotional and social behaviors.

Pendulum Swing from Autocratic to Permissive

Before the 1960s, the predominant leadership style of parents was autocratic. When hard and fast rules were not obeyed, the consequence was often harsh punishment. Then the hippie subculture did what had been unthinkable: it questioned authority. Young people rebelled against their parents' and grandparents' rules, roles, and values, and insisted on "freedom." This movement reshaped culture, music, politics, and families.

Since this era, the predominant parenting style has been permissive. The parenting pendulum swung as younger parents rebelled against the rigid structures and often "cruel" punishments of their childhood, preferring a new style of parenting that gave their children lots of freedom with few (if any) rules. Fewer limits were set—and often, unfortunately, children were not held accountable for misbehavior. These young parents helped usher in a new epoch for families based on a permissive leadership style, which has become the widespread norm half a century later. Today's vigilance in protecting free speech and personal freedom has engendered a tolerant "whatever" society—in some ways for the better, but in many ways for the worse.

Put that together with the experience of culture shock, culture fatigue, and future shock, and we have generations of overwhelmed parents without the language, skills, or confidence to be the authority their children need. Often feeling out of their depth, these "whatever" parents raise children that crave authority and limits.

A Screen in Every Room

Our human brains crave information, interaction, and the presence of other human beings. We are hardwired for story, and we learn from drama.

The media has brought us more of these good things than anyone could ever have imagined, with no signs of letting up. Yet our transition to a technological society has happened so quickly that we do not yet know how to handle the abundance of information.

The 1930s and 1940s were the Golden Age of Radio, and people regularly tuned in to their favorite music, comedy, adventure, and other programs. Television became the dominant media trend of the 1950s. In the 1980s, computers and video games arrived, and in the new millennium, families logged on to the Internet. Now more than ever before in history, children are looking at a multitude of screens—they are being raised by the media. Through entertainment, advertising, and shared interests, TV, pop radio, and social networking define culture and values, manipulate desires, and teach—or undermine—morality.

Cradle-to-grave marketing targets everyone, even toddlers and babies. Predatory marketers don't care if they cripple children's development and undercut their chances of becoming healthy, happy adults. They care only about increasing profits. Kids learn from commercials to nag for toys, creating conflict and divisiveness in the family while undermining parental authority.

Little children are open, innocent, trusting, and vulnerable—ready and eager to learn from any and every source. Yet disturbing images appear randomly at all times of day. Murders, missing children, and massacres from around the world appear on the news and bring fear and chaos into our homes. The average child watches twenty-eight hours of television per week, and 70 percent of day care centers have the TV on during a typical day.[3]

Based on studies on the effects of TV violence, the American Academy of Child and Adolescent Psychiatry concludes that children become immune, or numb, to violence as a result of watching television. They begin to identify with violent or victimized characters, imitate what they see, and may psychologically accept violence as a legitimate way to solve problems.[4]

Children see, and children do. They imitate the behaviors—pushing, punching, put-downs. They have not yet developed perspective, judgment, discernment, and self-regulation. They must be taught that TV is not real, not trustworthy, and even potentially dangerous to their health; the Internet even more so. As screens proliferate from one per household to one per pocket, it becomes harder and harder for parents to supervise and manage their use. Television and high-tech devices have put families at risk in ways we still do not fully comprehend. Surveys show over and over again that watching too much television is associated with mild depression, and that obesity goes hand-in-hand with screen time.

Potentially our best teaching tools, screens are even taking their toll with regard to education. Research shows a correlation between screens in children's rooms and obesity, poor sleep, poor reading habits, poor grades, and smoking[5]; cell phones and iPads in school make it easier to cheat; and middle school teachers have to deal with all the drama that kids bring to class from the previous evening on Facebook.

Perhaps the biggest changes brought on by the proliferation of screens have to do with privacy. Not only do we lose privacy with cameras on us all the time, and with spam and hackers in our online accounts but also we gain privacy in other ways, and our children do as well. When you see young people across the room looking at a screen, you don't know if they're doing homework or viewing pornography. The shows a mother restricts on the living room TV are available online when her back is turned, or when her child's friends are over playing quietly in the child's room.

High-Tech Tools and Toys

Parents have been blindsided by the technological tsunami that has opened the floodgates for anonymous writers and producers who do not necessarily have the healthy development and well-being of young users in mind.

In the past, children's lives and brains were shaped by spending most of their time with real-life people who provided practice for complex relationships, both nurturing and challenging. Now, for the first time in history, children are spending most of their time with interactive devices—computers, electronic toys, iPads, and video games. In the form of smartphones, progress has brought us miniature "everything machines" that take photos, send messages, tell time, make and play recordings, call friends, play movies, hold libraries full of books, and give us access to anything we can imagine over the Internet.

Eighty-nine percent of school-age kids own video games. Video games are designed to hold the attention of kids at every age, with clear objectives and built-in reward systems. In general, the games are also designed to be addictive, with another level to achieve after each one is completed, and no natural stopping points. In general, these fast-paced, adrenaline-pumping experiences are shaping children's brains, behaviors, and values in new ways.

Video games may be fun distractions or "stress relievers" for children and teens, but parents have to be wary of the uncaring, materialistic values they can instill; many games model disrespect, nasty put-downs and sarcasm, aggression, and violence. Kids in the past made guns out of sticks to imagine shooting bad guys or hunting, but today they no longer need to imagine.

First-person shooter games let kids freely express their anger and fear by fighting, shooting, and killing other human beings. They feel a thrill with such actions—but worse, they learn to shoot and kill casually, with no feelings of compassion or remorse. Killing has become morally easy for all ages, and there are no consequences for killing or getting killed; you can simply restart the game. One human development textbook states that "the amount of television viewed at age 8 and the preference among boys for violent shows predicted the severity of criminal offenses at age 30."[6]

The award-winning children's educational program *Sesame Street* has been broadcast in more than 140 countries. For over forty years, it has addressed positive development, such as social competence, tolerance of diversity, and non-aggressive ways of resolving conflict. Despite its popularity, more and more young children start school without having learned respect, civility, and manners. Although many learn social skills from their family, they also learn attitudes and behaviors, as well as racial and sexual stereotypes, from television and video games. And many "whatever" parents allow M-rated video games in their homes for all ages to play.

Overwhelmed by the prevalence of these games in their children's lives—often presented as gifts by other children or relatives—

"whatever" parents are unaware of the rating systems (such as "M" for "mature") provided by the Motion Picture Association of America and the Entertainment Software Rating Board, or evaluation tools such as Common Sense Media.

Stress: The New Normal

Let's step back now and take a look at a typical American dinnertime. It's Tuesday night, and the family is preparing to have a rare meal together during the hour between when Mom and the kids get home, and Dad has to leave for the night shift. Mom cuts open two bags of frozen food and sticks them in the microwave as she sets the table and puts medications out, Dad talks on the phone while he prepares for work, and their youngest turns on the living room TV and opens a bag of chips. The evening news on the kitchen TV reports stories about global warming and a school shooting, which Mom is glad her older son doesn't hear: he has his headphones on listening to music while he texts his friends and does homework.

Mom calls the family together, but her teenage daughter announces she's going out shopping with a friend for a dance dress instead (and needs money). Mom says okay, relieved that her daughter is finally making friends, and kisses her goodbye, but Dad grumbles about credit card debt as the daughter leaves. Mom opens a Coke to calm her headache, and remembers she has to do some online shopping after the kids go to bed and before her show comes on. Dinner discussion, before the kids start fighting, centers on a video game a friend has that the two boys want. Dad yells at the boys to watch their language at the table. Mom wonders whatever happened to her babies.

In this book, we talk a lot about brains. Humans are born with an excess of brain cells and neural connections that die off if they are not stimulated. "Use it or lose it" may be a cliché, but it is also a basic neurological fact. Children's early years are the most important for brain development, and we have to be aware of what may happen to a child's brain when he or she is not able to "use it." When parents don't shape their kids, their kids will be shaped by outside forces that don't care what shape they are in.

Therefore, we need to make sure we are not derailed from the things we value. We must make sure we cultivate what matters the most. A *Time* magazine poll on happiness reports that the major sources of happiness are relationships with our children, relationships with our friends, and contributing to the lives of others.[7] Of the three, relationships with our children are the most important and require the most attention, especially during the first five years of their lives. What happens early on in their lives has an enormous effect on what happens later on. Comforting and loving, listening to, teaching, and protecting a child are a parent's best investments for that child's healthy future. If we hug our children daily, they will one day hug our grandchildren. This concept in economics is called the "multiplier effect." A small investment early on will multiply and bring a huge return over time.

This is only one of the many aspects of positive parenting, but it is the essence of it. If we shower our kids with love, and build a family where each person really matters, we can avoid many of the illusions, booby traps, black holes, and dead ends that the changing world keeps putting in front of us.

Enormous Challenges . . . Enormous Rewards

For all the challenges that change has brought upon us, we must not be discouraged. One hundred years ago, women could not wear pants in public, much less vote. In the last century we've increased sanitation, cleaned up rivers and air, conquered many childhood diseases, and lengthened lives with seat belts, smoke detectors, and speed limits. After the Second World War, the Universal Declaration of Human Rights was adopted by the United Nations, defining human dignity for all to understand and aspire to. Broader civil rights were extended in the United States, both to people of color and to women. And many people have gained a more fundamental understanding of racism, sexism, and religious intolerance, and are more keenly aware of discrimination and injustice.

We have learned so much, and we keep learning more. We have overcome so much . . . and we can overcome bullying.

3

. . . .

Problematic Childrearing Practices

What's done to children, they will do to society.

— KARL MENNINGER

Behind all of the overwhelming statistics, at the heart of all of the sweeping societal changes are the unique stories of millions of families. Each one of these families is made up of parents with their own personal stories, raising children full of potential. One fact about parenting is that we all figure it out as we go along. One fact about being human is that our old experiences shape all of our new experiences.

Wouldn't it be great if bullying had a quick and easy, five-minute solution? The great thinker Albert Einstein once said that if he had one hour to save the world, he would spend fifty-five minutes defining the problem and five minutes finding the solution. Rick Hanson, author of *Buddha's Brain,* states it more simply: "To make any problem better, you need to understand its causes."[1] If we take the time to understand why our youngsters are likely to bully and get into other risky behaviors, we can understand the complexity of the problem, which has been developing over centuries. Then perhaps a five-minute fix will be obvious.

Many families, both past and present, have faced a number of culturally accepted hardships such as domestic violence and alcoholism. Whatever our heritage, knowing the stories of our parents and ancestors helps us develop compassion and new understanding. Putting our family into context gives us insight into the gifts and booby traps that shaped us. This hindsight becomes a mirror in which to better see ourselves. If we face the truth about our past—positive and negative—and work on healing the trauma, we can be better parents to our children.

This is a good time to consider the legacy of hardship, since in fact, much research has been done on understanding the connection between our ancestral brutality and schoolyard and cultural bullying today. Intelligent, motivated, educated, and caring individuals and organizations have invested a good deal of time, effort, and commitment into understanding the big picture of the bullying dynamic with the hope of resolving our imbalances. The time has come for all caring adults to bring the research together and put solutions into action. The time has come for parents to understand their key role in creating a bully-free future.

The fact is that many parents—without knowing it, without intending it—are actually contributing to problem behaviors. They may be shocked to discover, after doing what they thought was "the right thing" for a long time, that something is not right. They may notice that their kids are not turning out as expected, and suddenly find themselves lost, on the wrong road. Feeling anxious and worried, they want to figure out what went wrong. Applying insight to hindsight will help. They *will* figure it out.

Negative vs. Positive Parenting

Before we explore problematic childrearing practices, let's touch base with a core part of our message: *Bullying isn't fair.* We believe in fairness.

Every sport has rules. Those rules are usually clearly stated and become social agreements. When a rule is broken, when a player goes out of bounds, or if there is a foul, the action stops. There's often a flag, a penalty, a time-out; a player is given another chance, someone is thrown out of the game, or the game is forfeited. There are appropriate and repeatable penalties and consequences for breaking the rules.

It's different in families. When a baby is born, parents are not handed an instruction manual or rulebook. There are rules and laws and books, but unfortunately, instructions on how to take the "high road" toward a healthy and happy family life aren't provided to new parents. Parents are most often guided by social norms, which vary greatly from family to family, neighborhood to neighborhood, and subculture to subculture.

What do parents on the "high road" know that other parents don't know? Somewhere in life they learned and remembered certain positive behaviors; the luckiest ones learned them in childhood by experiencing positive parenting from their own mothers, fathers, and other caregivers.

The Three Rules of Positive Parenting

Positive parents are certainly not perfect; no one is perfect. They are distinguished by a commitment, however, to giving their child a loving, good start in life that sets him or her on a positive trajectory—an upward spiral. If there were a rule book for positive parenting, the three rules might be the following:

1. **Show up**. Be there. Be engaged. Be present for your children. Be available when they need you, period. This means physically, by phone, emotionally—any way you can. Follow this rule and your children will never be neglected.

2. **Do no harm.** Based on the Hippocratic oath, this is a fundamental principle of medical ethics around the world. Follow this rule and you will never abuse your children.

3. **Be the parent you wish you'd had.** This is similar to the Golden Rule that many major religions embody: *Do unto others as you wish be done unto you.* Follow this rule and your actions as a parent will be shaped by compassion and respect.

Abiding by these three basic (though not simple) rules guarantees an enormously positive payoff of caring, cooperation, and connection within your family.

Breaking the Rules: Negative Parenting

When these rules are broken, negative consequences—both short-term and long-term—can result. The following "negative parenting" behaviors would be considered "fouls" by a referee, and they come with real-world penalties:

- **Neglect.** Neglect of an infant, toddler, or child disrupts basic developmental processes that build security, confidence, and the ability to self-regulate. Neglect interferes with the mental and physical health of children, and it leads to problems in school and with peers, including bullying or being bullied. Neglect comes in many forms, from abandoning children to ignoring them when they need attention; lack of nurturing and withholding love are highly destructive. Not loving or valuing our kids and not taking care of their emotional and physical needs are forms of neglect. Isolating children, excluding them, and ostracizing them are also forms of neglect. Permissiveness in the form of lack of rules or structure also constitutes neglect, as does not holding kids accountable.

- **Abuse.** Abuse, marked by punishment and/or violence, starts with disrespect and violation of boundaries. Cruelty damages trust and causes overwhelming shame and humiliation. Abuse communicates to the child that the parent does not love him or her, no matter what the parent may say afterward. The emotional confusion and insecurity that comes with abuse creates bullies and victims alike.

  - **Emotional/psychological violations** include verbal instances of disrespect (being "dissed"), disgrace, dishonor, and being treated with contempt; taunting, mocking, and ridiculing; being treated as if a person is insignificant, unimportant, or worthless. Chronic, recurrent humiliation is the most destructive.

  - **Physical violations** include threats, slaps, spanking, hitting, and assaults with hands, weapons, and other objects.

  - **Sexual violations** include a range of behaviors from inappropriate comments and touch to rape and incest, a taboo in nearly every society. Even exposing a child to mature content or inappropriate sexual behavior on TV violates the child's innocence.

- **Exposure to violence.** A witness to violence is a victim of violence. Children who are exposed to violence can become cognitively, socially, and emotionally impaired. Most children identified as bullies have been exposed to violence—in the home, in the media, or in both. With violence, there are no innocent bystanders. When a violent event occurs, be it a terrorist attack or a mother slapping a child in public, all witnesses are affected in some way.

- **Alcoholism.** The American Medical Association recognizes alcoholism as a disease that affects the whole family. People who are drunk or high are capable of doing things they would never do in their right mind, including all of the behaviors mentioned above.

When adolescents get into trouble with the law, there is an intake interview as part of the juvenile justice system. Over and over again these youngsters report abandonment, abuse, neglect, anger at not having a father or mother, or being abandoned by a parent.

As childhood victims of poor treatment, these emotionally overwhelmed youth may lash out in violent rage, intentionally causing damage and harm, or they may simply stumble foolishly into bad situations without truly knowing any better. If they get sent to prison, the economic costs to society can be enormous. Childhood damage begins a negative trajectory for life and harms many others in an outward spiral. The way parents treat their kids can set the stage for the bullying dynamic.

Nine Ways Parents Bully Their Kids
Some parenting practices can clearly be considered "bullying." Parents teach their children to be victims by habitually dominating them, having the last word, discouraging their children from being assertive or sharing their feelings, and by claiming parental authority. Parents bully kids by

1. Constantly telling them they're wrong
2. Targeting them or permitting their siblings to single them out

3. Teasing them in a mean way—and/or not protecting them from mean teasing

4. Sexually abusing them

5. Shaming them

6. Calling them names

7. Insulting them

8. Threatening them

9. Hitting and spanking them in anger

Adverse Childhood Experiences (ACEs)

Juvenile delinquents are not the only ones who have suffered from negative parenting practices. Many other children do too, yet they grow up to lead productive lives. But their experience plays out in other ways. Physician and author Gabor Maté points out, "What happened to us when we were kids really does affect us dramatically in the here and now, especially if 'negative' emotions like anger were repressed and love was poorly expressed. And early trauma leaves an impact like a wrecking ball hitting delicate crystal."[2]

A major research project concerning childhood trauma—the largest of its kind—was initiated by Dr. Vincent Felitti, the former chief of preventive medicine at Kaiser Permanente in San Diego, and his partner Dr. Robert Anda. The survey asked 17,000 middle-class patients of diverse ethnicity with the average age of fifty-seven, "How did childhood trauma affect your health decades later in life?" The surprising results demonstrate the connection between traumatic childhood experiences and medical problems, mental health issues, and addictions throughout a person's lifetime. The study reveals a clear relationship between our childhood experiences and our physical and mental health later in life. In fact, adverse childhood experiences (or ACEs) can convert into organic disease later in life.[3]

Furthermore, these early negative experiences are often blocked from memory or are hidden and denied because of social, cultural, or family norms.

Unfortunately, ACEs tend to also be passed on to one's children and grandchildren in the form of deep unconscious feelings of fear, shame, guilt, powerlessness, low self-esteem, isolation, and difficulty trusting others. Unless parents are aware of this intergenerational legacy and commit to resolving the issue, they tend to do to their kids what was done to them, despite their good intentions.

Sample Survey Questions

Here are a few of the questions from Felitti and Anda's survey: Before your eighteenth birthday:

1. Did a parent or other adult in the household often or very often . . .
   - Swear at you, insult you, put you down, or humiliate you?
   - Act in a way that made you afraid that you might be physically hurt?

2. Did you often or very often feel that . . .
   - No one in your family loved you or thought you were important or special?
   - Your family didn't look out for each other, feel close to each other, or support each other?

3. Did you often or very often feel that . . .
   - You didn't have enough to eat, had to wear dirty clothes, and had no one to protect you?
   - Your parents were too drunk or high to take care of you or take you to the doctor if you needed it?

People who answered four or more questions (out of ten) as "yes" had a much higher likelihood of life-threatening health problems.

Categories of ACEs

Eight categories of ACEs were studied. The prevalence of each category from the sample is stated in parentheses:

1. Recurrent and severe physical abuse (11 percent)
2. Recurrent and severe emotional abuse (11 percent) (Most destructive is chronic, recurrent humiliation such as calling children "stupid" and "worthless")

3. Contact sexual abuse (22 percent)

Growing up in a household with:

4. An alcoholic or drug user (25 percent)

5. A member being imprisoned (3 percent)

6. A mentally ill, chronically depressed, or institutionalized member (19 percent)

7. The mother being treated violently (12 percent)

8. Both biological parents not being present (22 percent)

To learn more about ACEs and to get your own score, visit www .ACESTooHigh.com. The website includes articles about how people all over are using this study to change society for the better.

Interestingly, researchers in the Felitti and Anda study observed that the follow-up appointment was profoundly important to the research subjects. Even though subjects had "confessed" their deepest, darkest secrets, they still felt accepted by the researchers. An elderly woman said, "Thank you for asking the questions! I feared I would die and no one would ever know." We'll talk about the reasons for this response in part 3.

Overall Findings

The data reveals staggering proof of health, social, and economic risks that result from ACEs. Enormous medical and societal problems originate early on in the home. In fact, the data shows that ACEs are a major public health problem. Some of the major findings reveal the following:

- Although concealed and unrecognized, ACEs are surprisingly common.

- Fifty years later, ACEs still have a profound effect, although transformed from psychosocial experience into disease, social malfunction, and mental illness.

- ACEs are the most important determinants of the health and well-being of our nation.

• Primary prevention is ultimately the only realistic solution.

This information is distressing. However, it is also enlightening: it shines a spotlight on where we need to go and what we need to do. It also highlights the tremendous power parents have to shape the lives of children.

One researcher states, "In all our history, ours is the first generation to recognize the ravages of child abuse and neglect and begin to do something about it. We are also the first generation to begin to heal ourselves physically and psychologically from the harmful effects of ACEs."[4]

Shining a Spotlight on Solutions

The implications of Felitti and Anda's study on the medical world are tremendous. No amount of biomedical research will find a gene for calling a child "stupid" or "worthless," or a drug that treats imprisonment or divorce. This study shines a brighter and broader beam on the search for solutions. Examining the bigger picture—the biological-social-psychological-spiritual model—we can discover the underlying root causes. By focusing on the whole child, the family, and other influences, we have a greater perspective and find more creative, deeper, and more effective solutions.

Complex problems call for an interdisciplinary, integrated approach that will point to realistic solutions, such as improving the understanding and skills of parents and child-care providers. This is where positive parenting comes in.

Parenting's Troubled History

As we learned from the ACE study, negative childhood experiences are often kept secret, downplayed, or repressed because of our powerful desire to put such things behind us. Unfortunately, our minds and our brains don't work that way. Patterns can play out automatically, no matter how hard we try to suppress them.

Just as it is important to know family medical history (e.g., diabetes or tuberculosis), it is equally important to know about our social inheritance.

What is your social ancestry? What destructive patterns did your parents and grandparents overcome? Think back to your childhood, to how you were disciplined. What were the consequences of this disciplinary action in the short term? In the long term?

Here is a chilling quote from author Lance Morrow in his book *Heart:* "Generations are boxes within boxes; inside my mother's violence you find another box, which contains my grandfather's violence, and inside that box (I suspect but do not know) you would find another box with some such black secret energy—stories within stories, receding in time."[5]

Punishment and Fear-Based Leadership

Authoritarian or autocratic leadership, predominant in early twentieth-century European countries, was also the predominant style in the United States before the 1960s. Many families and subcultures in America still abide by this style. The primary goal of authoritarian parents is obedience; their tools are blame, shame, guilt, threats, force, and abuse. They desire control, and their greatest tool is punishment.

Punishment appears to be an easy fix in the short run, but it can actually cause bigger problems in the long run—instilling fear and distrust, and resulting in a damaged relationship. Youngsters also learn that it is okay to bully to get their way. Furthermore, punishment causes great confusion for a child: "How can the most important people in my life, who should be loving and protecting me, be attacking me?"

Research shows that punishment increases aggressiveness and behavior problems, and lowers IQ and academic performance. Punishment provokes anger and the desire for revenge. When backed into a corner, humans may revert to their basest instincts.

The American Psychological Association states that "corporal punishment is violent and unnecessary, may lower self-esteem, and is liable to instill hostility and rage without reducing the undesired behavior."[6] The APA adds, "Corporal punishment . . . is likely to train children to use physical violence."[7]

Yet many parents still rely on punishment, holding beliefs such as

- "My parents used it and I turned out okay."
- "My parents never punished me, and I didn't turn out okay."
- "You have to beat your own kid or the world/the police/others will beat him/her."

But punishing does not feel good, nor is it good for anyone; it can physically destroy bodies and brains, and it harms families. In a fear-based parenting style, children become compliant or defiant, shutting down their emotions and avenues to problem solving. They are then likely to become bullies or to attract bullies, since they are taught a rigid, narrow view of right and wrong. They may appear to be confident, but they are controlled by fear.

Breaking Their Will

Parents generally love their children and have the best intentions for them. If punishment feels wrong and has such negative consequences, then why do parents do it?

The age-old belief behind harsh punishment is that children are wicked by nature and parents must break their child's will in order to turn him or her into a decent human being. Furthermore, generations of parents who were not formally educated relied on superstition and false beliefs.

Murray A. Straus, a well-respected researcher on family violence in the world, explains this dynamic. "Stemming from the Christian belief that babies are born with 'original sin,' children may be perceived as innately bad. Consequently, parents may believe they have the duty to rid children of their evil and willful tendencies. Strict physical discipline may be considered necessary to teach children to be good, and to beat the devil out of them."[8]

This belief continues to influence many parent-child relationships. These days it is considered extreme for a parent to "beat the devil out of a child," but distressingly more normal to strike or spank a child for acting out. Parents still resort to punishment to break a bad attitude, a willful streak, or "brattiness." But those who punish, even with the best of intentions, harm the child, their relationship with that child, and themselves.

"Breaking their will" does, in fact, damage or destroy a child's sense of self, the core part that can experience an authentic connection with life, spirit, and/or God. And when children don't know who they are or what they want, they look to others—often choosing unhealthy influences.

For Your Own Good

Often referred to as "the most significant thinker in psychiatry today," prolific author Alice Miller was obsessed with trying to understand how a Hitler could happen. In her books, she portrays children who had been abused and silenced, then later became destructive to themselves and to others. That was Adolf Hitler's story.

Hitler's father was quick-tempered and demanded blind obedience. Adolf was viciously beaten by his father and emotionally abandoned by his mother. Adolf learned to accept daily beatings with unquestioning compliance, numbing himself to the pain. He learned to be obedient. He also learned to be cruel. Many years later, he took revenge on the cruel world that had shaped him.

The predominant parenting style of turn-of-the-century Germany used violence to instill absolute obedience (dubbed "poisonous pedagogy" by Miller). Without this parenting style, there might not have been a Hitler. If his countrymen had not experienced that same sort of upbringing, Hitler might not have had the psychological sympathy of millions of followers, and consequently, millions of victims.

And yet, according to Miller in her book *For Your Own Good,* there was a basic tragic assumption that this treatment was, and is, good for children:

> Most of today's parents and teachers were physically punished as children. Society's argument to justify this phenomenon is that being beaten, especially by a parent, prepares children for life and helps them learn to be

obedient; indeed, we are all familiar with the exhortation to "beat some sense into him/her/them."[9]

Because children are often not allowed to talk about their mistreatment, enormous damage can ensue. The pain, according to Miller, is stuffed deep inside the psyche and morphs into neurosis or psychosis. Being told it's for "their own good" is degrading and confusing for children, and leads to negative effects later in life. On the other hand, when children can express their feelings and pain, they can begin to release and heal the trauma.

The phrase *for your own good* has confounded countless children who need to believe in and trust their parents, but these children have to deny their own reality in order to do so.

The Rights of Children

The United Nations, which set forth the Universal Declaration of Human Rights in 1945, created the Convention on the Rights of the Child (CRC) in 1989 with the awareness that people under eighteen years old often need special care and protection that adults do not. This document outlines in detail the basic rights of every human child, including the right to survival; the right to develop to the fullest; the right to protection from harmful influences, abuse, and exploitation; and the right to participate fully in family, cultural, and social life. This document inspired hundreds of countries to uphold the human dignity and harmonious development of every child. It states clearly that children have the right to be protected from abuse and harm.

After Canada ratified the CRC in 1990, researchers in that country attempted to find positive consequences of physical punishment and found none.[10] Dozens of nations have now passed laws against hitting children, including parental spanking. Parents who break these laws are not punished for hitting their children; instead, child-care experts visit them to help them learn better childrearing skills.

Many progressive nations in Europe, Africa, and Asia have improved their family systems and the overall wellness of their children. In some European countries, children have "wraparound" support from the government, wherein mothers are given paid leave of three years for each child, and families are provided with free health insurance and free preschool programs. In addition, older children care for younger ones in school to improve their caregiving abilities. When these older children become adults, they are then able to relate more peacefully with others, which has contributed to more stable societies.

Every country has ratified the CRC except two: Somalia and the United States. Somalia had a good reason: it didn't have a government.

One of the reasons the U.S. Congress has not ratified the CRC is that one small section of it recommends that "a clear prohibition of torture or other cruel, inhuman or degrading treatment or punishment, as well as the ban on corporal punishment in the family, be reflected in the national legislation." Many Americans, particularly in Southern states, strongly believe that parents have the right to spank their children; they consistently elect congressional leaders who agree with this. America is home to some of the strongest voices for children's rights, but many parents feel it is their right and responsibility to spank or beat their child. One California teacher who got a job in Texas was shocked that parents respected her less because she did not physically punish her students—their children.[11]

Physical and psychological punishment (as opposed to discipline and guidance) constitute mistreatment and degradation of children. Sooner or later they have destructive consequences, whether visible or concealed. Children who are treated well, who are allowed to feel nurtured and free and strong in childhood do not tend to humiliate or harm others. To create a bully-free world, we need a clear definition of bullying and wide social agreement on healthy childrearing methods.

Slippery Slopes

Even without being harsh or punishing, today's parents often pass on values to their children that pave the way for bullying issues.

Most parents who pick up this book tend to worry about their children in school. Schools are where the values that parents teach their children become apparent. Here are some of the things parents commonly teach their children that teachers see played out in the drama of bullying:

- **"Hit them back."** Parents are correct in teaching their children to stand up for themselves, but they are often mistaken as to what "being assertive" means. The problem with the "hit them back" approach is that it becomes an eye-for-an-eye escalation process. When a child is hit at school, it is better to teach them to yell "Stop" and go get a teacher.

- **"Don't be a tattletale"** misguidedly teaches children not to ask for help when they need it. A better response when it seems a child is tattling is to ask, "Do you need help solving your problem?" Children develop problem-solving skills over time with guidance and practice, and need to be taught or shown ways to defuse and resolve issues. "Don't tattle" has evolved into "Don't snitch," which is rule number one in gang life. "Don't snitch" empowers bullies, while keeping ugly dynamics hidden. *Instead of tattling, children should be taught the importance of "telling" a parent or adult when something is wrong.* Tattling means trying to get someone in trouble. Telling means trying to get you or someone else out of trouble.

- **"My little prince/princess."** Parents have good intentions of building self-esteem in their child with this idea, but some parents overdo it, giving their child the impression that he or she can do no wrong. Children who are placed on pedestals feel superior to other children and disrespect adult authority. There is a slippery slope to narcissism when children feel so entitled that they can't meaningfully engage with others.

- **"You should know better than that."** Adults come down hard on children for making mistakes, but it's hard to learn if someone is yelling at you. You can't tell kids something once and expect them to learn it, any more than you can show dogs a trick once and expect them to learn it. What builds knowledge and understanding is repetition and good modeling. Children should be forgiven for forgetting . . . and then taught again.

- **"He's just a child."** On the opposite end of the continuum, adults let children off the hook and let them make mistakes without learning from those mistakes. Kids can learn a lot more when we give them opportunities to self-manage and self-regulate. This phrase goes along with "boys will be boys" in terms of making excuses for children and enabling them to avoid accountability.

One of the most widespread and dangerous things that many parents practice, however, is allowing hate speech in the home. When adults have hostile outbursts—yelling and screaming—that are irresponsible, threatening, and/or without empathy or regard for others, they give their children permission to do the same outside the home. Children see, and children do. When children bring hate speech to school, they bring family conflict into society. And when school leaders fail to see labeling, name-calling, harassment, threats, and hate speech as a continuum, they perpetuate the problem.

Rudeness Is Antisocial

In previous generations, rude behavior by children was noticed, complained about, and corrected by adult members of society. But today, so many adults are themselves disrespectful, rude, and uncivil that children are confused. This epidemic of meanness may seem casual, but it threatens everyone. Casual rudeness and "cute" nastiness are unfortunate parts of a permissive and open society, one that allows and welcomes comedy that is often at someone else's expense.

Peter, Paul, and Mary had a popular song called "If I Had a Hammer." It's a wonderful song about social justice, and it makes a charming metaphor as well. You don't give children a hammer, since they'll hammer all over the house. When rude speech and antisocial behaviors are permitted, they are like hammers . . . that hammer all over the land.

Antisocial behaviors escalate into bullying and violence; pro-social behaviors do not. Children are especially at risk when they grow up thinking that put-downs, swearing, and bullying behaviors are "normal." They have to unlearn and replace their habits if they are to have satisfying and successful relationships in their adult lives.

Rude speech is powerful, and—although it can be seen as harmless or funny when used by rock stars and comedians—when it comes out of the mouths of children or is directed at children, a downhill slide into trouble can result. Mild disrespect can turn to incivility, rudeness to meanness, complaining to blaming and threatening, and from there to physical harm. Slaps, spanks, hitting with hands, hitting with objects are all steps on the path of abuse, violence, harm, and damage . . . even killing.

On a societal scale these disrespectful actions are an abuse of power, and they may show up as date rape, domestic violence, gang fighting, torture, and war. This "hammer" slope can escalate into enormous pain and suffering, destruction, and humiliation. Some of the consequences can be predicted; some are unforeseen and come as a surprise.

In reality, there are numerous tools, unlimited strategies, and an abundance of non-damaging, pro-social approaches that many parents simply don't know about. Every parent needs to have a toolbox packed with effective strategies, motivators, and disciplinary tools that can solve problems and bring out the best in all relationships. If one approach doesn't work, there are many more (non-injurious) options.

Pro-social tools and skills are based on the second rule of positive parenting: *Do No Harm.* Positive outcomes result from caring and respect, pro-social values, and a moral compass. Positive social skills strive for win-win resolutions that benefit everyone.

It is the job of parents, caregivers, teachers, and adult friends to teach youngsters respect and other pro-social behaviors. Day-to-day positive interactions between adult and child shape a child's brain positively. It is also the responsibility of caring adults to evolve from their own negative patterns of the past and develop and re-create positive habits. Keeping "civil" in our civilization is everybody's business. (See chapter 12 for how to build these skills.)

Repatterning Families

*If we could change ourselves, the tendencies
in the world would also change.*

— MAHATMA GANDHI

We are all products of our upbringing. Innocent, trusting, and not knowing better, as children we accepted everything as "normal." We developed our own individual patterns, and we also downloaded common cultural patterns. The attitudes, feelings, and behaviors we learned early in life are our hidden social inheritance. Later on we learned that some patterns are positive, while others are negative. There are truly beneficial and effective ways to treat our children—and ourselves—that could solve many of the world's problems.

Mostly we are unaware of our patterns until we get a wake-up call. This might happen as a flash of insight out of the blue, or a memory from a dramatic incident. A mother in Louise's workshop confessed why she was there: While spanking her young son, she spotted her angry red handprint on his bare bottom. It shocked and appalled her! Flashing back to when she was hit as a child and how much it hurt her, she blinked back tears, embraced her son, and swore she would change. "Never again," she vowed. The next day she registered for the class to learn better ways to deal with her stress and his frustrating behaviors.

Bare-bottom spankings were a pattern she had learned when she was young, as the "normal and right" way to raise kids. With her awareness came new choices. Her courageous commitment and heroic follow-through helped her change the harmful pattern and put her son's life on a more positive trajectory. It has also helped other parents with similar experiences who have heard her story.

The past still lives inside of us all. Once we wake up and understand that patterns can sneak up on us, we can watch for them and are empowered to break the cycle. This is not about blaming anyone. Our ancestors did not know any better. But we have many advantages they didn't. We know better. And we can do better.

Interrupting Patterns

Patterns are like the computer operating system of the brain—the software that supports the basic functions of the "hard drive." During the first five years of childhood, we built this operating system by processing every bit of information that came in through our senses. Later we encountered difficulties—bugs, viruses, glitches in our original operating system, and software conflicts when we tried to run adult programs like relationships, work, and finances. As adults we now have the opportunity to evaluate what's working and what's not working, and to consciously upgrade our personal operating system.

All adults need to know about the power of hidden patterns and tendencies that can drive their lives and sabotage their best intentions. And, equally important, adults need to know that they are not destined to do to their children the harm that was done to them. No parent is doomed to transmit damaging patterns to the children he or she loves. Anyone at any age can change attitudes, behaviors, and habits. Anyone can make new choices that begin to change the family trajectory. Getting on the higher road is hard work, but positive parenting can develop into the most fulfilling job on the planet.

It is true that we are products of our upbringing, but we are also so much more! We have *free will*. We can interrupt and transform the old programs and patterns. We can make our lives—and consequently, our children's lives—better.

Prevention Is the Best Policy

As we have learned, early trauma has devastating consequences. Kids don't "just get over it" as we wish they would. Repressed emotions remain in the body. They take on a life of their own, as was proven with the ACE study, and show up later in life. The most important question to ask is, "Will what I am about to do or say deepen or rupture my connection with my child?"

The more parents scold, scream, and spank to control behavior, the worse the child's behavior can become. Parents who focus on deepening connections with their children, however, have fewer battles than those who focus on controlling their kids. Pam Leo, author of *Connection Parenting,* has a famous motto: "Connect before you correct."[12] (Chapter 11 is all about connection!)

The best way to prevent discipline problems, explains Leo, is to build a stronger connection. Set up opportunities to connect more often and more fully with your children. Spend time together every day to develop and maintain a strong positive connection. The benefits of this connection are multiple: parents and children understand each other better, work together better, and respect each other more. And the bottom line: love flows.

Rewriting History

All the world is full of suffering. It is also full of overcoming.

— HELEN KELLER

It is possible to alter self-limiting patterns, to learn positive parenting skills, and even to rewrite family history through insight, connection, and understanding. We cannot change the past, but we can do better today and in the future.

A new choice can begin an upward spiral away from struggling and toward thriving. New choices, commitment, and tenacity bring changes and hope, little by little. The plasticity of the brain makes transformation possible. (More on that in chapter 16.)

Many people who were not effectively parented as children because of alcoholism, ignorance, or other trauma did not learn how to be good parents. If these folks do to their children what was done to them, the same story and pain will repeat. But if, instead, these parents learn new information and skills and—most importantly—befriend other parents who are on a positive road and ask for support, they can change the course of their family's future.

Positive Discipline

There is a difference between discipline and punishment that many are not aware of. *Punishment* is penalizing for an offense through pain or humiliation. The word *discipline,* on the other hand, has the same root as the word *disciple,* meaning pupil or learner. The purpose of discipline is to teach in a way your children can learn.

Louise began her first book, *The Winning Family,* with an analysis of the saying "spare the rod and spoil the child," which is often quoted by parents as justification for punishment. What most parents don't know is that the rod was a tool used by shepherds to guide sheep, in conjunction with the staff, which was used to pull them back. What shepherds would want to beat their sheep?

Kids are not mind readers. They need to be taught appropriate behaviors, what's right and wrong, what is acceptable and what is not. Kids generally want to live up to high standards and expectations if they are attainable; they don't want to disappoint you.

But parents aren't always present to tell kids what to do.

The ultimate goal of discipline, therefore, is self-discipline and self-responsibility, so that children will do the right thing even when you're not present, even when no one is watching. Positive discipline is neither punitive nor permissive.

- Positive discipline is based on mutual respect, firmness, and kindness.

- Positive discipline is proactive, not reactive; you give the situation your full attention before you speak.

- Positive discipline is about teaching, preparing, skill building, and getting to effective solutions without harm.[13]

Jane Nelsen, author of the *Positive Discipline* series, has created a network of educators who help parents find their way. In chapter 9, we will discuss positive discipline as it relates to family climate.

From Reactive to Proactive

We have talked about negative vs. positive parenting, antisocial vs. pro-social approaches, and punishment vs. discipline. Another contrast to keep in mind is reactive vs. proactive actions, which is similar to the difference between hindsight vs. foresight.

It's easy to be reactive, but not helpful. Yelling about spilled milk does not clean it up or help the spiller figure out how to keep it from happening again. We cannot change the past, but we can learn from mistakes and do better in the future.

It takes more time, more patience, and much more self-control to be a proactive parent. Yet by being proactive, one can avoid the drama and trauma of knee-jerk reactions and the negativity that surrounds a bullying dynamic. Being proactive means using foresight to prevent the "bad stuff" from repeating.

It is not easy to become a proactive parent when you are in the habit of being reactive, since we often react out of a deep sense of self-protection. Self-protection may be a habit that we picked up as children for some reason or another, or that was passed on to us from our parents. There is nothing wrong with being self-protective, but if we can understand it better, we can heal our scars instead of hiding them, and learn to truly care for ourselves while we care for our kids.

Healing the Wounds of History

The more we heal ourselves, the less our children
will have to heal themselves.

— MICHAEL BROWN, *THE PRESENCE PROCESS*

As much as history is about humanity's progress, it is about humanity's pain as well. The deep legacy of abuse in cultures contributes to an endless cycle of emotional insecurity and turmoil. But we also contain within us a deep well of possibility and the ability to heal. Over the centuries, religion has taught us faith as well as fear, and now science confirms that there is hope for healing from trauma and emotional pain. Until recently, it was believed that our brain cells grew until we were five years old and then began to die off, but this has been proven to be untrue. Our bodies build new cells constantly, and our brains can grow and change as long as we are alive. It is possible to move from insecurity to confidence as parents, and to build confident children in our ever-renewing relationships with them.

On an everyday basis, parents and caregivers are called upon to comfort their youngsters and heal their cuts and bruises. Kisses and Band-Aids may help, but carefully listening and offering comfort can actually help children release their pain, recover their balance, and strengthen their ability to manage mishaps in the future.

When we endured trauma as children, we may have had no one to listen to us, comfort us, soothe us, and support us during the hard times, but that is in the past. It's now up to us to release and heal the pain, to let the past go and move forward. The fact is, life continually presents us with opportunities to heal.

Trauma remembered is trauma ready to be dealt with, to be resolved, to be healed. But when trauma is blocked from our awareness, fragments of these past experiences may color our present and future interactions with our children and partners. Once we bring awareness and understanding to those old wounds and patterns, we can move toward healing and releasing them.

Trauma is a fact of life. But so is resilience, and so is healing. When trauma is accepted as real—not denied, minimized, or discounted—and when it "can be expressed, processed, ameliorated, or 'metabolized' in a healthy way," says an author discussing the ACE study, "eventually few or no lasting detrimental effects remain."[14]

Healing calls not only for huge changes in the way we see ourselves but also for a *mindshift*—a shift in our beliefs and mindset. A mindshift requires supportive people around us, plus new skills for regaining health, personal power, and sovereignty over our lives.

· · ·

PART 2

Focus on Bullying

A new government agency dedicated to the problem of bullying (www .stopbullying.gov) defines the issue as "unwanted, aggressive behavior among school-aged children that involves a real or perceived power imbalance." Other programs include *persistent, focused*, and *repeated* in their definition of aggressive bullying behavior in all age groups.

Dan Olweus, a pioneer in bullying research who is quoted widely in this book, has discovered that, contrary to popular belief, bullying behavior is not "normal" behavior, nor is it "just a stage" that kids "get over." When bullying occurs, someone always gets hurt, and some even die; therefore, it is a problem we *must* solve. Fortunately, bullying is a problem we *can* solve. There are complex reasons why kids bully, and there are effective approaches to ending it.

Directions are badly needed to solve the bully problem! Talk shows and news programs commit short features or entire episodes to the issue without discussing, or even touching on, solutions. The documentary *Bully* was all about targets and victims, and it showed adults at a loss about what to do to change the situation. Social skills expert Corinne Gregory, who has made the phrase "putting *civil* back into *civilization*" her rallying cry, justifiably complains that we focus too much on "anti-bullying" when we should be talking about "pro-social skills."[1]

The next three chapters of this book are about directions. Chapter 4 looks at all the directions bullying can take, tracks how bullies develop, and talks about bullying targets. Chapter 5 explores ways of interrupting and preventing bullying, and includes a new direction for bystanders to take in standing up against bullies. Chapter 6 discusses upward, downward, inward, and outward spirals as a way to focus on our path toward a bully-free culture.

Raising the Bar

"Raise the bar" is a phrase used for raising standards and expectations. In the last forty or fifty years, the ideals of the free speech revolution—which called for a higher quality of interaction, deeper thought, and understanding—have become lost in a culture of lower expectations. Given the freedom to be whoever they choose, children have lost out on the important lessons of propriety and wandered down a slippery slope into "acceptable" disrespect, put-downs, incivility, bullying, and violence.

What is the "high road" we aim for today? Our children dream of lavish material wealth rather than a life of learning and contributing. These dreams are supported by social structures and the media, who confusingly glorify and reward glamour and profits rather than personal growth and the common good. At one time, houses of worship were the places where social and personal standards were held high, where hearts turned to values and service. But congregations have dwindled nationwide, and some televised clergy have even become mouthpieces for hate speech.

Parents have always had an obligation to guide their children to higher standards, and today more than ever we need to raise the bar for our communities as well. We need to be on high alert for ways society dumbs our kids down and give support and attention to societal structures that help direct our children away from self-absorption and toward concern for the greater good.

In and Out

Let's start with looking at two basic approaches to solving bullying.

Outside-In

An "outside-in" approach is about authorities—be they parents, teachers, principals, police officers, or judges—enforcing rules and laws, and holding kids accountable in order to change behavior. Appropriate behaviors are taught outside-in when these authorities send clear and consistent messages that bullying is not tolerated. Bullying stops when authorities don't let bullies get away with it. But this is only half of the solution.

Inside-Out

An "inside-out" approach is about educators—parents, teachers, principals, counselors, and clergy—helping children develop attitudes, values, and skills that empower them to have respectful relationships based on rights and responsibility. When appropriate behaviors are discovered through insight and logic, they become truths that shape an individual and, therefore, a culture. Bullying simply does not have a chance to grow in a deeply developed culture of respect and caring. Ideally, an inside-out approach starts very early in life, but it can even be learned after the path has become difficult.

When seeking any solution, especially when parenting, both approaches should be developed and implemented. The next three chapters provide examples of how both are used successfully.

. . .

4

. . . .

Understanding Bullying

The vast majority of violence is learned, and it can be unlearned.
This is not therapy, it's education.

— SUNNY SCHWARTZ, *DREAMS FROM THE MONSTER FACTORY*

In the 2011 documentary *Bully,* there is a scene in which a school's vice principal is trying to help two boys resolve a problem. She tells them to shake hands and make up. One boy puts out his hand promptly and forthrightly; the other hangs back. At first we assume Cole, the one who is reluctant to shake hands, is the person who bullies, since he is being rude. But we soon learn he is the one wronged. Cole is finally pressured into shaking hands, and the other boy is sent to class. But Cole is still in trouble. The vice principal insists that, because he didn't accept the boy's apology, he was also at fault. "Except I don't hurt people," Cole protests.

"By not shaking his hand, you're just like him," the vice principal says, wanting the problem to go away.

"Like someone who pushes you into a wall, threatens to break your arm?" Cole asks. "Threatens to stab you and kill you? Shoot you with a gun?"

Suddenly we understand the dynamic. By appearing confident and cordial, the bully is making his target look like the one at fault. But the insensitive vice principal does not understand. "He apologized," she says. "If you can accept his apology, I can see you two being good friends some day."

The adult in this situation is apparently unable to relate to this child's situation, much less his feelings of fear. If she were a police officer, and the two kids were adults, she would ask Cole, "Would you like to press charges?" Threatening bodily harm is a crime. But in day-to-day life, children's relationships are hard to compare to, or measure by, adult interactions. Brothers wrestle, sisters spar, and best friends fight and resolve issues so fast it makes a grown-up's head spin. A parent or teacher doesn't want to take sides. He or she wants children to learn to work things out on their own.

There are so many more reasons why it's hard for adults to fully grasp the scope or depth of bullying. As we see in the movie, a target is often reluctant to talk about the situation, not wanting to upset a parent or appear weak—so the parent doesn't know what is going on. When adults hear about incidents of bullying, they don't always know how to respond. Parents have their own experience of bullying or being bullied, which creates a filter of judgment. They may be in denial, not wanting the bad news to be true. They may not know what to say. The ways in which bullying can occur have multiplied, expanding as fast as the ways information can be shared. And finally, bullying doesn't always look like bullying.

It is essential for adults to understand the issue. Bullying has escalated into such a powerful force that kids have committed suicide at the suggestion of their peers, or out of feelings of desperation and helplessness. Had Cole's school had an anti-violence policy that included verbal threats, his bully would certainly have faced disciplinary action.

The authors of this book are of the opinion that the movie—although well done, timely, and appropriately provocative—was misnamed; it should have been called *Victim*. The documentary shed little light on why the bullies were as mean as they were, what made them tick, or what made them think it was okay to speak to other kids the way they did, to treat them so badly.

The website for the *Olweus Bullying Prevention Program* (www .violencepreventionworks.org) defines bullying as "aggressive behavior that is intentional and that involves an imbalance of power. Most often, it is repeated over time." Bullying may involve one child bullying another, a group of children against a single child, or groups against other groups. It may include a variety of behaviors, such as derogatory comments and name-calling, physical harassment (hitting or kicking, pushing, spitting, etc.), social isolation, telling lies and spreading rumors, stealing or damaging another's property, or other threats. It can be targeted toward race, religion, gender, sexual orientation (or perceived sexual orientation), body type, or any number of characteristics.

We will explore the nature and dynamics of bullying in this chapter, as well as some solutions. At the end of the chapter, we celebrate a growing cultural movement against bullying.

The Bullying Continuum

Like many other issues, bullying lies on a continuum. On one end is a cold and misguided individual who commits acts of violence and aggression so horrible we see this person as evil. In the middle is a social manipulator who thinks nothing of cutting others down for his or her own gain. On the other end is the clumsy, lonely, confused individual who has not yet learned good social skills and acts out to get attention. Most bullies think they're in the right to act as they do. Some regret their impulsivity and wish they could control their tempers, but find it hard to stop bad habits.

It is important to recognize both ends of the spectrum, since the biggest bullies are a danger to society, and the smallest bullies need understanding and help. But in the wide middle are individuals—and here we mainly focus on children and teens—who act intentionally and repeatedly to exert power over others.

Characteristics of Bullies

Bullying refers to words or actions expressed to gain power over another person, as in the saying "Might makes right." This urge to dominate, to be superior, underlies child abuse, date rape, domestic violence, workplace violence, and hate crimes. The need to dominate contributes to the imbalance of power.

Bullies can be characterized in a number of ways:

- aggressive bullies who are hot-tempered, strong, impulsive, and confident
- passive bullies who are insecure and have personal problems; they tend to follow the lead of aggressive bullies
- bully-victims who have been bullied, then bully others
- pure bullies who are well adjusted but just enjoy dominating others

Some bullies are children who themselves have been bullied, although that's not true for all. For some, bullying might be a way of dealing with situations at home that they're having trouble coping with. For others, they may have poor social skills or learning disabilities, making it hard to fit in with other kids; for these children, bullying provides a sense of control to satisfy their own sense of powerlessness.

Characteristics of Targets

Any child can be bullied, but there are often some common characteristics of targets:

- passive victims who are anxious, fearful, and socially withdrawn (sometimes with good reason), making them appear vulnerable. Experts have named many types of passive victims, such as
  - vicarious victims who feel vulnerable, sympathetic, and guilty when there is bullying around them
  - false victims who feel they are being bullied, even when they are not
  - perpetual victims who have been bullied so much that it becomes part of their psyche
- provocative victims who arouse negative responses from those around them
- bully-victims (see above)

In this book, we use the terms *victim* and *target* interchangeably. But there are subtle differences between the two terms.

Victim vs. Target

Victims, many have observed, seem to attract bullies, as though they have a "kick me" sign attached to their back. They lack self-esteem and self-confidence. They victimize themselves in their self-talk and can't imagine any other way of being. They are perceived to be different, and may be considered outsiders. They are seen to be weaker, timid, and quiet, and are socially less competent. Habitual victims draw the conclusion, usually from some early childhood experience, that they deserve bad treatment.

Targets tend to be in the wrong place at the wrong time. Targets may be chosen arbitrarily, or they may simply have qualities that irritate the bully.

The word *victim* can carry a real self-esteem wallop, since it implies that the person being bullied is part of the dynamic, which is sometimes but not always the case. The word *target* shines a different light, pointing out that bullying is about an aggressor choosing a likely receptor for his or her actions. Alex, the central subject of the *Bully* movie, had a very unusual appearance. He was systematically bad-mouthed by nearly every boy he encountered for almost anything he said or did. Even his father criticized him for "being a victim."

The difference between the two words is subtle, and perhaps immaterial. Every child is different, as is every situation. When deciding which word to use, choose whichever word gives your child a greater feeling of strength and understanding. Also, keep in mind the difference between *naming a problem* and *labeling a person.* Naming a problem gives you the power to discuss it, and to bring it to light. Labeling children diminishes them by defining them as bullies, victims, etc.—with all the accompanying baggage. Separating the person from the behavior gives everyone the opportunity to choose different behavior.

Children who are more prone to be picked on tend to have the following characteristics:

- low self-esteem
- emotional insecurity
- lack of social skills
- inability to pick up on social cues
- tendency to cry or become emotionally distraught
- inability to defend or stand up for themselves

Children who have congenital differences are easily targeted. Any physical difference—be it a birthmark; cleft palate; big feet, ears, or nose; glasses; or even being an ethnic minority or having unusual eyes or hair (which may later be considered beautiful)—can be perceived as a vulnerability. Cognitive or developmental differences are harder to see, but children with Asperger's syndrome, autism, high or low intelligence, attention deficit disorder (ADD), or AD/HD, or who are simply more sensitive, are also picked on. A child who is known or suspected to be LGBT is often a target.

Some very sensitive children may even appear to provoke their own victimization. Children who are not adept at reading social cues, for example, may tease bullies and make themselves vulnerable by egging the bullies on. Seeking attention, these sensitive children may not know when to stop. When the balance of power turns, they may not know how to effectively defend themselves.[1]

The Bully/Victim Dynamic

Studies of interpersonal relationships have provided us with a model of conflict styles that sheds light on the bully/victim dynamic. Imagine a half-circle diagram, somewhat like a speedometer. On the left side is the Passive style, and on the right is the Aggressive style. These are both ways of dealing with conflict—either by giving up or by dominating. (On the far left is Avoidance, and on the far right is Passive-Aggressive. Both of these are ways of completely avoiding dealing with the problem.) In a bully/victim interaction, as you can imagine, the arrow will swing from one extreme to another with painful and unsatisfying results. The optimal area in the bully/victim dynamic is in the middle—the Assertive style, which allows both sides to win.

Of Mice and Monsters

In her best-selling children's book *The Mouse, the Monster and Me: Assertiveness for Young People*, Dr. Pat Palmer teaches three communication styles using a fun metaphor that kids quickly relate to.

Since the main characteristic of bullies is their need to gain control over others, the metaphor of an aggressive, forceful "monster" is used to describe how bullies get what they want without consideration for the other person's rights or feelings. And because the main characteristic of victims is their inability to stand up for themselves, the metaphor of a passive, timid mouse is used for this style. "Mice" behaviors include crying, whining, begging, pouting, hinting, getting sick, and hoping someone can read their mind. "Mice" can be nice, but sometimes they get stepped on.

Palmer shows how timid, unassertive "Mice" are afraid to express their opinions or stand up for their rights. Passive people want to avoid conflict and may keep their feelings bottled up inside, but they are often very angry. Conversely, "Monsters" express their feelings, but do it aggressively and without regard for others, hurting others in the process.

The "Me" communication style that Palmer describes is assertive. "Being assertive means you are letting yourself and others know what you want, not in a pushy way like monsters do, or a scared way like mice do, but in an honest way by just being YOU," she writes. "When you use mouse or monster ways to get what you want, you feel bad, and so does everyone else around you."[2]

Both victims and bullies—everyone, in fact—can benefit from learning assertiveness and other social skills. And everyone needs support before and after bullying incidents.

Many people who are involved in bully/victim dynamics have not heard of the word *assertive,* or they confuse it with something else. Yet it's a very important word describing a very important skill that can change lives. Chapter 14 is all about building assertiveness.

Forms of Bullying

Bullying can be an isolated mean or cruel act, or it can be a series of verbal, written, physical, or electronic actions intended to inflict discomfort or pain, or cause humiliation and social exclusion. (The Olweus program defines bullying as an act that is repeated over time, but adults should intervene even if it happens only once.)

Children, like all humans, have basic emotional needs. They need to be accepted, to be liked, to feel safe with peers, and to have good friends. Unfortunately, however, they are constantly judging and being judged by their peers. They want to fit in but are often hyper-aware of their differences.

Toxic verbal attacks can pierce their hearts: "Fat." "Ugly!" "Fag!" "Nobody likes you." "No one really cares about you." "I hope you die!" When believed and internalized, these negative messages can result in self-hatred and create the misguided belief that "No one likes or cares about me."

Bullying comes in many forms:

- **Verbal** bullying is the most common form, and includes name-calling, taunting, malicious teasing, and threatening.

- **Nonverbal** bullying includes making faces or gestures, or excluding someone from groups or activities, which is one of the most damaging forms of bullying.

- **Physical** bullying includes pushing, spitting, kicking, and taking someone's belongings.

- **Psychological/emotional** bullying includes spreading rumors, intimidation, and manipulating social relationships.

- **Sexual harassment or violation** may include the other forms of bullying, but focuses on the target's body, self-image, perceived sexual orientation or sexual activity, or other aspect of sexual identity.

- **Cyberbullying** involves verbal, psychological, and sexual bullying through the use of technology. The emotional outcomes of cyberbullying are similar to other bullying outcomes, but the reach of the damage can be enormous—being humiliated by thousands of anonymous "friends" who saw a text or read a Facebook post can feel many times more painful than being humiliated in the presence of others. People who are cyber-bullied can feel trapped, since the injury exists in cyberspace long after an apology is issued. Fortunately, cyberbullying is a crime in many states.

Even young children are caught up in this wave; 7.5 million children under the age of thirteen are illegally using Facebook. Bullying expert Rick Phillips says, "Bullying and other forms of mistreatment are occurring at younger ages, getting meaner, and becoming more acceptable in youth culture. These incidents are also more difficult for adults to identify because students are becoming 'experts' in electronic aggression via text messaging, social network sites, cell phone pictures and videos to bully, harass, and humiliate their peers."[3]

Boys, Girls, and Blurry Lines

There was a time when the word *bully* denoted a tough boy who used his fists or picked on girls. Although boys still tend to bully more than girls, girls are more and more willing to get into the act.

For a long time girls had been taught, "If you don't have anything nice to say, don't say anything at all." But today it seems as if girls are not educated about the power of their words. Or worse yet, they *are* taught the power of their words, and then proceed to wield them with cruelty. Movies and TV shows are full of examples.

In her book *Queen Bees and Wannabes*, Rosalind Wiseman uncovered the world of girls' friendships and conflicts. She revealed secrets about how girls manipulate each other with power plays—from fake apologies to paying boys to ask targets out then dump them.[4] A few years later, Tina Fey produced *Mean Girls*, a movie partially based on Wiseman's book, about a girl infiltrating an all-girl circle of bullies, exposing them, and then reckoning with whom she had become in the process.

Bullying can be boy-to-boy or girl-to-girl. When it's boy-to-girl (and sometimes even when it's girl-to-boy), it's sometimes mistakenly called sexual harassment. And for some reason, many boys/men and girls/women feel comfortable picking on the approximately 10 percent of the population whose sexuality falls somewhere outside of traditional "straight" heterosexuality. Gender and sexual orientation is an issue in many forms of bullying.

One major theme of bullying is gender difference and sexuality. Jessie Klein, author of *The Bully Society*, discovered the following in her research of school shootings over the last three decades:

- 10 percent of the shootings involved boys targeting other boys about ex-girlfriends.
- Over 20 percent had to do with males feeling rejected by females.
- About 50 percent were related to boys whose masculinity was being challenged for not meeting stereotypical expectations.
- Almost 10 percent were related to name-calling based on real or perceived sexual orientation.
- 15 percent of the shootings had to do with dating or domestic violence.[5]

What, in a nutshell, does this research show us? It means we need more safe discussion about gender: about masculinity, femininity, and identity. As we will explore further in part 3, if you talk it out, you don't have to act it out.

Myths That Confound and Confuse

Many adults grew up with myths about behavior that did not help prepare them for today's bullying realities. Some of these myths include the following:

- "Sticks and stones may break my bones, but words will never hurt me." This is a lie. Words can cause great harm. This saying should be rewritten: "Sticks and stones may break my bones, but words can break my heart."
- Many of today's adults grew up hearing "boys will be boys" or "kids will be kids." Parents who believe this myth tend not to hold kids accountable, letting them instead get away with

unacceptable behaviors. Bullying can happen right under these parents' noses.

- Some people believe that "bullying is a harmless rite of passage," that "bullying is a normal part of life," or that "you've just got to accept it." This belief disempowers targets and prolongs their pain and suffering. Although teasing and hurtful speech do happen naturally as children grow and learn, *bullying* is not a natural part of growing up. It is an unacceptable social behavior that must be taken seriously and stopped.

- Many see violence not as a problem, but as a solution to a problem. People confuse strength with domination; words or actions are used to overpower and victimize others into submission. This belief is at the root of many conflicts, including war.

- "Kids are more mature these days." Many middle school teachers feel they are losing the battle against foul language and sexual horseplay because children are exposed to movies, TV, and video games beyond their level of innocence. But this does not mean children are comfortable with what they have seen, or what they know, or what they feel is "the right way to be." Kids pressuring each other into sexual behaviors or using expletives with each other is not maturity; it is disrespect.

What Bullying Is Not

Culturally, there are instances when bullying is built into the social fabric. One example of this is when newcomers to a group are tested.

It would be wonderful if, when we find ourselves in a new group of strangers, they would consistently welcome us with open arms. This happens sometimes in religious congregations where inclusion is a value; in some academic, volunteer, or work environments; and ideally in many families.

But life doesn't always work like that. Even when there is good will, it takes time to get to know people. And in situations where a high level of trust and bonding are essential for survival, such as in the military, the testing can get rough.

Initiation Rituals

When children start at a new school, a certain amount of social testing occurs. Kids come from different backgrounds and have to feel each other out, especially in middle school. A lot of mistakes and misunderstandings are made as students get to know and understand each other. They may challenge each other, insult each other, scare each other, or worry each other until they know where the other person is coming from or what he or she is "made of."

Many groups, especially in college environments, have initiation rituals that push the limits of appropriateness, safety, taste, and good judgment. Other more forward-thinking groups create positive trials—games, ropes courses, or other challenging events—to build trust and teamwork.

Adults need to be aware of this testing dynamic, which has been around since cave-dwelling days, and indeed is the dynamic of every social animal. Horses, lions, wolves, birds, and even house pets need to figure out who the leader of the pack is, who is "in" and who is not, and who can be trusted in times of trouble.

Parents need to guide their children to seek out social groups and environments where positive interactions are the norm. Teenage boys especially need to be encouraged to trust their intuition, carefully evaluating whether social ribbing and put-downs feel stimulating, warm, fun, and trust-building—or cold, mean, and demoralizing. All of us would do better to ask if the leaders we follow are principled individuals, since we are all capable of being manipulated by the groups in which we participate.

College kids are subjected to hazing in fraternities, sororities, bands, sports, and other on-campus groups and clubs. Parents should demand oversight of college hazing, as dangerous rituals frequently occur. Initiation rituals need to be monitored by adults to ensure things don't get out of hand.

Sibling Rivalry

There is a fine line between sibling rivalry and bullying. Although parents may want to let their children work things out between themselves, they must also be alert to situations that need intervention. Bullying within families is very common.

But what is the difference between bullying and playful teasing? Normal teasing, which bonds children to each other, is characterized by acceptance, playfulness, and fondness, and it comes and goes. The power balance is usually even. But teasing takes a wrong turn when one person stops having fun.

Caution signs for sibling bullying include

- one sibling using his or her power to hurt or scare a younger or weaker child
- one child being in control and the other feeling helpless
- one child intending to do harm
- persistent and predictable negative interaction

Typically, it is an older, stronger child who bullies a weaker, younger one. But power and strength can be social or psychological as well—not just physical. The basic rule of thumb is this: Behavior that would be unacceptable between two unrelated children is unacceptable between siblings.

Safe Words and Zones

One strategy parents can use to discourage bullying among siblings is to enforce a family-wide "safe" word or phrase for when things go too far. This can be straightforward, such as *stop* or *I mean it.* Or it can be creative, like *Mango.*

Parents can also create a safe zone where respect and kindness rule. This place, be it the dinner table, Mom and Dad's bedroom, or a stairway, can be a comfort zone for calming and balancing energy. Children will know they can retreat to this sacred space and get support when they need to repair hurt feelings, recover from trouble, or just calm down.

Family Tone

Parents can go a long way toward creating a positive family tone and expectations for their children. Parents who compare one child to another encourage competition and negative feelings between children. But parents who create traditions of cooperative accomplishment will nurture friendship and good feelings. (See chapter 9.) A well-known guide to promoting cooperation between family members and preventing lifelong grudges is *Siblings Without Rivalry* by Adele Faber and Elaine Mazlish.[6]

Fair Fights

To be clear, bullying involves a physical, verbal, or psychological attack or intimidation that is based on an imbalance of power. When two people of equal strength are trying to victimize or attack one another, the situation may be violent, but it is not bullying. These "fair fights," however, sometimes make victims of bystanders, who may be traumatized by what they see and hear. (More about bystanders in the next chapter.)

Consequences and Costs of Bullying

Bullying can have grim consequences for bullies and targets alike; depression, poor school performance, anxiety, and low self-esteem can persist for years. If the problem is not addressed early on, bullies are more likely to drink, smoke, use drugs, commit crimes, become violent, and raise children who become bullies. Without intervention, antisocial kids can find themselves on a downward spiral toward meanness, delinquency, assault, sexual harassment, abuse, domestic violence, abuse of their own children, and prison. If bullies are not given skills to deal with their inner conflicts, they may stuff their anxiety and fear, avoid conflicts and struggle, and/or drug their pain and depression. This spiral is troublesome and costly.

Students who watch as their peers endure the verbal or physical abuses of another student can become psychologically distressed by the events, just as the victims themselves are. Bullying expert Jonathan Cohen, president of the National School Climate Center, confirms that "there is a lasting, undermining, toxic impact on the witnesses to the bullying behavior."[7]

As discussed in chapter 3, adverse childhood experiences can begin a negative trajectory for life. ACEs can also spiral outward to involve and hurt others in a cascade of negative consequences.

Hidden Social Costs

In eighth grade, Danny got knocked down at school by Trevor, a kid who in the past had repeatedly called Danny names and pushed him around. After knocking Danny down, Trevor snatched a video game system out of Danny's hands and ran off. The vice principal gave chase, but Trevor escaped onto a bus. Danny was emotionally shocked, and physically and spiritually hurt.

Instances of bullying don't just affect the victim. Trevor's selfish impulse triggered an outward spiral of collateral damage in the following hours, weeks, and months. Danny's mom had to take the afternoon off work to go to the school. The vice principal used his personal time to contact Trevor's father in a failed attempt to do some restorative justice.

Suddenly entering the real world of crime and punishment added emotional stress at Danny's home, and spoiled the family's weekend plans. His father was angry, and his mother was torn between compassion and anger. Unable to contact Trevor's parents to seek understanding and resolution, Danny's mom and dad both lost nights of sleep.

Back at school the following week, the principal and the vice principal had to divert their attention away from academics to suspend Trevor and file paperwork to get him the help he needed. A few weeks later, on the day of the disciplinary hearing at the school district office, both the vice principal and Danny's mother had to miss a morning of work, and Danny missed a morning of classes. Trevor's father had to miss time at work as well. The academic judge and the vice principal had to do a few extra hours of paperwork at a cost to the school system. The police also had paperwork to do. They were all grateful, however, for the chance to get Trevor into the system early, since it would flag him as available for services he and his family needed, and hopefully deter him from the idea that he could get away with criminal behavior as he grew older.

This was a small crime that was handled responsibly by the school, yet it is easy to see how the costs added up: hundreds of hours of lost productivity by adults, cancelled weekend plans, emotional damage to families and friends, and $170 to replace the video game system. But multiply those damages by the millions and you can see the costs to society of jealousy, poverty, poor impulse control, and desperation caused by a culture of violence.

Financial Cost of Bullying

Some costs of bullying can actually be calculated. Schools across the country have paid millions in damages or out-of-court settlements to compensate students, parents, and teachers for injuries, both physical and mental, stemming from bullying and the school's lack of a suitable response policy. Beyond the cost of stolen toys, torn clothing, or broken glasses, the real financial cost to school systems and communities is significant.

Bullying is not just a problem with kids either. It is also found in athletic clubs, in the military, and in workplaces. One business journal cited a study of 9,000 federal employees that calculated the cost of workplace bullying at $180 million over two years' time. Some of the reasons cited were high employee turnover, stress-related illnesses, absenteeism, and loss of customer loyalty due to the negative feelings of harassed employees. "National statistics also show a sharp increase in workplace harassment and violence since the 1980s," according to this article. "Human resource managers are beginning to realize there is a real productivity cost to these kinds of things."[8]

Bullying and the Brain

The first five years of life are critical for language development and for the healthy development of emotions, such as empathy, compassion, caring, remorse, and guilt. Love shapes the brain positively; fear shapes the brain negatively. Mistreatment of young children has far-reaching, pervasive effects on brain development. Violence disrupts basic developmental tasks. Repeated trauma actually changes the architecture of the brain; the brains of traumatized children can actually become smaller. When the neural networks are buzzing from trauma, the brain is unable to focus on other important things, or to learn from experience. A child gripped in the fight-or-flight mode is not able to grasp what he or she did wrong, and is therefore likely to do it again.

The damage is even worse when the cause of the trauma is the parent or other trusted caregiver who should be protecting the child. These traumas change people's brains and can cause individuals to become chronically fearful, to not fear at all, or to decide to hurt someone before they themselves are hurt. It's bad news.

In other words, trauma and violence disrupt basic childhood developmental tasks and interfere with the mental and physical health of children. Critical developmental skills and competencies can be severely disrupted. (For further information about the brain, see chapter 16.)

Media Violence

Unfortunately, fear has a strong hold on today's children, and this fearfulness is reinforced by the media. We call this "the tentacles of trauma."

There is an axiom of psychology that says, "A witness to violence is a victim of violence." Social workers who work with children raised in homes where adults batter one another can attest to the wounds these children carry. And students who watch their peers being bullied can become as psychologically distressed as the victims, if not more so.

A witness to violence is likely to repeat/perpetrate it. According to the American Academy of Pediatrics (AAP), previous exposure to violence is the strongest single correlate of violent behavior. There is also a strong correlation between media violence and aggressive behavior.[9]

A recent Kaiser Foundation study discovered that today's children between the ages of eight and eighteen spend more than seven-and-a-half hours a day "being entertained" with various forms of media, more than any other activity besides sleeping.[10] This is cause for alarm, considering the following:

- The highest proportion of violence is often in children's shows.
- Violent content has increased over the years.
- The media portrays aggression as "normal" and acceptable.

- Violence is glamorized, glorified, or trivialized, without showing the real human cost and consequences—the broken bodies, hearts, and homes, and prison sentences.

- Violence at an early age teaches antisocial and aggressive behavior.[11]

According to the AAP, exposure to media violence is also linked to a variety of physical and mental health problems for youngsters, including aggressive behavior, desensitization to violence, depression, fear, nightmares, and sleep disturbances. Children younger than eight years old are especially vulnerable because they cannot discriminate between fantasy and reality; they think what they see is real, they believe it, and then they internalize it. It all registers in the brain.[12]

At this time of intense brain development between the ages of two and eleven, children are not only becoming desensitized to (and conditioned to be excited by) violence but also seeing more than 25,000 advertisements a year on TV alone. (See chapter 18 for more on technology.)

A Culture of Pain and Disrespect

For thirty-five years, prison psychiatrist James Gilligan interviewed criminals in search of what motivated them to commit violent acts. He reported, "The most violent prisoners had been humiliated repeatedly throughout their childhoods, verbally, emotionally, and psychologically (taunted, teased, ridiculed, rejected, insulted). They had also been physically humiliated by means of violent physical abuse, sexual abuse, and life-threatening degrees of neglect."[13]

During his extensive research with prisoners, Gilligan asked murderers why they had killed someone. Over and over again he heard: "Because he disrespected me/my mother/my sister . . ." or simply, "He dissed me." Revenge for perceived disrespect is one of the engines of our bully culture, a solution that always "seems to make sense at the time."

Overwhelming feelings of disrespect, humiliation, and shame are at the root of many violent behaviors. Disrespect includes being insulted, ridiculed, or rejected by others, or being treated as inferior or unimportant. In other words, violence is always a desperate and risky attempt to gain or regain respect, attention, and recognition for oneself or one's group.

Destructiveness and violence are intense hostile reactions to disrespect and rejection. Shame sparks anger, which triggers retaliation.

When bullies lack emotional intelligence—skills for managing emotions—violence is a common reaction. And bystanders and targets who lack skills for defusing violence or helping bullies "save face" often find themselves making problems worse.

Unfortunately, there is cultural support for hostile reactions. Generations of teaching young men "don't back down" has left a legacy of "the culture of honor," which leaves them prey to their emotions and sets them on the slippery slope of violence.

A Culture of Violence

What else causes people to be cruel? To injure others? To kill? Dr. Bruce Perry, a leading researcher on trauma and brain development, has identified six conditions that precipitate violence and bullying. (The last two factors listed have emerged over the last few generations; they contribute to the escalation of social damage experienced in the United States.) The following discussion is adapted from Dr. Perry's article "Why Does Violence Happen?"[14] Also included are ways to turn this culture of violence around.

Desensitization

Studies have shown that violence increases when people become desensitized to violence, death, or killing. The United States has one of the highest rates of violence and crime in the developed world today. Kids are exposed to violence on television, in video games, and in movies—often without seeing the true consequences of the violence. The average American child spends fifty-three hours a week with various types of media. Among parents of eight- to eighteen-year-olds, 54 percent have no rules about TV use.[15] By the age of eighteen, the average young person will have viewed 200,000 acts of graphic violence on television alone.[16] Violent events are also repeatedly rebroadcast into our homes via news programs.

Turn it around: According to the AAP, kids under two years of age should not watch *any* TV! Those older than two should watch no more than one to two hours of quality programming per day.[17] Also, never have a television in a child's bedroom. Use TV programs as opportunities to have open discussions, to find out what children think, and to share your thoughts. Help kids learn the real consequences of violence, the harm and the heartbreak. Teach empathy: "How would you feel if that happened to you?" Pay attention to ratings systems, and never take young children to violent movies. Keep the remote in your hand and turn off a violent program when children of any age enter a room. As a bonus, limiting screen time frees up time for other enriching activities.

Detachment

Kids who don't feel connected to others are at risk. Violence increases when people feel detached from family, friends, and community. The thinking becomes "If nobody cares about me, I don't care about nobody." Those who feel disconnected, isolated, and marginalized are more likely to be aggressive and violent, and less likely to feel empathy.

Turn it around: Humans are hardwired for connection. Kids need to be engaged with parents who will nurture, guide, and protect them, and with peers who will allow them to be themselves. Parent-child connectedness is *the* most important protective factor; it can protect kids from anxiety disorders, depression, alcohol and drug abuse, and violence. Feeling respected, feeling valued, and feeling a sense of belonging help build a strong sense of self. Parents need to help children nurture close friendships, and for some kids, parents need to arrange playdates to help children learn to get along.

Prejudice

Violence increases when we view certain groups of people as different or bad—as "them." Personal prejudices lead to misunderstanding, fear, and even hate crimes. Violence is often related to racism, misogyny (hatred of women), anti-Semitism, LGBT bashing, and negative attitudes about liberals, conservatives, Catholics, Mormons, jocks, geeks, etc. Sometimes it's the kids across town, a rival gang. Or people from the North . . . or South. When groups of people are dehumanized, we can feel justified in our prejudice. And when we prejudge, we can feel disrespectful and hostile toward others even before we meet them.

Turn it around: Children pick up the values and prejudices of their elders, and to end bullying, we must teach children tolerance. Every man, woman, and child deserves to be treated with respect, even if they are different from us, and even if we disagree with them. Learn about and respect other religions, cultures, and lifestyles, and share this attitude with your children. Do not allow jokes and actions that belittle, put down, dishonor, or humiliate others. Encourage children to reach out to kids who are different or isolated. Encourage them to connect with people who have different cultures and beliefs and to discover what they all have in common.

Substances

Violence can increase when alcohol or other drugs are involved. Alcohol and other drugs can affect people's judgment and even make them violent. A huge percentage of knee-jerk violence occurs when someone is under the influence. Teenagers do not have fully developed judgment skills, and they often don't know when enough is enough. With little experience measuring the effects of alcohol, adolescents often drink too much, too often, and in the wrong places. Particularly dangerous is the combination of drinking (or drugging) with driving.

Turn it around: Children are likely to copy our habits and lifestyle, including alcohol and drug use. If you use drugs, consider quitting for your children's sake, and getting help if you're unable to quit on your own. If you drink alcohol, do it safely, modeling restraint and talking with your children about your choices. Teach them the facts about drugs and alcohol so they can make good (and informed) choices. Avoid people who use too much or who use irresponsibly.

Violence as Entertainment

Unfortunately, over recent generations, children's play has drastically changed. Kids who play video games and simulated war games are practicing violence. Glued to monitors, they have fun killing virtual people. Where once children played cops or superheroes who put robbers or bad guys in jail (rather than killing them), kids are now regularly experiencing the fight-or-flight adrenaline rush and being rewarded for virtual murder and annihilation. One teacher calls this "ouchertainment." Killing is not entertainment. Kids should spend their time developing their virtues, gifts, and talents, not practicing ways to kill people by remote control.

Turn it around: Monitor children's activities. Limit the amount of time spent playing video games. Discuss video games with the parents of your child's friends to support and reinforce each other. Think carefully before letting younger children play violent games with older children, and always check video game ratings. Go to www.common sensemedia.org and www.esrb.org to learn about these ratings. (For more about technology, see chapter 18.)

Availability of Weapons
The availability of guns increases the probability of lethal violence. Guns can be deadly weapons when someone is scared or upset, drunk, hateful, or angry. A fistfight can turn into murder. Here are some statistics from the Law Center to Prevent Gun Violence:

- Americans own an estimated 270 million firearms—approximately ninety guns for every one hundred people.
- In 2009, guns took the lives of 31,347 Americans in homicides, suicides, and unintentional shootings. This is the equivalent of more than eighty-five deaths *each day* and more than three deaths *each hour*. Eight children under the age of nineteen die from guns every day.
- More than 1.69 million kids (under the age of nineteen) are living in households with loaded and unlocked firearms.
- A 2000 study of U.S. households that contained both children and firearms found that 55 percent of these households have one or more guns in an unlocked place.[18]

The news is full of stories about anger turning to tragedy when weapons are easily accessible.

Turn it around: Parents have a profound influence over the lives of their children, especially early on. Teach your children to resolve problems and conflicts peacefully—the earlier in their lives this is taught, the better. Teach your children about the consequences of gun violence and what to do if they ever encounter a gun (don't touch it, and tell an adult). If you own a gun, keep it unloaded and locked in a secure place, and store ammunition in a separate locked location.

Managing Emotions

When people do not know how to manage their emotions, control their impulses, delay gratification, and ask for what they want, their feelings can trigger a hostile reaction, sending them into a rage. If there is a backlog of unprocessed anger, fear, or anxiety left over from previous events, the situation can become complicated, making the person more susceptible to hostile, impulsive reactions. This inability to process feelings does not go away until emotional skills are learned, practiced, understood, and made a habit. Managing emotional responses is part of *self-regulation.*

Many parents sign their energetic children up for karate classes, hoping they will learn self-discipline. One martial arts teacher we spoke with said, "In twenty-five years of teaching martial arts, I've noticed a gradual slippage in the way kids relate to other kids—and to adults—a sad trend away from kindness. Bullying is epidemic, even in my students now. What kids lack is impulse control, empathy for others, and respect for authority."

But why do so many children lack these essentials? Why don't kids who are adored and loved and catered to with stickers, toys, and trips to Disneyland get the social and emotional learning (SEL) they need? As usual, parents hold the key. (See chapter 12 for more information about SEL.)

The Powerful Role of Parents

Parents have more power than anyone else to prevent bullying and other risky behaviors in their young children. There is great power in a parent's love and ability to connect. Parents have the power to protect, nurture, engage, teach, and put their children's feet on the right path—and redirect them when they stray.

Parents may not know it, but they have the ability—and more importantly, the *authority*—to create a positive climate based on respect, belonging, connection, and the Golden Rule ("Do unto others as you would have them do unto you"). They have the authority to establish family rules, such as "Disrespect is not acceptable" and "Bullying is not tolerated." Parents have the authority to teach morality, what's acceptable and not acceptable, what's right and what's wrong.

Parents have tremendous power to build inner strength and self-esteem that protect children against hurtful comments and behavior.

Parents have more power than they realize to prevent or encourage bullying behaviors. The difference can be confusing, since common parenting practices that actually support bullying are prevalent and considered to be "normal." These practices are so common that parents don't even realize they are teaching the bullying dynamic!

How "Regular" Parents Unknowingly Raise Bullies

Considered by many to be "the father of anti-bullying programs," Dr. Dan Olweus has studied the causes of societal problems and their solutions for more than thirty-five years. He discovered and confirmed that certain widespread childrearing practices are linked to the development of what he calls "hostile reaction patterns" and other antisocial behaviors in children. These very common patterns can be found at all levels of income, and in all races. They include the following:

- **Negativity on the part of the primary caretaker.** When a caregiver exhibits a negative emotional attitude instead of the warmth and involvement that healthy child development requires, children become emotionally insecure. This increases the risk that the child will become aggressive and hostile toward others.

- **Permissiveness of aggressive behavior by the child**. If the primary caregiver is generally permissive and "tolerant" without setting clear limits on aggressive speech and behavior, the child's aggression level is likely to increase. This means that parents who don't curb aggressive speech and behaviors are tacitly teaching that hostility and aggression are okay.

- **Use of "power-assertive methods."** When parents don't know what else to do, they commonly try to resolve conflict with power, aggression, and violent emotional outbursts. Spanking and physical punishment are typical of the autocratic leadership style, but children raised with these methods are more likely to become aggressive.[19]

For more information about restructuring family power, see chapter 15.

Those parents who were raised in a healthy way are indeed called upon in society to assist those who were not. They can do this by spreading the word about Olweus's three characteristics of families that nurture bullying, and share ideas about changing patterns by

1. Having a positive attitude toward their own and other children

2. Setting limits on aggressive speech and behavior

3. Finding better tools than physical punishment and emotional outbursts to change a child's behavior

A Growing Cultural Movement

Fortunately, a growing cultural movement supports this shift. Positive action is being taken to stop bullying and create safer environments for kids.

At a large youth gathering against bullying in California, 6,500 students from forty-nine Los Angeles schools watched the documentary *Bully.* Afterward, director Lee Hirsch told students that he had been bullied "really badly" as a child. Now he wants to give voice to the countless youth who are bullied every day. He encouraged students to use social media to write about their bullying experiences and how they are working to stop bullying. "This is where change begins—right here today," he said. "Each and every one of you are change-makers."[20]

We are lucky to be living at a time when change-makers are speaking up. In 2011, President Obama and the First Lady hosted a daylong White House Conference on preventing bullying, and launched www .stopbullying.gov. In his opening remarks to this first-ever event, the president denounced bullying as an inevitable part of growing up.[21]

At this time in history, more research is being done on the psychological mechanisms of violence than ever before. We are working hard to break old patterns, and we need to apply everything we learn toward a better world for our children and all of humanity.

. . .

5

. . . .

How Parents Can Interrupt
and Prevent Bullying

*Bullies are made not born. If we're serious about stopping bullying,
it has to start in the home.*

— CRAIG AND MARC KIELBURGER, COFOUNDERS OF FREE THE CHILDREN

A local post office clerk was called in by her son's principal because he was bullying a group of younger students. At the meeting, the mother's heart sank for the little kids. She asked them, "Is he scaring you?" They nodded. In front of her son, she said, "I promise you he will never do that again. If you need any help, or someone else is ever bullying you, he will be the one to go to."

That experience changed the young man. Through programs at the school and working with his mother at home, he ultimately became a friend to those children. The school security guard bumped into him one day and asked how he was doing. "Great!" the boy replied. "Love school. And I'm getting good grades." The surprised guard joked with him: "I thought I would see you in juvenile hall by now!"

"Now, he is a sweetheart," the boy's mother boasts. "He will even be speaker at his graduation!"

Bullying is a huge problem that begins in childhood and can continue throughout a lifetime if it is not stopped. Yet by taking the right approach, parents can raise children who won't harm others, won't be bullying targets, and won't be silent bystanders.

There are countless ways that parents can exert their power and influence. The most important ways are to build a warm and loving attachment to their child and to create a peaceful home based on respect and responsibility. Children with good emotional health and pro-social skills are less likely to be bullied or to attract bullies; they are more likely to have good relationships and use their energies for constructive things such as reaching out to their communities, expressing their creativity and intelligence, and positively influencing the world around them.

Interrupting Bullying Behavior and Providing Support

Parents, teachers, and other school professionals sometimes feel annoyed by a child's complaints about being picked on. They send the child back to class to work it out for himself or herself. They accuse the child of tattling, implicitly blaming him or her for the problem. But it's dawning on all of us that today's bullying has serious consequences and needs to be taken seriously. Children need more support.

Bullying often comes in the form of a crisis that leaves parents breathless and shocked, wondering what to do. It may be the discovery of a pattern of bullying, or a sudden, onetime event. It may even be a situation in which the child is being "tested" for inclusion in a group. (For instance, one teacher complains about the energy she spends in initiating intervention procedures, only to find the kids are fast friends the next day.)

Bullying others tends to peak in late childhood/early adolescence. The years leading up to middle school are especially important for teaching values as well as social and emotional skills, and for bolstering children's inner strength to prepare them for the challenges of their teen years. (We will talk more about this in part 3 of this book.) Many middle school teachers and counselors have a great deal of experience in dealing with bullying behavior.

Parents can more effectively work with the school by

- keeping a written report of bullying incidents, including dates, times, locations, and names of those involved
- meeting with their child's teacher and explaining their concerns
- asking if the teacher has witnessed bullying and what he or she intends to do

- following up with teachers and administrators if the behavior continues

What to Do When Your Child Is Bullied

Most parents who pick up this book will do so because their child may be dealing with bullies. Part 3 of this book is full of strategies to build children's internal and external supports that will superpower and protect them for life. But if there is a crisis and your child is bullied, here are some things you can do right away.

What Not to Say

A study of 3,000 children who were bullied reported the following kinds of advice that did *not* help them resolve their problem:[1]

1. "Don't tattle and just work it out on your own." This makes children feel abandoned.

2. "Pretend it doesn't bother you" and "Don't cry" convey the message "Change who you are." They do not help.

3. "Tell them to stop it" and/or "Tell the other person how the behavior made you feel" doesn't work; bullies don't care.

4. "What did you do to encourage it?" and "Were you asking for it?" These questions imply that it's okay to be hurt or that kids want to be hurt. It also implies that there is something wrong with the child who was bullied.

All of these responses somehow blame the victim, and we now know that someone being abused should not—and must refuse to—take responsibility for the abuser's behavior.

How to Help Victims/Targets

After a bullying event has occurred, here are nine things you can do to help victims or targets. The following is adapted from a list by the U.S. Department of Health and Human Services:

1. **Take them seriously.** Do not dismiss their story because it "happens to everyone," seems insignificant, is inconvenient for you, or makes you uncomfortable.

2. **Listen to them intently and patiently.** Stop what you are

doing and give them your total attention. It may take them some time to get the whole story out. Let them know you are available if they think of more to say.

3. **Help them express their feelings.** Ask questions if you need to, but let them say the words if they can.

4. **Do not diminish the event.** See #1. Also, as much as you might want them to shift toward feelings of "I'm okay," be careful not to tell them how to feel.

5. **Comfort them and let them know they are not at fault.** Help them see this from a bigger-picture perspective. Help them see that the bully is the one who was in the wrong, not them.

6. **Emphasize that they do not deserve bad treatment.** Nobody does.

7. **Teach assertiveness skills by role-playing.** This can help heal insecurities.

8. **Talk to other adults who understand the situation and can help.** It always helps to talk to a teacher, principal, or another parent who knows the kids involved, knows the social situation, or knows the age group.

9. **Report it.** Let a teacher, principal, or other school official know what happened. Most schools have a protocol to follow when bullying is reported. If necessary, report it to the police. These adults can help you determine the appropriate course of action and next steps.[2]

Many things can be done to prevent (or curb) victimization, such as the following:

• **Nurture positive self-regard.** Do what you can to build the child's self-esteem and sense of worth.

• **Develop self-confidence.** Help the victim/target identify and appreciate his or her inner strength.

• **Display acceptance of the child and model self-acceptance.** Model that it's okay to like yourself, that when you feel accepted you can be who you are—authentic. When you are not accepted for who you are, you think you have to be who you're not.

- **Affirm that it is okay to be different.** Over time, uniqueness becomes a source of strength, pride, and power. Let children know it's okay to reach out and ask for help. Assure them that they are not alone, and that over time they can be who they really are—themselves.

- **Assure them that they deserve to be treated with dignity.** Everyone deserves this.

- **Help them develop empathy** by understanding that everyone has the same basic needs for acceptance and dignity.

- **Help them create new narratives** by talking the story out and finding their power. For example, help them ask the right questions, shifting from "What's wrong with me that makes people call me names?" to "What is wrong with people who call others names?"

- **Teach them self-calming skills.** "When we ask anxious young people who've been mistreated if they'd like to learn a way not to cry in the face of abuse," one therapist reports, "they often say yes, even though we explain that this may not change the behavior of their tormenters."[3] Teach your children some relaxation techniques, such as quiet meditation or breathing exercises—anything that might allow them to take control of their emotions and soothe their hurt.

- **Help them find their passions.** Social isolation is profoundly difficult. Having a task or job that contributes to something they care about is a huge self-esteem builder. (For more on this topic, see chapter 17.)

- **Teach assertiveness skills.** Instructing children to tell a bully to "stop it" is not the same as teaching them true assertiveness. Being assertive is a great way for children to save themselves from bullying. Whether it means speaking up and saying, "Get away from me" or telling a teacher their side of the story, assertiveness changes the dynamic. According to the *Middle School Journal*, "Victims of bullying who developed assertiveness skills experienced reductions in bullying. When victims respond assertively, bullies will be more likely to stop bullying or find another, less assertive victim."[4] (There is more on assertiveness at the end of this chapter and in chapter 14.)

What to Do When Your Child Is a Bully

Aggressive behavior doesn't happen in a vacuum. There is a reason bullies act out. Typically bullies are angry, have themselves been victimized, lack empathy, or don't understand the implications of what they are doing. Sometimes they need help with an undiagnosed issue that affects their perception or impulse control. Often it's all of the above. Use an inside-outside approach (that is, look at the situation from the child's point of view) to find out what else is going on in their lives. Try to get to the bottom of it while being compassionate and understanding.

Teach bullies that what they did is unacceptable, and that they are responsible for the damage and the consequences. Then help them find the words and actions to make amends.

At its core, bullying is a learned behavior that is often an attempt to gain superiority or control over someone else. Because of their poorly developed social skills, bullies might imagine threats where none exist. They might judge others as being hostile when they are not. Because of their poor impulse control, bullies might become aggressive.

Bullies tend to have the following things in common:

- immature social skills
- poor impulse control
- watching aggressive TV programs and playing aggressive video games
- lack of compassion and empathy

Parental intervention is powerful. The postal clerk who talked to her child's targets had a strong, clear, and supportive approach to turning the problem around. A variety of approaches can help improve social interactions. The following are eight ways to help bullies stop their behavior:

1. **Talk about empathy.** Talk about it daily, model it in your own behavior, and in every possible situation point out the good it does.

2. **Teach perspective-taking.** Bullies often see themselves as victims. Acknowledge this, but then help them see things from the point of view of the victim. Compare situations.

3. **Help kids learn to name/identify emotions in themselves and in others.** This builds emotional literacy. Naming our emotions is the first step to properly managing them.

4. **Teach anger management, stress reduction, and conflict resolution.** Bullies often act as they do because they don't know a better way.

5. **Teach self-control and self-restraint.** Help bullies learn to think before they act. Help them become aware of the steps they go through mentally and physically as their tension builds: for example, their face getting hot and changing color, their fists clenching, and their body shaking. Becoming conscious of their emotional process can engage their rational brain, and disengages the fear-control center, the amygdala. (For more about the amygdala, see chapter 16.)

6. **Help kids change their behaviors.** Praise and reward them any time they cool down or make good choices rather than lash out.

7. **Limit TV and violent video games.** Talk to kids about the images they see; help them make connections between how they feel before and after they see violence or play violent games. Help them choose better sources of entertainment. If they *talk* their feelings out, they don't have to *act* them out.

8. **Teach assertiveness skills.** Being assertive is the middle ground between being passive and being aggressive. Assertiveness

allows children to confidently seek what they need without being aggressive or manipulative, and it enables children who are bullied to stand up for themselves.

All of these topics will be addressed more fully in part 3 of this book.

What to Do When Your Child Witnesses Bullying

When Kristen's son started middle school, he was astonished by the behaviors of kids who came from the other elementary schools. These kids would eagerly gather around a fight, something that would have been unconscionable in his upbringing. They would even pull out their cell phones and record fights. One day there was a fight on a balcony where two girls were trying to push each other off. "I could have witnessed a murder," Kristen's son said later, worried and emotionally shaken.

As we discussed in the previous chapter, a witness to violence is a victim of violence. When your child is exposed to bullying, he or she needs a special kind of support. Following are eight things you can do to help children who are witnesses to bullying:

1. **Give them a chance to talk.** They may need to tell their story over and over as they try to make sense and integrate the experience. Or they may not want to talk about it. Spend time together doing something that allows them to talk if they feel like it.

2. **Help them express their feelings.** Ask questions if you need to, but let them say the words if they can.

3. **Do not diminish the event.** You may want them to "get over it" since it happened to someone else. But as much as you might want them to shift toward feelings of "I'm okay," be careful not to tell them how to feel.

4. **Comfort them; they are not at fault.** Help them see this from a big-picture perspective. Help them see that bullies seek a target because of their own personal problems, not because of who their victim is.

5. **Help them feel safe.** Seeing someone get hurt makes you think it could happen to you. Address real and imaginary fears. Talk about what might be done in imagined scenarios.

6. **Teach assertiveness skills by role-playing.** This can also heal insecurities. Talk about what they could have done, or might do, in future situations if they witness bullying: for example, they could not join in, call the child being bullied away from the situation, run or walk away and get a teacher, etc.

7. **Talk to other adults who understand the situation and can help.** Let other parents, teachers, and school counselors know what you learned. There may be other children who also need to talk.

8. **Report it.** Just because your child wasn't involved in the event directly doesn't mean you shouldn't let a school official know about it—officials may not have heard, and they will want to know. Inquire about whether your school has a bullying prevention program that involves both parents and teachers.

From Bystanders to Upstanders

The world is dangerous not because of those who do harm, but because of those who look at it without doing anything.

— ALBERT EINSTEIN

In a typical bullying event, there is generally one bully, one victim, and a group of bystanders. Traditional thinking puts the burden on the victim for handling, reporting, solving, permitting, or even causing the bullying. As more is learned about the dynamics of bullying, this way of thinking is shown to be unjust and unhelpful in truly solving the problem. Then when you consider how deeply bullying affects bystanders, and the profound and sometimes tragic influence a bully has on the culture, it's clear that it's in every bystander's best interest to become empowered.

Bystanders make a decision to either actively or passively support the bully. An "upstander," on the other hand, recognizes that he or she has a choice and decides, "I can and will do something to help make things better."

It is important that all children realize they have this choice. Some children who are not chosen as victims or targets have strong social skills and conflict management skills. Because of this, they can play an important role in changing a bullying dynamic. They are more willing to assert themselves without being aggressive or confrontational. They can suggest compromises and alternate solutions. They tend to be more aware of people's feelings and can be very helpful in resolving disputes, as well as encouraging others to get help.

Youngsters are more likely to bully when they can get away with it, and when there are no consequences. Upstanders make a difference by getting help, speaking up, and reporting what they saw; consequences naturally follow.

The Power of Upstanders
Upstanders have great power to

- curb a bullying event and diffuse the drama
- support the victim and reduce the trauma
- model assertiveness
- set an example of doing the right thing
- ask for help when a victim cannot
- set healthy boundaries
- encourage others to be compassionate and also stop bullying

If witnesses *do not* take action to stop bullying, a tacit message is sent that bullying is permissible.

When witnesses *do* take action, it sends a strong message of disapproval. When upstanders intervene correctly, bullying situations can be stopped before they start. Children can be taught to be upstanders by

- not supporting the bullying
- supporting the target in private and also talking privately to the bully

- supporting the target in front of the bully
- asking for help from an adult

A Community of Upstanders

The upstanders movement is widespread, effective, and catching on like wildfire. Search "upstander" on the Internet and you will find many different programs that support this idea. Here are some examples:

- In 2010, the "It Gets Better" Project was started to combat suicides by LGBT adolescents. Short video clips of successful, happy adults reach out to kids to say, "I've been there" and "Hang in there." (See www.itgetsbetter.org.)

- To empower youth and inspire bravery, Lady Gaga announced the Born This Way Foundation in partnership with the Berkman Center for Internet & Society, a major interdisciplinary center at Harvard Law School. (See http://bornthiswayfoundation.org.)

- All sorts of celebrity upstanders are making personal commitments to end genocide and crimes against humanity—governmental bullying of the highest degree—at the Enough Project (www.enoughproject.org). In 2011, students from ten high schools stood up for human rights in the "Child Soldiers and Bullying: Taking a Stand against Genocide and Hate" conference.

- Bullybust: Promoting a Community of Upstanders is a project by the National School Climate Center (www.schoolclimate .org/bullybust). It provides a "virtual wall" online where visitors can post thoughts and feelings.

- During the National Day of Silence, students across the country take a vow of silence to call attention to the silencing effect of anti-LGBTQ bullying and harassment in schools. (See www.dayofsilence.org.)

The next chapter is about other programs that help to interrupt and prevent bullying. But first, let's think about the fluidity of personal and interpersonal interaction.

Spiraling into Control

The idea of an upstander or a victim putting a stop to bullying is inspiring. In our society today, we see so many examples of situations spiraling out of control. Indeed, life is full of downward and upward spirals, and we do have the ability to shift directions.

The spiral is a compelling shape that shows up frequently in nature—in tornadoes and hurricanes, in the shape of a nautilus shell, and in the DNA molecule. There are five giant gyres in the world's oceans, made of spiraling currents of water.

We can live life on an upward spiral with good things getting better, or on a downward spiral with bad things getting worse. Sometimes people are caught in a downward draft that seems to swallow them up.

Yet at any point on the downward spiral, a positive change can occur—a new person or experience, a change of heart, a new choice, a "stroke of luck"—that will start a shift into an upward spiral.

When Kyle Rooker was in the eighth grade, the kids thought he was gay. He was pushed down the stairs at his school and urinated on. Bullying and name-calling continued for three years, until he decided enough was enough.

It started in sixth grade for Damian McGee-Backes, when a group of kids learned that he had two dads. By the eighth grade, fed up with being labeled a "faggot" and being assaulted, Damian was determined to fight back.

These two boys, along with four other students who had also been bullied and subjected to vile behavior, filed a lawsuit against their school district. As a result, the district took action to establish a comprehensive, district-wide plan to counter and prevent harassment of students perceived to be gay, lesbian, bisexual, or transgender.

Their courageous actions stopped the downward slide and opened the way for better lives—for upward spirals—for themselves and their classmates. At a standing-room-only ceremony to honor the six students, McGee-Backes said, "We are hearing from kids in the . . . district that there is no bullying."[5] Talk about *Zorgos*!

Downward Spirals Are Easy

Negative emotions and beliefs can trigger a damaging and self-perpetuating downward slide. Narrowing thoughts and actions fueled by repeated experiences of isolation and sadness can create a tightening inward and downward spiral, leading to further isolation, self-doubt, relationship struggles, and even suicide.

The trouble with a downward slide is that not just one person is affected. We are social creatures—our actions affect others and ripple through our communities. One child's downward spiral into bullying behavior can create an outward spiral of fear and negativity throughout the playground and the school. One young man makes a choice to commit a crime, and his whole family suffers. One adult in a position of power makes a selfish decision, and thousands can be affected.

Yet this happens all the time, as if things are "supposed to be" that way. And there's a reason for that. Taking a look at how our psyches process positivity and negativity reveals great insight into downward and outward spirals.

The Brain Tilts to Fear and Negativity

Have you ever noticed how a hundred people can give you a compliment, but the words of a single critic are what stick with you? We sometimes beat ourselves up for being too obsessed with the negative; yet this is a natural state we can sink into, unless we work hard to avoid it.

During the evolution of the human brain, a "negativity bias" developed that tilts toward survival and fear about dangers that could suddenly appear. In fact, the brain is designed to hold on to the bad stuff, and allow the good stuff to fade from memory. It is tilted *toward* anxiety and fear, and *against* personal happiness.

In order to level our internal playing field, it is essential that we counter the negative tilt of our brains. In order to help our children, we need to manage the negative messages of the media and the culture. We must declare—outwardly so it can be heard—an optimistic tilt toward the positive, toward good feelings, toward positive experiences.

The downward spiral is characterized by a depressive state with narrowed pessimistic thinking and ever-worsening moods that erode psychic energy. Abuse, adverse childhood experiences, and bullying can all fuel a downward slide that ensnarls aggressors and victims alike. Negative emotions weigh down the spirit and endanger psychological and physical health.

A Shift to Positivity

Positive emotions, even if they are fleeting, can tip the scales toward a flourishing life. In her book *Positivity*,[6] Barbara Fredrickson published the results of twenty-five years of groundbreaking research about positive emotions and overcoming negativity. This distinguished award-winning professor, at the forefront of the positive psychology movement, helps us to understand and embrace the hidden strength of positive emotions, to overcome negativity, and to thrive.

The Grand Purpose of Positive Emotions

Positivity is essential to health and happiness. Positive feelings help create more positive feelings, building to the point where good days can become the expected standard. Positive feelings can undo the damage of negativity and have far-reaching effects. When bad days happen, they are dealt with and resolved, so that life can return to the customary, positive tone. Positivity increases optimism and feelings of resourcefulness and resilience, and it can counter pain and trauma. Positive emotions can be life-giving.

There is convincing evidence that when life or safety is threatened, negative emotions narrow the scope of people's thinking and attention, sharpening their focus and preparing them for fight or flight.

Positive emotions, on the other hand, lead people to be more open, expansive, creative, and flexible. In other words, positivity broadens the scope of attention and opens us to more options.

Fredrickson's "Broaden-and-Build" theory describes how positive emotions evolved from the ancestral brain and how, today, they vitally shape people's health and well-being.

Increasing positive emotions creates an upward and outward spiral. Over time, positive emotions tend to become bigger, leading to increased frequency in the future, even developing a life of their own. At an interpersonal level, positive emotions increase trust and people's sense of "oneness" with those close to them. Upward spirals, in effect, are more social than downward spirals.

Positive emotions build a reservoir of self-esteem and resilience that sustains and strengthens, feeds the heart and soul, and acts as a buffer to reduce the impact of future distress. In other words, even though emotions are fleeting, the effect of positive emotions is cumulative and durable, and can fuel resilience.

Furthermore, upward spirals of positive emotions can undo negative emotions, offset downward spirals, and prevent a slide into an emotional/psychological vortex with painful consequences.

The 3-to-1 Ratio

The 3-to-1 (or 3:1) ratio is another one of Fredrickson's conclusions: *It takes a 3:1 ratio of positive to negative emotions over time to generate the elevating and expanding growth of the "Broaden-and-Build" theory.*

"We need three positive emotions to lift us up for every negative emotion that drags us down," states Fredrickson.[7] A steady stream of respectful, kind, encouraging words that build positive emotions can stop a downward spiral and activate an upward and outward spiral in most situations.

Going above the 3:1 ratio can "spark flourishing dynamics characterized by goodness, generativity, growth, and resilience," Fredrickson says. When people have lower than a 3:1 ratio of positive emotions to negative emotions, however, they don't function optimally but instead may feel distressed, impaired, and unfulfilled.

Positive emotions appear to "undo" or dismantle the body's fight-or-flight reaction, and make a reasoned response more likely. When something bad occurs, countering it with three times as much comfort and soothing can actually halt a downward slide and even undo negativity in the process. Every parent knows that comforting a crying child is crucial to soothe the pain, begin the healing, and get back to normal. So it is with bullying behavior as children grow older. Encouraging positive thoughts and feelings will increase a child's ability to rationally deal with negative experiences.

Self-Generating Positive Emotions

But what happens when we just don't feel positive? Fredrickson teaches us that it's possible to self-generate positive emotions in the face of negativity—to soothe, encourage, comfort, and support ourselves. In fact, this skill is an active ingredient for resilient coping, an important factor in preventing bullying. It's nice when someone says or does something to uplift our spirits, but it's not necessary to wait and hope for that to happen. Learning how to generate our own positive emotions can put us in charge of our moods—and therefore our happiness.

There are many ways to lift our spirits, to turn negative energy around. Sports and physical activity, music, dancing, singing, good conversation, mindfulness exercises (a form of meditation)—all of these things can help set a positive tone for problem solving.

As you might guess, this has everything to do with interrupting bullying. Positive kindness and being mindful of others can stop bullying in its tracks. Give kids tools to calm their brains and bodies, let them experience kindness and connection firsthand, and you set them on a positive spiral upward.

Positive emotions help youngsters and adults alike to become more resilient—able to bounce back from adversity, ward off negativity, and continue to grow.

Upward and Outward Spirals

Simply put, positive emotions expand people's mindsets in ways that, little by little, literally reshape who they are.

Children tend to have a lot of positive emotions, and their delight and joy bring amusement and positive emotions to parents. When children feel safe, they reach outward and become expansive by broadening and exploring.

All the positive emotions parents share with their children—through respecting, nurturing, playing, laughing, being silly—cultivate trust and attunement (a harmonious and responsive relationship). Positive emotions build a reservoir of self-esteem and resilience that sustains, strengthens, and fuels the heart and soul. In other words, even though emotions are fleeting, the effect of positive emotions is cumulative and durable and can fuel resilience. Positive emotions can act as buffers to reduce future distress.

Furthermore, behavior is an expression of how people feel about themselves. Kids who bully are taking their anger and other negative feelings out on others. When kids are feeling good, they're not likely to hurt others—or themselves.

Positive feelings can interrupt negative feelings, therefore, and keep us on a path toward strong mental, emotional, and physical health.

Eyes on the Prize: Mental and Emotional Health

Nature's goal for human growth is for the eventual maturation of a self-motivated, self-regulated, and self-reliant adult.

—DR. GABOR MATÉ

Everyone wants authentic happiness, mental health, and well-being for themselves and their children, but few have learned how to achieve it. What do those few who have figured it out know that others don't? What makes it seem easy for some parents to put their children on the right road? What does it mean to be mentally healthy?

Mental or emotional health refers to how you feel about yourself, your ability to manage your feelings and deal with difficulties, and the quality of your relationships. Generally, it describes your overall well-being.

Just as not feeling bad is very different from feeling good, good mental health is much more than *just* the absence of mental illness. The ability to manage one's thoughts, emotions, and impulses is referred to as *self-regulation*.

Characteristics of People with Good Mental and Emotional Health
We are all human, and we have all had struggles in life that kept us from flourishing. No one has all the characteristics of good mental health all of the time. But the following list describes characteristics of people who seem able to participate in life to the fullest extent possible.

1. They have self-confidence and self-esteem.
2. They are able to manage their feelings.
3. They have the ability to build and maintain strong and close relationships.
4. They feel content with themselves and comfortable with others.
5. They have a zest for living and can laugh and have fun.
6. They respect themselves and others.
7. They are able to handle disappointments.
8. They can deal with stress, meet life's demands, and bounce back from adversity.
9. They make their own decisions and create balance between work and play, activity and rest.
10. They shape their environment whenever possible, and adjust to it when necessary.
11. They enjoy a sense of meaning and purpose in their activities and in their relationships.
12. They are flexible and open to learning new things, and adapt to change when it occurs.

Presuming that adults with good mental health can raise children with good mental health, let's look at how, exactly, these people parent their kids.

Key Qualities of Parents and Teachers Who Prevent Bullying in Children

During decades of research, psychologist Dan Olweus found a set of key qualities of the adults in school and home environments that prevent bullying problems in youngsters:

- They convey warmth and positive interest.
- They set firm limits for unacceptable behavior.
- They use discipline positively and consistently when dealing with unacceptable behaviors and rule violations.

- They are positive role models who act as authorities responsible for the child's development, including social relationships.

Parents have the authority to make rules—"Don't run into the street," for example—to ensure the survival, safety, and positive development of their children. Children need parents to be authorities, since they are often unable to make good decisions for themselves. When parents don't know how to use their authority wisely, kids are more likely to become bullies.

When, on the other hand, parents *do* use their authority to teach children and guide them in a positive direction, children's personal assertiveness increases, along with their confidence. Parents who are comfortable with authority know how and when to gradually turn it over to their children as they are ready for it.

Assertiveness and other pro-social skills are common traits of strong and confident adults and kids who know how to interact without being aggressive or passive. These skills can be learned at any time, and are the foundation for the win-win communication style of parents who are good leaders. (For more about these skills, see chapters 13, 14, and 15.)

What Every Child Needs to Be Physically, Mentally, and Emotionally Healthy

Promoting a child's emotional health is the most successful approach available to fighting violence.

— DR. BRUCE PERRY

It is easy for parents to identify physical needs: nutritious food, clothes, and bedtime at a reasonable hour. However, a child's mental and emotional needs may not be as obvious. Good mental health allows children to think clearly, become socially competent, and learn new skills. Additionally, positive relationships with adults, good friends, and encouraging words are important for helping children develop self-confidence, high self-esteem, and a healthy emotional outlook on life.

Mental health and emotional well-being are shaped by one's experiences. Early childhood experiences are especially significant.

The Essential Core Strengths for Healthy Development

The last chapter mentioned award-winning child psychiatrist and author Dr. Bruce Perry and his ideas about what contributes to a culture of violence. Perry, a leading expert on children's mental health, child maltreatment, neurological development, and youth violence, details six core strengths that are essential in order for kids to become respectful, resilient, and socially and emotionally healthy. These strengths build on one another. When children do not develop these core strengths, problems inevitably follow. This chapter on interrupting bullying concludes with a peek at these core strengths, since ways to teach them will make up the third part of this book.

1. Attachment

Attachment is the capacity to develop and maintain healthy emotional relationships. A child's attachment bond with his or her parents is crucial and foundational to all other strengths. This powerful connection helps the child to love, to learn empathy, and to choose friends wisely.

Attachment is the primary love bond that sets the tone for all future relationships. It helps prevent aggression and antisocial behaviors.

When there are attachment problems, children tend to withdraw, act out, feel isolated, and have few friends. They are at an even greater risk when they are exposed to violence. If empathy is not developed, bullying can follow.

2. Self-Regulation

Self-regulation involves pausing between an impulse and an action. This is necessary throughout life for self-confidence and success.

Help your children to think before they act; mindfulness can help them turn knee-jerk reactions into deliberate responses. (For more about mindfulness, see chapter 12.) Also, delaying gratification (e.g., "Not now, dear") may frustrate children, but it helps them develop self-regulation and patience.

Children with self-regulation problems (such as some kids with AD/HD) are reactive and impulsive and can unintentionally hurt others. They are easily overwhelmed by threats and violence.

3. Affiliation

Affiliation refers to the ability to form relationships, to join in. It starts from strong emotional bonds with family, then with others. Every child needs good friends. Support your child's affiliation by helping them nurture strong and positive relationships. Children with affiliation problems have difficulty forming friendships, and their fear and social pain can be turned inward (resulting in depression and self-loathing) or outward (resulting in aggression and violence).

4. Awareness

Awareness is being considerate of others—being tuned in to their needs, interests, and values, and being able to see their strengths. Help children move from "me" to "we" by being attentive to the values and needs of others. Awareness is best taught and modeled by adults, who look for strengths and qualities in those who are different, and include them in activities to break down prejudices. Youngsters with awareness problems can be self-absorbed and have immature thinking and stereotypical prejudices. They are likely to exclude others, tease, and act in mean or violent ways.

5. Tolerance

Tolerance refers to accepting differences in people, finding out how they are unique, and being flexible and adaptive. The Golden Rule helps teach tolerance and respect for others. Parents teach this most effectively by modeling it in their own behavior (e.g., not making comments about those who are different, not using derogatory slurs, treating neighborhood kids and classmates with equal respect, etc.). Children with tolerance problems are likely to tease, lash out, bully, and be violent. They also tend to intimidate and exclude others.

6. Respect

Respect is at the heart of caring and is an essential part of *Zorgos*. Respect means appreciating the worth of oneself and others. Respect replaces fear. If you treat your children with respect, holding them in high regard, they learn self-respect, self-worth, and self-acceptance. Make respect for the rights of others a fundamental value in your family. Children with respect problems tend to be fearful and quick to criticize. Because they don't respect others, they cannot respect themselves, and this can develop into a lifelong issue that robs them of love and satisfying relationships. Parents who lay the foundation for a stable, caring family full of empathy and compassion foster respect and resilience, and raise socially and emotionally healthy youngsters who will not bully.

. . .

6

• • • •

Toward a Bully-Free Culture

If there's one goal . . . it's to dispel the myth that bullying is just a harmless rite of passage or an inevitable part of growing up. It's not.

— PRESIDENT BARACK OBAMA

In a recent student workshop designed to create a community of upstanders at one middle school, participants all gathered on one side of the room. There was a line down the middle of the floor. The facilitator called out a statement, and those who identified with it would cross the line to the other side.

- "I was born in another country."
- "My parents are not together."
- "I have been in a fight."
- "Someone close to me died this year."
- "I have seen someone die."

When the facilitator read the sentence "I have a family member who has been to jail," all of the remaining students crossed the line.

This exercise was a way for students to build empathy and understanding for one another without needing to have a face-to-face conversation. The students in this group had been selected by teachers as potential leaders because they always seemed to be in the middle of the action in a school known in the district as being a "school of hard knocks."

"Climate change" is on all of our minds these days. When we talk about "school climate," however, we are actually talking about "school culture." Bullying exists where an environment supports it. A culture is a collective agreement about what behaviors are accepted, expected, or considered normal. Cultures vary from country to country, city to city, church to church, school to school, class to class, and family to family. School, community, and family climates or cultures overlap.

This chapter focuses on the big picture—how parents, schools, and communities can work together to create a more respectful, child-friendly, bully-free culture, both in and out of school. Joining hands—with other adults and kids—is more powerful and effective than pointing fingers.

The Three Tiers of Prevention

An ounce of prevention is worth a pound of cure.

—BENJAMIN FRANKLIN

The skills for good mental and emotional health are best learned early on in life—before too many mistakes, bad choices, pain, and suffering occur. That is why prevention is crucial, especially from birth to age five.

There are three "tiers" to prevention that, when understood by families and society, can save a lot of "tears" down the road. Primary, secondary, and tertiary prevention are what the experts call them, but using the language of medicine, we will call them the following:

1. **Building immunity to bullying.** The saying "As the twig is bent, so grows the tree," illustrates primary prevention. Parents and teachers who nurture, protect, play, and guide a child's developmental stages are investing in future well-being.

2. **Remedies for bullying.** The saying "Nip it in the bud," describes secondary prevention. When caring adults notice behaviors that open the door to the bullying dynamic, they can intervene and redirect. Schools, mental health professionals, and community programs are essential for this tier, since it's often a signal that parents need a little help and/or support.

3. **Recovery from bullying.** If there is a saying for after bullying

has occurred, it's "Today is the first day of the rest of your life." When a kid gets to juvenile hall, it is often too late to undo what was done. Life is now about repair: picking up the pieces, dealing with the consequences, and trying to mend the damage. This is the realm of doctors, lawyers, police officers, courtrooms, and social workers.

Anti-Bullying Programs

Most bullying occurs in environments with lots of children, and most groups of kids are found in schools. This chapter presents some of the programs schools are implementing to change the school culture. We've organized these programs in light of the three tiers of prevention.

Anti-bullying programs can take many different forms. Some are created by teachers, students, or parents; others are available "out of the box" complete with materials, curricula, and expert training. Some cost nothing, and some cost hundreds or thousands of dollars.

Not all programs are equally effective, and it's important that parents who advocate for the implementation of a certain program in their school or community seek programs that are evidence-based, that is, the program is based on research, has been independently tested, and has shown positive results.

Programs That Build Bullying Immunity (Primary)

Primary prevention stops problems before they start. Parents, more than anyone, are perfectly positioned for primary prevention. They have the opportunity—and responsibility—to nurture and care for children at the beginning of their lives, and to set them on the path to a wholesome and fulfilling future. Taking care of children's needs and promoting emotional health throughout their childhood is *the most effective approach to preventing violence.*

A new study links maternal nurturing with healthy brain development. Preschool children whose parents love and nurture them have better-developed brains when they reach school age than other children. This very powerful evidence has tremendous implications for public health.[1]

Parents who are loving and nurturing are engaging in primary prevention, proactively growing strong and confident children who are on a positive life trajectory.

The following are some notable programs that support primary prevention.

Olweus Bullying Prevention Program (OBPP)

This "gold standard" of evidence-based bullying prevention programs is actually both a primary (prevention) and a secondary (intervention) program. It's used in thousands of K–12 schools, and has over thirty-five years of research behind it. *OBPP* is a whole-school program that provides a blueprint and guidance for system-wide change. Based on studies on aggression and the bully/victim dynamic that date back to the 1970s, it was developed by Dan Olweus, a distinguished Swedish psychologist and researcher whom we quote widely in this book. His work has played a key role in the mindshift occurring in many countries—from seeing bullying as a natural part of school life to seeing it as a solvable social issue.

OBPP starts with a school-wide questionnaire that provides ways to plan and gather resources, and it is followed by certification of the staff. Trainings and support are provided at the individual, classroom, school, and community levels. This program has been proven to prevent and reduce bullying in countries all over the world.

OBPP recommends the following simple list of four rules pertaining to bullying:

- We will not bully others.
- We will try to help students who are bullied.
- We will try to include students who are left out.
- If we know that somebody is being bullied, we will tell an adult at school and an adult at home.[2]

Harlem Children's Zone's Baby College

"One of the most ambitious social-service experiments of our time," to quote the *New York Times*,[3] the Harlem Children's Zone Project is a unique, holistic approach to primary prevention, rebuilding a community, and changing the culture. It promotes an enriched, educational, and supportive environment to counter the "toxic popular culture that glorifies misogyny and antisocial behavior" in a one-hundred-block area of Harlem.[4]

The Baby College begins with a two-month workshop for expectant parents and others with young children up to the age of three. These free programs bolster a strong foundation for educational success during the critically important first years. Over the past two years, this program has taught almost one thousand parents positive discipline skills (verbal correction, not physical punishment) and the importance of reading to their children.

This program has been so successful in strengthening a community that it is being replicated by inner cities throughout the continent. The truth is, this project mimics independent communities everywhere that support a safe, nurturing environment for mothers and babies. Some health providers offer pregnancy, birth, and parenting classes. New parents anywhere can seek out classes and join or start mothering co-ops that bring in experienced parents and experts who can teach them what they need to learn.

Tribes

Schools that build social skills and teach community building have less bullying than schools that don't. One of the oldest and most successful of these programs is Tribes, which originally had children create mini-communities within the classroom. Activities in class meetings and morning circles build trust and respect among teachers and students. Tribes Learning Communities create a culture in which inclusion, respect, collaboration, and taking responsibility are upheld by everyone.

Safe & Caring Schools

The Safe & Caring Schools program is designed so that teachers can easily incorporate social and emotional learning (SEL) into daily academic instruction for children in pre-K through eighth grade. The program's fun and exciting activities build self-awareness, social awareness, relationship skills, and responsible decision making. When children have better skills in these areas, bullying, harassment, and violence decrease, and academic success can be the focus. One superintendent writes, "A particular advantage we see from our use of SEL is the time it saves teachers and frees them up to do more instruction. This is because of what we do to promote the kids as decision makers and problem solvers."[5]

Squash Circles

In the absence of school-wide standards, many kids experience how some teachers create a culture of calm while others allow chaos into their classrooms. One clever teacher invented a unique structure for conflict resolution with the help of her kindergarten students.

The classic preschool rule "Use your words and not your fists" teaches children to think before they act. But using words is difficult when you don't know how!

"I kept seeing conflicts arise on the [school] yard and in the classroom among both boys and girls," said Stacey Norman, Louise's granddaughter's kindergarten teacher. "I blurted out one day, 'Well, let's squash this problem,' and it stuck. Silly term, I know, but the kids love it and connect with it."

Norman had noticed children fare better in conflicts if they are able to express themselves to their peers and feel they are genuinely being heard. "I quickly realized that well-intentioned, teacher/adult intervention was quite useless, as they tend to just talk at children and tell them what their problem is, rather than encourage kids to discover and solve the problem on their own. Putting words in the kids' mouths, and putting adult perceptions on a conflict, always seemed to cripple a child's ability to truly solve the problem at hand."

She provided her students with a common language and simple techniques for when they felt wronged. The children sit in a large circle—a "Squash Circle"—and raise their hands if they want to "squash" a problem with a classmate. One child then calls on a child he or she felt wronged by. The two stand in the middle and begin the scripted dialogue:

Victim: "I didn't like it when you (called me a name, hit
me with a ball, stepped on my toe)."

Aggressor: "I'm sorry. What can I do to make you feel better?"

The victim responds with suggestions appropriate to the situation—be it, "Could you play with me tomorrow?" or "Tell my toe it's going to be okay."

When the children feel they have "squashed" their problem successfully, everyone claps their hands and shouts, "Squashed!" The process usually ends with a hug. The kids in Mrs. Norman's class can take these problem-solving skills with them throughout school and life, using them to create upward spirals wherever they go.

Roots of Empathy

Because families tend to be smaller these days, many children miss out on the opportunity to get acquainted with babies and learn how their brains work. A unique award-winning program makes this connection possible in classrooms.

Founded in 1996, Roots of Empathy is a classroom program that measurably reduces levels of aggression among school children, while increasing empathy and raising social and emotional competence. During the school year, a loving neighborhood mother of an infant is selected to make three forty-minute visits to a classroom of five- to eight-year-olds with her baby. A trained instructor guides the children as they observe the mother-infant relationship, identifying and coming to understand the baby's intentions and emotions. These interactions help young students identify and reflect on their own feelings, as well as the feelings of others. Research on this program shows an increase in kindness and other pro-social behaviors, and a significant decrease in aggression. Called "Canada's olive branch to the world," Roots of Empathy has been adopted on three continents and continues to expand.

In Scandinavian countries where bullying prevention programs were instated decades ago, it is now the norm for older children to routinely spend time with younger children, which helps build understanding and caring, and lessens the isolation of each age group.

Many American schools have "Reading Buddy" programs, where a higher-grade class will "adopt" a lower-grade class and spend some time each month reading to the younger students. This promotes literacy at both ends of the spectrum, and it bonds younger and older students together to strengthen the cultural fabric of a school.

Enrichment Programs
Traditional programs and activities such as school bands and choirs, sports groups, dance groups, student government, and drama clubs have helped youth build social skills for decades. With a common focus on a collective goal, children's attention is elevated from the emotional drama of bullying dynamics. They are provided a chance to socialize and build trust in a supervised environment. Especially in the arts, children can work out their emotional issues without acting them out. The fact that bullying has increased during a time when art and music programs have been cut from school budgets is no coincidence.

Community Programs
Community programs tend to promote positive youth development as well. After-school programs, scouting groups, service activities, and church groups all provide opportunities for children to develop healthy social skills.

Big Brothers, Big Sisters is a model program that nurtures children and strengthens communities. For over one hundred years, this mentoring program has helped youngsters ten to sixteen years of age realize their potential and build their future.

Youngsters need continued exposure to positive experiences, settings, and people to help them to learn and develop life skills, positive assets, and qualities, and to continually discover new opportunities for themselves.

Programs That Build Remedies for Bullying (Secondary)
When we get sick, we need medicine. When bullying happens, we need secondary prevention to intervene, to fill in the pieces that earlier opportunities missed, and to restore emotional health. Like medicine, intervention is essential to keep things from getting worse. Patterns of

bullying and victimization may be established as early as ages five and six. Child-care providers and preschool teachers, therefore, can have a powerful influence on children's development, redirecting negative behaviors before they blossom into problems, and teaching positive behaviors and interactions when the moment is ripe. The school programs we look at in this section are of the intervention type, focusing on smaller groups of students who missed developmental steps and perhaps are already on a rocky path.

Bully Guards

When the locker of a fifteen-year-old San Antonio high school freshman was broken into, sprayed with deodorant, and his shoes stolen, the school counselor was alerted to trouble. During her investigation, she learned that the student was being taunted and teased in class and at the bus stop. Approaching the bullies didn't work; they blamed the boy for "crying to the counselor."

While brainstorming on "some compassionate muscle," the counselor had an epiphany. She asked the high school football coach to recommend some players to help her out. Three seniors agreed. They memorized the fifteen-year-old boy's schedule, met him after each class, and walked with him to his next class.

"He was so by himself," eighteen-year-old right guard Ryder Burke said compassionately. "Us three [football players] were already great friends and . . . he just got tossed into the mix."

The freshman, who was also struggling with adjusting to a new language and new culture, outgrew his shyness and was able to adapt to the school, thanks to the seniors' kindness. The counselor's epiphany grew into a successful program using peers as allies to solve problems. Three months after she called the coach, the bullying of the freshman had been stopped so effectively that the Bully Guard program expanded to a dozen football players who guarded four more besieged freshmen. For the next school year, eighteen Bully Guards had already signed up to protect eight incoming freshmen.[6]

Safe School Ambassadors (SSA)

In the wake of the 1999 student massacre at Columbine High School outside Denver, Colorado, an organization that studies school violence designed a program to keep such a thing from happening again. Safe School Ambassadors are chosen from the socially influential leaders of a school's various cliques and groups, then trained to calm potentially explosive situations before they escalate. The thinking behind this program is that students have a better sense of what and where the problems are than the adults do, and that bystanders can and should be empowered to influence their school culture. SSAs are trained in powerful, nonviolent communication and intervention skills, which are modeled for other students. The SSA program has been implemented in approximately 1,000 elementary, middle, and high schools in thirty-two states. Safe School Ambassadors is a project of Community Matters.[7]

Trauma-Sensitive Schools
A new approach to bullying is getting to the root of the problem in a handful of schools across the nation. It's based on two principles that underlie much of our children's bad behavior.

1. Adverse childhood experiences (ACEs) create severe and chronic trauma that causes emotional stress.
2. Stress traps kids in a *fight, flight, or freeze* mode of survival, which physically damages the developing brain, making learning difficult or impossible.

Jim Sporeleder, a principal at an alternative high school in Washington State, learned about ACEs and then attended a lecture by John Medina, author of *Brain Rules*. After twenty-five years of practicing "discipline with dignity," Sporeleder said that a lightbulb went off in his head. He suddenly understood that *punishing misbehavior just doesn't work.* "You're simply adding trauma to an already traumatized kid." At his high school, he initiated a new approach to school discipline—and the suspension rate dropped by 85 percent.

Here is an example of his approach: When a student swears at a teacher, instead of giving an automatic suspension, the principal sits the teen down and says quietly, "Wow. Are you okay? This doesn't sound like you. What's going on?" He gets even more specific: "You really look stressed. On a scale of one to ten, where are you with your anger?"

In most cases, this respectful and caring inquiry disarms the teen, who then feels free to talk about the problems he's having. Perhaps his father is an alcoholic, causing trouble at home. The teen feels listened to and realizes he shouldn't have blown up at the teacher. In most cases, he goes back and apologizes to her, without any prompting from the principal.

Natalie Turner, from Washington State University's Area Health Education Center and an expert in creating trauma-free schools, explains: "Teens who live with complex trauma are walking post-traumatic stress time bombs. The smallest incident can push them into a full-blown meltdown. Some kids run away. Some explode in rage. Some just mentally check out. In flight, fight, or freeze mode, survival trumps everything else."[8] In such "Trauma-sensitive schools," "Trauma-informed classrooms," "Compassionate schools," or "Safe and supportive schools," adults have accepted the proven fact that kids who are experiencing the toxic stress of severe and chronic trauma cannot focus on learning.

It's not that bad behavior has no consequences in these schools; it's just that punishment is no longer one of those consequences. Principals and teachers learn how to make a child feel safe, and then those children can make better choices. With positive, caring adults to help them, these teens continue to build their resilience and their character.

The climate in these schools is based on acceptance, caring, and honesty. Kids talk about their ACE trauma scores, and they learn that "Resilience trumps ACEs." Their ability to regulate their emotions has improved dramatically, interactions are more subdued, and emotional explosions and suspensions are far fewer.

Recovering from Bullying (Tertiary)

Picking up the pieces after bullying can be a very difficult process requiring therapy and legal action. The harsh truth is that many children who have been victims of bullying become bullies them-selves, and sometimes end up in the criminal justice system. There are new programs that work toward healing the wounds of bullying.

Restorative Justice

Used around the world to heal wounds caused by crime, violence, and even genocide and civil war, Restorative Justice is a new way of think-ing that is currently being adopted in schools, as well as in prisons and with child welfare issues. The intention of Restorative Justice is to keep communities whole, which can be difficult for the victim at first, but ultimately rewarding.

When a toy or tool is borrowed and then broken, a friendship can also be broken, and in a functional community, elaborate steps are taken to repair and apologize for harm after it has occurred. Restorative Justice operates under the same principle, giving bullies a chance to repair the damage they have caused. For example, if a child steals a lunchbox and destroys it, the child's family is asked to replace the lunchbox. Furthermore, the child who took the lunchbox might make lunch for his or her target and deliver it with an apology. Another great example is if a child spreads a rumor online, he or she must then distribute a retraction and an apology through the same channels, in addition to a personal apology.

Restorative Justice is more effective than punishment in rehabili-tating bullies and repairing relationships. It creates a space where vic-tims are empowered to confront their bullies, and bullies are required to listen and take true responsibility. With a full understanding of what they have done, the children who have bullied (along with their families) may take steps toward eliminating their violent behavior, thawing out numbed feelings of sadness, weakness, and shame. They learn empathy in the process, and try to find what drove their cruelty. When bullies are confronted with the consequences of their actions and beliefs, they often change.

Schools are now offering Restorative Justice as an alternative to expulsion, suspension, or other consequences. Teachers like this con-cept because so often they are put in the position of punishing a bully only to find another issue is at the root of the problem. A common feeling among teachers is "I don't want the bullies to be punished; I want them to change their behavior."

Justice can be restored through art, drama (writing and acting), dialogue, letter writing, chores, replacing what was lost or broken, or whatever other activity suits the situation. It can be more time-consuming than punishment, and in many cases a trained expert is required, since sometimes the parents of bullies and victims need mediation as well.

Anti-Bullying Policies

Central to any bullying intervention program is the establishment of rules and policies. Does your child's school already have an anti-bullying policy? All states now have laws requiring such policies, so learn what is available. Get involved in the PTA or another parent organization.

Does your child's school have a progressive discipline policy? This means a clear, step-by-step policy of consequences that increase in severity. For example, level one might list problems such as talking on a cell phone during class, which might result in the teacher taking the phone away for the day. Level three might include a list of behaviors that would call for expulsion.

Notice whether the policy is punitive or encouraging. The Center on Positive Behavioral Interventions & Supports, sponsored by the U.S. Department of Education, acknowledges that punishment, "including reprimands, loss of privileges, office referrals, suspensions, and expulsions," is ineffective according to a description of the program that appears on its website, "especially when it is used inconsistently and in the absence of other positive strategies." Instead, "teaching behavioral expectations and rewarding students for following them is a much more positive approach than waiting for misbehavior to occur before responding."[9]

Peer mediation or conflict resolution programs can teach children important problem-solving skills. It is desirable for schools to have these programs, as they can be appropriate and helpful for dealing with issues involving shared responsibility and equal power. Unfortunately, they are not adequate for dealing with bullying. Bullying is characterized by a power imbalance in which one party is more responsible than the other. Bullying should not be put on the same level as other disputes; treating it as such actually normalizes bullying.

The Politics of Policies

If your school does have a bullying policy, read it and talk to parents and teachers to find out if it is effective. Is it detailed? Is it meaningful? Is it consistently upheld by all teachers? As mentioned earlier, because of their religious beliefs some parents are suspicious of anti-bullying programs and policies that specifically prohibit anti-LGBT speech. But these are some of the most dangerous and pervasive bullying behaviors.

There are many downsides to zero-tolerance bullying policies. Often these policies are in place in schools that have few programs set up to help the child who bullies. These policies, originally designed to prevent weapons in the school, can sometimes be misused.

Bullying policies can also be enforced haphazardly. Check around to see how your school implements them. Are policies or rules (like the Olweus rules, above) posted in every classroom? Can students recite any of them? Does every adult at the school consistently enforce them? Or do some teachers make exceptions for their favorite students, letting those students routinely break school rules?

The bottom line: Is there a caring climate at your child's school? Look closely for answers to this question. Your school may seem like a cheerful place where kids dress nicely and their parents have good jobs. But is it a school where popularity drives social interaction? Is it a school where negative pop culture icons are embraced? Do children bring the "cute nasty" tone of TV shows and pop music into the classroom? Is it a place where it is okay to put others down, or do adults or other students step in?

A Caring School Climate

The ideal school is a place where all teachers see all students as "my students." It is a place where adults speak to all students, connect with them, and correct their behavior. In these caring schools, teachers can be responsive to the needs of the students without having their hands tied behind their backs by school or district policies. In the competitive, punitive atmosphere of educational funding programs that, in many cases, ignore the needs of teachers, achieving such a caring environment has become increasingly difficult. Teachers need time to prepare, collaborate, and grade work, and are increasingly expected to do so with inadequate pay and funding. Teachers also need smaller class sizes—particularly in lower grades—so they can give proper attention to each student.

Competitive Environments

In the workplace, a "tough management style" often isn't recognized as bullying, but a highly competitive environment can encourage abusive behaviors. Even positive consequences like promotions and bonuses can reinforce bullying in cutthroat atmospheres.

When you walk into your school's office area, do you see football trophies and cheerleading photos posted prominently? Does the school also highlight honor roll students and pass out bumper stickers to only these parents? All of these things are traditional positive reinforcements, but they also turn children into status symbols. Does your child's school celebrate *all* of its children, or only the "stars"? Start a conversation about this and look for solutions. Unbalanced power relationships are the cornerstone of bullying.

A Culture of Respect

Without feelings of respect, what is there to distinguish men from beasts?

— CONFUCIUS

There are many forms of respect: respect for parents, for children, for teachers, for elders, for diversity, for other's differences, for authority, for the earth. There is respect for human rights, for boundaries and laws, for values and customs, for beliefs and religions, for property, and for privacy. Respect is the first step on the path toward a more child-friendly, bully-free culture. Children first learn respect when they are treated respectfully by their parents and the other important adults in their lives. They learn *self*-respect—which is a source of self-worth and mental health—and respect for others. People with self-respect and respect for others are better members of family and society, and can be better friends. They also have the greatest possibility for happiness, satisfaction, and joy in life. Youngsters who have learned respect are aware of the feelings and needs of others.

Unfortunately, in many ways, disrespect has become the norm in our society. Tone of voice, body language (e.g., eye-rolling and offensive gestures), behaviors like slamming doors, and vulgar words—notably on the Internet, especially when the writer is anonymous—all convey a casual disrespect. It's difficult to know how our "respect deficit disorder" came about, but it is both reflected in and perpetuated by our sources of entertainment. Compare, for example, the language of Jane Austen's popular novels of a few centuries ago, where young men and women are elaborately careful not to cause anyone distress, with any of today's sitcoms, where put-downs and mean humor are accompanied by canned laughter.

Teachers often have to endure the common disrespect of students, with bullying and high-tech toys making classroom management a challenging and painful part of the school day.

Creating Expectations of Respect

Lightly create the mindset of positivity—be open, be appreciative, be curious, be kind, but above all, be real.

— DR. BARBARA FREDRICKSON

So many positive things begin with respect—holding others in high regard, honoring them, admiring them, and showing consideration for them, as well as having healthy self-esteem. We pay our respects when someone dies, but that's not enough; people need to be respected every day. Respect is one of our deepest psychological needs, and its absence is the root of our deepest troubles. One respectful relationship can multiply into many, spiraling out into our communities.

It's important to know how your school teaches respect, and to reinforce these methods and rules at home. This consistency between school and home simplifies kids' lives and strengthens them. As an example of these mutual expectations and responsibilities, here is a rules poster from Sequoia Elementary School in Oakland, California:

Respect Yourself and Others at All Times!

1. **Respect** the personal space and belongings of others.
   * Keep your hands, feet, and *all* body parts to yourself.
   * Aggressive behavior, fighting, and/or play fighting is not tolerated.

2. **Respect** the personal beliefs of *all* people.
   * Racial and homophobic slurs are not tolerated.
   * Bullying—physical or verbal—is not tolerated.

3. **Respect** *all* school and personal property.

4. **Respect** each other's property. Students must leave toys, cell phones, and *all* electronic equipment at home.

5. **Respect** your health and the environment. Students may not bring junk food to school.

Busting Myths about Respect

Unfortunately, the word *respect* can be twisted with a different meaning in the bullying dynamic. Here are some misconceptions about respect:

- **Respect can be demanded or forced.** Respect and fear are different; do not confuse the two.

- **Respect must be fought for.** Like trust, respect is freely given and received; it can also be earned.

- **Respect can be manufactured.** You can't respect others if you don't respect yourself.

- **Respect means having power over another.** True respect shares power; it does not dominate.

- **Respect must be earned.** In friendly relationships, respect is freely bestowed; this is an unwritten standard of positive social interactions. People are treated as valuable, important beings.

Respectful Communication and Conflict

From the first week they began living together, Kristen's husband insisted that they use "please" and "thank you" during the smallest interactions. At first this upset Kristen, since she assumed in a respectful relationship, "please" is implied when you say something like, "Hand me that towel." But she respected his wish. Two years, five years, and ten years down the road, she could fully appreciate this habit that had been woven into the fabric of their relationship. As years go by, it's easy to forget your manners. And in families, where the wheels must keep turning for years on end, manners are like the grease that keeps all the parts moving smoothly without stress or damage.

Respectful communication is easy when everyone wants the same thing. But bad feelings, bad behavior, bullying, and violence happen more easily when there is some sort of conflict. Assertiveness training helps prepare us for when this happens.

Assertive communication—which includes talking about and managing feelings, asking for what we want, and saying "no" to what we don't want—is the basis for respectful relationships. Assertiveness skills help targets of bullying behavior to appreciate and tap into their own inner strengths, to value themselves and realize that they deserve to be treated with respect, and to become more confident and avoid being the target of bullies in the future.

Assertiveness Training

Why does assertiveness training both interrupt and prevent bullying and victimization? Several studies have found the following reasons:

- Assertiveness is based on self-esteem, which increases with increased successful interactions.

- Assertiveness training is a process of learning to stand up for your rights without violating the rights of others, taking into account the other person's feelings. It is not negative confrontation.

- Assertiveness training emphasizes self-expression of one's feelings, beliefs, and opinions in socially acceptable ways; it is particularly appropriate at the beginning of adolescence.
- Assertiveness training can improve social skills and emotional health and well-being, enhance self-concept and locus of control, and lower self-abasement.
- Assertiveness training improves social coping skills, modifies aggressive behavior, and helps to prevent adolescents from using alcohol, tobacco, and other drugs.
- Assertiveness develops responsibility and a sense of personal power.
- Assertiveness skills enhance personal relationships and interactions between people.
- Assertive skills turn bystanders into upstanders.
- Assertiveness and other social and emotional skills can be like a vaccine and a remedy for the epidemic of mean and cruel behaviors of all kinds.

Children who learn assertiveness skills in elementary school enter middle school less likely to be bullies, victims, or passive bystanders.

Assertiveness is such a large part of positive parenting that we've devoted a whole chapter to it (chapter 14). Let's move on now to part 3, where we will learn more about positive parenting.

· · ·

Positive Parenting for a Bully-Free World

*It isn't enough to bring up children happy and secure;
you need to provide a decent world for them.*

— DR. BENJAMIN SPOCK

Positive parenting is about strengthening families and developing character, competence, and resilience in children. It's about fostering the astonishing transformation of a helpless infant into a capable and confident adult. Positive parenting focuses on helping kids discover what they are capable of, and actualize their potential through encouragement and empowerment. Positive parenting places them on a positive trajectory of confidence, service, autonomy, and healthy relationships and well-being.

Part 3 is about building children's "emotional immune system" in order to prepare them and protect them from aggression and bullying. It discusses pro-social skills and other life skills that reduce and even eliminate risks, increase resilience, and help youngsters flourish.

The important, overarching concepts of part 3 are

• balance

• a developmental trajectory

• developing resilient capabilities

Balance

*When the body is not disturbed by hunger, thirst, pain, or illness,
and when the mind is not disturbed by threat, frustration, or rejection,
then most people settle into their resting state, a sustainable
equilibrium in which the body refuels and repairs itself and the
mind feels peaceful, happy, and loving.*

— RICK HANSON, *YOUR WISE BRAIN* BLOG

Our bodies have wisdom. They let us know what there is too much or too little of in our lives. They let us know when it is time to drink, eat, put on a sweater, or go to the bathroom. Bodies strive to maintain and regulate a stable internal environment known as homeostasis.

In terms of parenting, balance is the key to equanimity, ease, and flow.

- We need to protect—not too little, and not too much.

- We need to nurture—not too little, and not too much.

- We need to give attention—not too little, and not too much.

- We need to balance self-care with caring for our family.

To have balance means to have a happy medium between too little and too much. Balance represents the optimal degree or amount that best fits your ends and goals. Balance improves our lives. Remember, however, that nothing is ever in perfect balance for more than a second or two.

Out-of-Balance Parenting

Parents lead very busy lives, and they often are so caught up in activities with their children—such as potty training them and enforcing bedtimes—that they lose touch with their own needs. Trying to cope with family and home and work responsibilities, plus phone messages, e-mails, Facebook, texting, and junk mail, can be absolutely overwhelming. Many parents are stretched thin with too many burdens and too little support.

Our emotions can throw us out of balance if we don't know how to manage them. Large and small psychological events can pull us off center.

When we are out of balance, life is more challenging. From time to time, therefore, rebalancing is called for—re-evaluating priorities, making adjustments, and rearranging schedules and routines.

When our children are "off"—acting unlike their normal, better selves—positive parenting invites us to figure out what's going on *underneath* the actions, to find out what they need. That information—perhaps through intuition or a hunch—can point to what will bring them back into balance.

Playing together can help to rebalance the energy, renew our hearts, and rejuvenate our souls. Other practices can help hold the balance and restore equanimity in the moment:

- quiet time—taking time to breathe, to rest, to just be
- being in natural settings such as woods, lakes, hills, or mountains
- rituals, such as telling stories around the dinner table
- routines, such as reading and snuggling before bedtime
- balancing indoor time with outdoor time, and work with play
- peaceful activities such as viewing a full moon, playing board games
- exercise, walking, yoga, mindfulness, or meditation

Don't hesitate to ask others for help or ideas. Befriending your neighbors, extending your family supports, carpooling, and sharing dinners can all help to reduce stress and incorporate balance and structure into your life. Attending to body, mind, and spirit helps maintain equilibrium.

Parents also need to balance their own needs and wants with responsibilities and desires. Out-of-balance parenting can be harmful to children. Here are some examples:

- Overparenting: Parents do for kids what they should be doing for themselves.
- Underparenting: Parents fail to provide structure or engage in the inner life of children. "Whatever" parents fall into this category.
- Overprotection: This parenting style is based on worry and fear. An example is "helicopter parents."
- Underprotection: Parents neglect the needs of children by not setting adequate limits or boundaries.
- Overindulgence: Giving kids much more than they need is actually a form of neglect, because it hampers their healthy development and well-being.

Adults need to be mindful of a balance between "too much" and "too little":

- We need to be flexible, but not too flexible.
- We need to be strict, but not too strict.
- We need to be in charge, but not overcontrolling.

In the space between the extremes lies the broad, "just right" middle way.

We will examine in chapter 15 the extreme leadership styles: the autocratic style with too much structure and too little freedom, and the permissive style with too much freedom and too little (or no) structure. We will explore the broad but balanced middle road between rigid and chaotic extremes. The democratic (authoritative) leadership style balances structure with freedom. This is the healthiest leadership style of positive parenting.

Moderate, level-headed parenting practices heal imbalance, stop the ping-ponging between extremes, and restore equanimity and satisfaction to family life.

A Developmental Trajectory

It's easier to ride a horse in the direction it's going.

— ABRAHAM LINCOLN

An acorn is destined to become a mighty oak. A daffodil bulb is destined to blossom. A baby is destined to become an autonomous, self-directed, thriving man or woman when given a nurturing environment.

The developmental trajectory from infancy to maturity in humans is about increasing responsibility and capability.

- **The first stage** is total dependence. Moms and dads are completely in charge of meeting the needs of babies and are totally responsible for their survival. After a year or two, a little voice insists, "Me do it!" as the child puts his or her shoes on, and then later proudly announces, "I can do it all by myself!"

- **The second stage** begins when children show signs of becoming more self-sufficient. Bit by bit, mothers and fathers turn over little responsibilities: For example, children begin to feed themselves and go to the bathroom without any help. The role of parents evolves to include more supervising, teaching, guiding, and empowering. Becoming coaches and cheerleaders, parents work *with* the child's natural developmental trajectory toward autonomy. Grandparents, child-care providers, and teachers also move children along the continuum of self-regulation, from telling them what to do (regulated by others) to consulting with and advising them (shared regulation). Youngsters eventually make good decisions and smart choices on their own—and become masters of their own behavior.

- **The third stage** is independence and autonomy. Youngsters at this stage have learned to make good choices, self-regulate, and use pro-social skills. As the child's responsibility increases, the parent's responsibility decreases.

The ultimate goal of positive parenting is to nurture and support the eventual independence and autonomy of children. When the process is successful, the parents have worked themselves out of a job!

Developing Resilient Capabilities

Resilience develops in children in ordinary circumstances, over time.

By stopping a child's unacceptable behaviors early on, parents help develop the cognitive (thinking) part of the child's brain that influences basic abilities like attention, memory, and motor skills for long-term benefits. Competent parents build resilience capability on a daily basis by being consistent and kind while developing self-regulation.

Psychologist Tina Daniels reports, "Today's children come to school with lower levels of self-regulation and early childhood teachers report that they are ill equipped to deal with these problems."[1]

Becoming a family is a journey, and it is also a destination. Part 3 will help you build positive emotions and therefore positive families. Chapters 7 and 8 discuss positive psychology and positive parenting—the foundational philosophies of this book. Chapters 9 through 19 cover related topics to help you superpower your kids in the twenty-first century—including how to handle some of the "booby traps" that make parenting challenging.

Regardless of their circumstances, all parents can promote positive development for their children. A child's family, in fact, has the most fundamental influence on his or her life and future.

. . .

7

· · · ·

A New Psychology

Raising children . . . is vastly more than fixing what is wrong with them.
It is about identifying and nurturing their strongest qualities . . . and
helping them find niches in which they can best live out these strengths.[1]

— MARTIN SELIGMAN

Since the days of Sigmund Freud, traditional psychology has mostly been concerned with the dark side of human existence, with diagnosing and treating mental illness and disorders. Yet toward the end of the twentieth century, the man at the helm of the American Psychological Association (APA), Martin Seligman, twisted the rudder and began steering this massive and powerful ship away from seeing humanity as a sea of disorder and disease, and toward a science of building strengths and virtues, happiness and optimism, positive emotion and resilience.

After spending the early years of his professional life "working on misery," shocking lab dogs until they learned helplessness, Seligman shifted his investigation to the dogs that did not give up. As a therapist, Martin Seligman listened over and over to people's stories of resilience, and later on in his career he discovered that teaching children optimism skills cut their rate of depression in half. A prevention focus, he realized, is so effective it could "save an ocean of tears."

Seligman's turning point came while weeding the garden with his young daughter, Nikki, who was instead playing, singing, and throwing flowers in the air. "Goal oriented and time urgent," Seligman just wanted to get the work done, so he yelled at her. She stopped, but later approached her father and sternly reminded him that she had given up whining on her fifth birthday. "If I could stop whining, Daddy, you can stop being such a grouch." A lightbulb went on in Seligman's head. He recognized her strength and ability to change her habits. He also realized that his job as a parent was to notice and nurture her strengths.[2]

That insight brought another epiphany. He realized that by focusing on suffering and trauma, traditional psychology was neglecting to focus on what makes life worth living: happiness, virtues, and strengths. After the APA elected him president in 1998, Seligman's mindshift changed the direction of the ship, as he almost single-handedly launched a new branch of the organization: positive psychology.

Positive psychology presumes people are doing the best they can to lead fulfilling lives, and that fulfillment is cultivated through building strengths and virtues such as love, courage, compassion, creativity, and self-control. Positive psychologists believe that institutions should study and support human strengths in areas such as justice, responsibility, civility, parenting, nurturance, work ethic, leadership, teamwork, purpose, and tolerance.

Changing Your Mindset

The good life consists in deriving happiness by using your signature strengths every day in the main realms of living. The meaningful life adds one more component: using these same strengths to forward knowledge, power, or goodness. A life that does this is pregnant with meaning, and if God comes at the end, such a life is sacred.

— MARTIN SELIGMAN

When Seligman changed his point of view, he discovered a surge of power. In his book *Learned Optimism,* he validates that personal change is possible through one's efforts, will, and choices. He also goes into detail about how optimists and pessimists have enormously different ways of explaining their troubles.

Explanatory Style

Explanatory style defines how we explain to ourselves why we experience certain events, either positive or negative. Listen to your inner dialogue—your self-talk—about how you explain or justify the experiences and events in your life. See if your explanatory style is more characteristic of a pessimistic or an optimistic mindset:

Temporary vs. permanent: When you experience a setback, do you perceive it as temporary, or something that will last a long time? Do you say, "This, too, shall pass," or do you say, "This always happens to me"? Pessimists tend to see bad situations as permanent. Optimists see them as temporary.

Pervasive vs. coincidental: Do you consider the event to be universally pervasive, or specific to one person, one event, one quality? For example, "I can't do anything" (universal) vs. "I am having trouble with math" (specific). Or, "The teacher was unfair" (specific) vs. "All teachers are unfair" (universal). Pessimists tend to see things as pervasive or universal. Optimists give the benefit of the doubt.

Personal vs. general: Do you feel "It's about me" (internal, attribution personal) or "It's about others" (external, attribution general)? Where does the fault lie? Do you blame yourself? Or do you blame someone else or blame the circumstances? You can probably guess that pessimists take things personally.

Pessimists think that they deserve the bad experiences. Everyone thinks pessimistically sometimes, but a habitual pessimistic style can damage our physical and psychological health.

As Seligman says: "Optimistic people tend to interpret their troubles as transient, controllable, and specific to one situation. Pessimistic people, in contrast, believe that their troubles last forever, undermine everything they do, and are uncontrollable." [3]

Here's the good news: We now know that people are not "born" optimists or pessimists. We know that explanatory styles are learned, and they can be unlearned. We know that we can discipline and train our thoughts, just as we can train our bodies to get into shape.

How We Acquire a Negative Mindset

Research shows that an explanatory style is primarily learned rather than inherited. To help us understand this, let's look at how a child explains adversity. There are three ways children learn their explanatory style:

1. *How their primary caregiver explains adverse events.* If the mother blames herself or the child when bad things happen, the child will notice and learn this pessimistic style.

2. *If the child is blamed.* When bad things happen, if children are blamed or criticized, or if their character, personality, or self are attacked, they quickly learn to blame themselves using personal, permanent, and pervasive explanations. (This could be a deep root of pessimism and self-bullying.)

3. *Tragic life crises.* If children experience a crisis—such as a house fire, divorce, abuse, war, or extreme poverty—they notice if these tragedies get resolved after a period of time, or if they persist forever. If the crisis gets resolved quickly, the child learns to believe that adversity is specific and temporary and can be overcome. If the crisis expands and never ends, the child learns to believe that adversity is permanent and pervasive.

The style children learn for explaining adversity tends to persist throughout their adult life. Pay attention to how you react to adversity and how you handle crises. Your children are watching and listening.

As Seligman says, how we learn our mindset is a matter of A-B-C, which we can see operating every day in our own lives:

A. **Adversity.** When we encounter adversity, we react by thinking about it.

B. **Beliefs.** Our thoughts congeal rapidly into beliefs, which may become so habitual that, unless we stop to focus on them, we don't even realize we have them.

C. **Consequences.** We act according to our beliefs, and then face the consequences. If we believe we are helpless, we give up.

If we believe we can make a difference, we take constructive action. Henry Ford once commented on the power of beliefs, "Whether you believe you can or believe you can't, you're right."

Fortunately, we can learn to dispute our pessimistic explanations.

Banishing Negative Thoughts and Pessimistic Beliefs

You cannot manage thoughts that you are not aware of. Awareness of negative thinking, therefore, is the first step in the process of shifting from a pessimistic mindset to an optimistic mindset. Observe your thoughts when responding to negative and positive events. Take note if you are seeing things as permanent, pervasive, and personal.

Once you are aware of those negative thoughts and pessimistic beliefs, there are two ways to deal with them:

1. Distract yourself. For example, you can change the television channel or start thinking about something else.

2. Dispute them. Argue against those self-limiting thoughts and replace them with positive thoughts. (This approach, in the long run, is more effective than distraction.) When pessimistic beliefs are successfully disputed, they are less likely to recur. (For more on this, see chapters 10 and 17.)

Positive psychology is like an immunization against stress. Children raised with positive psychology tend to have fewer emotional troubles. In fact, Seligman says, "Teaching children learned optimism before puberty, but late enough in childhood so that they are metacognitive (capable of thinking about thinking), is a fruitful strategy. When the immunized children use these skills to cope with the first rejections of puberty, they get better and better at using these skills. Our analysis shows that the change from pessimism to optimism is at least partly responsible for the prevention of depressive symptoms."[4]

According to Seligman's research, ten-year-old children who have learned to be optimistic and hopeful are half as likely as their peers to become depressed during puberty. And depression is linked to bullying.

Positive Principles for Raising Children

Life is meant to be happy. I know this is sometimes hard to believe, and I know that on many days it simply is not your experience, but it is true. You have all the tools right now to make this day, this moment happy.

— NEALE DONALD WALSCH

Here are Martin Seligman's **three principles for raising children:**

- The main task for the first six years is to **build positive emotion.** This is a time for children to *broaden and build* resources—social, physical, and intellectual—to draw on, like a savings account, for the rest of their lives.

- **Nurture positive emotions to start an upward spiral.** Positive emotions generate more positive emotions. When children are in a good mood, they are more likable, and connections are likely to improve. Furthermore, positive emotion is its own reward.

- **Notice positive traits** as being equally authentic and real as negative traits. Look for emerging strengths and virtues, like kindness, prudence, judgment, and fairness. Identify and build "signature strengths." Positive strengths can be buffers against negative emotions and misfortune, and lift life up to a more positive plane.[5]

Remember the spirals. Positive emotions and traits create upward and outward spirals. They have a ripple effect on families and communities.

Boosting Your Happiness

Although happiness is a natural state, it does not happen automatically to everyone. Happiness must be sought after, nurtured, and developed. Happy people are more caring, more socially engaged, more successful, harder working, and healthier than unhappy people.

Pursuing happiness is a skill that can be learned. Parents and children alike can take an uplifting approach, learn new skills, and see how different choices can create a better life. *Being happy is a choice.*

The positive psychology movement has ushered in the new "science of happiness." Contentment, satisfaction, well-being, joy, pleasure, gratitude, and appreciation are all expressions of happiness. More than two thousand years ago, Aristotle observed that "Happiness is the meaning and the purpose of life, the whole aim and end of human existence." Even the U.S. Declaration of Independence states that we have the right to pursue happiness!

The following **"happiness boosters"** are proven tools and simple strategies that will help you create happiness one day at a time.

- **Close relationships.** The most important factor in a satisfying life is having close relationships. Brain research tells us that humans are "hardwired for connection." Families are a perfect place to boost happiness.

- **Meaning and purpose.** Purpose consists of living a meaningful life and attaching to something larger, noble, and transcendent. The most obvious source of meaning is our love for our family.

- **Gratitude.** When we focus on the things that we are grateful for, the things that make us happy, these things tend to grow. Think of the people and things that make a difference in your life: for example, your health, a beautiful object, or a kind person.

- **Speaking the good.** At the end of each day, talk to someone about the positives. Ask children what they liked about their day. Then ask, "What was it about that (person or thing) that made it 'good'?" By doing those activities, children learn to create more good days for themselves. You can extend review into preview by asking, "What are you looking forward to tomorrow?"

- **Making time for pleasure.** It takes a huge amount of work to raise a family, and many families have very tight schedules. Make having fun with your family a high priority. Plan a special outing, or just drop what you're doing and take time out for play.

• • •

8
. . . .

Parenting for a Positive Present . . . and Future

Let's raise children who won't have to recover from their childhood.

— PAM LEO, *CONNECTION PARENTING*

Positive psychology stood traditional psychology on its head because one remarkable man, confronted by the honesty and earnestness of his beloved daughter, changed his beliefs on parenting. Something similar is happening in families from coast to coast and around the world: Parents are soul searching about their day-to-day interactions with their children.

Louise, as the mother of three young children in the 1970s, vowed not to punish as her mother did; she resolved to find a better, more positive way. Her daughter Kristen believes that was the best decision Louise ever made, and she passed along these positive strategies to her own child. Stories abound about how parents everywhere are learning better ways to raise their children. Blogger and author Becky Eanes, for example, writes:

> I didn't start out a positive parent. . . . It wasn't until my baby became a toddler and I had to figure out how to "make him mind" that I stumbled across this philosophy. I didn't buy into it overnight, either. I didn't use physical punishment because that felt instinctively wrong to me, even though I'd experienced it in my own childhood, but I certainly dished out the time outs, the threats, the bribes, the withdrawal of toys. **And it wasn't working.**[1]

As you can see from this quote, positive parenting is about finding a harmonious relationship with kids that is not related to controlling, dominating, or even necessarily "getting good behavior." Nor is positive parenting about being permissive and letting kids get away with bad behavior. Rather, moms and dads guide children toward good behaviors without blame and shame; individuals acknowledge their part, accept responsibility, set things right, and move on. With this encouraging and uplifting approach, children are healthier and happier, as well as more caring, cooperative, and confident.

Positive parenting can be approached from dozens, even hundreds of angles, much like positive psychology. And like positive psychology, positive parenting is about nurturing the best in people.

Being a positive parent means you intentionally and systematically cultivate empathy, dignity, responsibility, optimism, courage, authenticity, self-discipline, and perseverance. These virtues develop character and resilience, short-circuit bullying dynamics, and build *Zorgos*!

Positive, Not Perfect

Our job as parents is to prepare our children for the world, but we all have different ideas of what that means. In previous generations, it meant teaching girls to sit quietly with hands folded and legs crossed. Or it meant teaching boys never to look an authority figure in the eye. Traditions such as these were upheld because children could suffer societal consequences for breaking the status quo.

Since then we have learned there are dire consequences for expecting perfection from our children—and ourselves. Too many families have been ripped apart because their children feel like failures, leading to troubling behavior from bullying to robbery to addiction—even suicide. A sense of shame and disappointment clings to every perceived bad deed, and actual bad deeds can follow.

It is estimated that among the general population, 30 percent of us are perfectionists. Perfectionists can be judgmental, self-deprecating, shy, procrastinators, and workaholics; they can suffer anxiety, depression, mood swings, and migraine headaches. Furthermore, they can develop anorexia and bulimia, as well as obsessive-compulsive disorders.

Perfectionism, with its all-or-nothing thought patterns and self-defeating beliefs, can also affect one's parenting style. No matter how hard perfectionists work, no matter how good they (or their kids) are, they never are good enough.

Positive parenting begins with self-acceptance—a humility that we are human and don't know all the answers. Acceptance is at the core: we accept our children as being in process—yet perfect as they are, at every stage, moles and warts and all.

Positive parenting has nothing to do with being "perfect." There is no way to be a perfect parent, but there are a million ways to be a good one. Positive parenting is an uplifting, proactive, optimistic, nonpunitive approach that sets clear, achievable expectations, while *accepting* and *respecting* the ages, abilities, and differences of family members. Positive parenting is not a bar to measure ourselves against, but a set of skills to be learned, feelings to feel, and a joyful ideal to be creatively pursued.

Big-Picture Parenting

Building a family is like building a house. You start with a vision and plans. Then you build a firm foundation. Step by step, you move forward. If any steps are missed, there's makeup work to be done.

An optimistic vision can give meaning and purpose to the ongoing and often draining tasks of parenting. How you envision your life is extremely important because it plays into everything else. An inner vision of how you want things to be can guide you on a day-to-day basis toward desirable outcomes, and also sustain you through the hard times. All the "little things" you do on a daily basis contribute to the success of your "big picture."

What is your optimistic vision for your children? What kind of adults do you want them to become? In Louise's workshops, parents have expressed wishes in their "grand vision" for their children. Parents wish for their children to

- be happy
- be well-adjusted
- be successful

- be respectful
- be responsible
- be in touch with nature
- be true to themselves
- be open to the world
- be loving
- have high self-esteem and self-worth
- love learning
- contribute to society
- be cooperative
- be wholesome
- be able to express themselves
- not have to spend their adult life recovering from their childhood

A "grand vision" for a family is an unfolding love story that brings out the best in everyone.

Reframing: Shift Your Focus from Half-Empty to Half-Full

One frustrated teenager made a statement to her counselor that speaks to children, other teenagers, and even adults everywhere: "When people are so focused on what's wrong with you, it's hard to discover what's right with you." She was fed up because her parents saw only half the picture—her flaws and pimples, her shortcomings and problems. They completely overlooked her strengths and positive qualities. The result of their "half-empty" perception was a discouraged and disconnected girl with low self-esteem.

Children's behavior improves when we evaluate them from a "half-full" perspective rather than a "half-empty" one, when we focus on their strengths rather than on their flaws, when we lift them up rather than put them down. Once we identify our perfectionist thoughts, and let go of impossible standards and beliefs, connections and self-esteem improve, and families have more fun. As Glennon Melton says, "Don't let yourself become so concerned with raising a good kid that you forget you already have one."[2]

Bring Out the Best

Expectations have great power. That's because your children don't want to disappoint you. They will live up to—or down to—your expectations. However, when expectations are too high (as in perfectionism), or too low (as in prejudice), youngsters are set up to fail. To be effective and fair, expectations must be reasonable and attainable—and age appropriate.

Expecting and modeling positive behaviors will inspire the good behaviors you want. You will notice the desirable behaviors increase, while undesirable behaviors fall away and disappear.

Why is a positive focus important to parents, especially parents of children who get into bullying dynamics?

- You and your child will both begin to notice and talk about good things you had previously overlooked.

- Seeing only faults and failings is unfair, and damages self-esteem. A negative self-concept triggers negative peer interactions.

- Flaw-fixing is not the best way to promote optimal human development. Even when flaws are overcome 99 percent of the time, the 1 percent still feels defining.

- A negative focus perpetuates negative behaviors, while a positive focus encourages more positive behaviors.

- When you acknowledge good behavior with praise or attention—a smile, a pat on the back—you motivate your child to exhibit more good behavior.

This does not mean you let kids get away with unacceptable behavior. People must be held accountable for unacceptable behavior—by acknowledging responsibility, setting things right, and moving on. Guide your child toward good behaviors while maintaining a respectful, loving connection.

Attribution: Who Is to Blame?

In the last chapter, we talked about the explanatory style, and how optimists and pessimists make sense of difficulties. When things go wrong, do you blame yourself? Do you blame others, including your child? Do you blame the circumstance? It's easy for us to point fingers and cast blame on others, especially when we are stressed.

The brain can play tricks on us. Our minds can make assumptions and tell us stories that make it easy to jump to false conclusions and take things personally.

One mother of a class bully, for example, was talking to the principal. She said, "He's just trying to get back at me for leaving his dad." This mom may have had her finger on the correct issue, but she was telling herself a story that put all the responsibility on the child; she was unfairly blaming the child.

As a matter of fact, a lot of our thoughts can be untrue, or misinformed, or unfounded assumptions. When, for example, we imagine that someone is judging us or intends to harm us, our imagination is making up that story; it may be the furthest thing from his or her mind. Instead of reacting, evaluate the situation. Is your assumption true? Is it a fact? The child in the story above was grieving, and his pain was made worse when his mother mistook his feelings of confusion for hostility.

Even in the best relationships, careless words can trigger feelings that are different from what were intended. Watch out for innocent mistakes that might escalate into big problems.

The next time you notice "bad behavior," don't react. Pause and breathe deeply to calm down. What is underneath the behavior? What unmet needs or upsetting feelings are being acted out? Remember that children (and adults) are all doing the best they can with the brains they were given. (For more on how to slow down reactions, see chapter 12.)

Naomi Aldort, author of *Raising Our Children, Raising Ourselves,* writes, "The reason a child will act unkindly or cause damage is always innocent. Sometimes she is playful and free spirited, and other times, when aggressive or angry, she is unhappy or confused. The more disturbing the behavior, the more the child is in pain and in need of your love and understanding."[3]

Positive parenting doesn't look for something or someone to blame, or pathologize the problem. Instead it looks for solutions, asking, "What steps are missing in normal, healthy development? How can we make sure our children take those steps?"

Red Flags

Sometimes it's difficult to reframe our thoughts, especially the negative and persistent ones. But we must do that in order to help our kids develop in a healthier way. Negative thoughts can sabotage us, make matters worse, and cause disconnection and loss of trust.

When you are having a parenting challenge, remember: "Misbehavior" is not a challenge to your authority, but an unmet need, a reaction to unrealistic expectations, or an expression of pain. *Do not take uncooperative behavior personally!*

When you are having the following dangerous "red flag" thoughts regarding your child or children, you need to stop and reframe the situation:

- "She just wants attention."
- "He is manipulating me."
- "There is no good reason for this behavior."
- "They need to know they don't always get what they want."
- "He's just trying to control me."
- "She's doing this on purpose to get me mad."

Replace these "red flag" thoughts with the following "green flag" thoughts to calm yourself down. Remind yourself that your child's brain will not be fully developed until his or her mid-twenties. Then, breathing deeply, address the emotions underlying the undesirable behavior. Look for your child's best intentions by telling yourself the following:

- He's doing his best with the brain he has.
- This child is a good person.
- She is really feeling the emotions she is showing; she must be really upset.

- He is emotionally dependent on me and is affected by what I say and do and how I interact with him.
- She's only a baby/child.
- I love my child.
- He's not yet emotionally mature.
- She's overwhelmed by emotions, and is "out of her (rational) mind."
- He needs more practice controlling his emotions; how can I help him?
- Being reasonable is not yet an option; I can wait.

After calming yourself, you are better able to calm and soothe your child. Try these three simple steps:

1. **Listen** to your child's words and/or nonverbal cues. Encourage your child to *talk it out,* so he or she doesn't have to *act it out.*
2. **Comfort** your child. Connect. Show that you care.
3. Try to **solve** the problem that is upsetting him or her.

Always acknowledge your child's best intentions. Find ways to build on those positive intentions while letting go of any negative thoughts, words, and actions. Most importantly, treat your child kindly and with respect as you tune in to his or her feelings and try to get to the root of the problem. Our children give us the opportunity to reframe our thoughts about many situations in life.

An Authentic Connection

A teacher friend of ours came up with the unscientific and nonmedical diagnosis "connection deficit disorder" to describe the kids who arrive at school desperate for connection—any kind of connection, whether positive or negative. When there is a lack of connection (from neglect), interrupted connection (a parent leaves), or connection to the wrong things (screens, drama, obsession, addiction), children and adults alike seem to lack what in the old days was called common sense.

Another teacher explained that twenty years ago, she might have had one disconnected child in her class every few years, but now she has four or five of them in every kindergarten class. She used to be able to take the one child under her wing, but now she is pulled in all directions.

Children who get involved in bullying or other risky behavior often do so because they feel disconnected from others, and from themselves. Kids who have trouble with family relationships have trouble with other social relationships. Kids who feel a strong connection with a parent, however, have a powerful advantage. Now and then they may have trouble, but they can rely on two things: a basic inner security, and support when they need it.

Therefore, part of an optimistic "big-picture" vision for a family must include a deep connection with each child, and authentic relationships between the children. *Authentic* means the real thing. Authentic relationships are transparent and purely loving; they honor the soul of each person. Authentic relationships are "touchstones" that you can return to again and again to remember who you really are.

Parents need to make authentic connections a high priority, and society needs to find ways to support them in this effort.

Parent-child connectedness, in fact, has been defined as the "super-protective factor" against negative outcomes in adolescence.[4] A close, connected relationship with a caring adult who is attentive to feelings and responds to needs builds a strength that continues in different ways throughout the child's lifetime. (For more on connection, see chapter 11.)

The Three Jobs of Positive Parenting

Positive parents work to develop trust and competence; identify and encourage strengths and talents; maintain loving connections; and create fun, joy, and happiness. In a nutshell: positive parents comfort, play, and teach.

Most new parents have little knowledge of how to raise a child and feel acutely unprepared when their baby arrives. A Canadian organization boiled it down to three simple tasks that can help new parents keep their minds focused on the positive in the important role they play in their child's early years.

Comfort, Play & Teach: A Positive Approach to Parenting is a research-based approach that can "transform everyday interactions from the ordinary to the extraordinary." Developed by Invest in Kids/Canada,[5] this simple recipe for parenting young children strengthens family bonds, builds confidence, and establishes the foundation of lifelong respectful and warm relationships. It also helps parents with children of all ages re-establish good connections.

When parents engage their child in these three ways, healthy development is supported. And when parents see positive responses, their confidence increases.

Win-win practices enrich the present moment and can open a world of possibilities. This positive approach to parenting will help you discover your child's unique personality, enhance bonding and a strong connection, and set a foundation for a respectful and warm relationship for life.

Comfort Your Children

Children need to feel loved and nurtured. If they do not feel loved and cherished, little else parents do will have much of an influence. Comfort is the primary necessity of babies and children, especially when they are sick, tired, upset, or hurt.

We comfort our young ones with our touch—by holding, hugging, and caressing them. We comfort them with reassuring words when they're scared or confused. We comfort them with eye contact that is accepting and caring. When we comfort our little ones, their bodies and their hearts feel safe and protected. They feel secure, loved, and valued.

Why is comfort the first thing on the Invest in Kids/Canada list? Because it is most important. Babies must be comforted in order to learn to self-soothe. Soothing alters brain chemistry and builds neural connections so that babies can learn to soothe themselves. Soothing teaches them that their emotions are manageable, and not to panic. Being comforted is just as important to your baby's development as being fed and diapered. In fact, comfort is important throughout childhood.

Play with Your Children

Play is the "work of children." Through play, children learn about themselves as they explore their world. They learn different ways to think, solve problems, and communicate, and moms and dads are their favorite playmates. When you join in, building a tower, throwing a ball, or pretending to be a king or a princess, you can enjoy a few moments of being a kid again. When you make it a habit, you are taking care of everyone, including yourself.

Play has far-reaching benefits beyond *fun*. The spontaneity, creativity, imagination, and connection associated with play stimulate brain growth and learning of all kinds. Play builds mastery, which in turn builds self-esteem. Playing outside is great exercise, and playing together builds great friendships. Lots of important things happen beneath the surface while playing.

According to the American Academy of Pediatrics, "Play is important for healthy child development. Free play contributes to the cognitive, physical, social, and emotional well-being of children and youth and offers parents an opportunity to engage fully with their children."[6] Play increases health, happiness, and harmony in families. It creates bonds and enhances self-esteem. Furthermore, play today builds memories to draw on as time goes by. To quote parenting author Vicki Lansky, "You will always be your child's favorite toy."

Teach Your Children

Teaching helps develop the architecture of the brain. Talking with children and reading to them develops their vocabulary and helps them learn about life. Sharing your observations and commenting on situations helps them understand new things, solve problems, and make sense of the world. The more they learn, the better their brains perform and the more confident they become.

Teaching can be proactive. For example, teaching good table manners (napkin on lap, don't talk with your mouth full) before you go to a restaurant can spare you from difficult moments later. Teach appropriate behaviors; model, encourage, and support.

When you tell your children something in a direct, kind, and respectful way, they take it to heart. In other words, kindness improves their ability to hear. With teaching, you let children know what you *want*, rather than reacting to what you *don't want*. Reacting is not the end of the world, however; you can always follow a reaction by teaching: "... and this would be a better way to do it next time."

Teaching gives kids standards to uphold and values to abide by; teaching right from wrong instills a moral compass. What you teach your children develops their character and makes them who they are.

Loosening the Grip of Negative Patterns

Become the parent you wish you'd had.

— LOUISE HART, *THE WINNING FAMILY*

Our children's experiences routinely take us back to our own childhood memories. That personal history can carry unexpected power in determining the kind of family we will have. Yet negative childhood experiences do not have to determine our fate and the fate of our children.

Once we become aware of the patterns we inherited, once we evaluate and discern whether they were for our own good—or not— we can begin to change our personal family story. We can do better, and be better.

Daniel Siegel, coauthor of *Parenting from the Inside Out*, says, "If you had a difficult childhood but have come to make sense of those experiences, you are not bound to re-create the same negative interactions with your own children. Without such self-understanding, however, science has shown that history will likely repeat itself, as negative patterns of family interactions are passed down through the generations."[7]

Patterns Are Predictive

Parents of old—like parents today, but possibly more so—were flying by the seat of their pants when it came to raising a child . . . much less

146

ten children. Large families of the past had life-and-death challenges, economic pressures, and no books, classes, or therapists to help them reflect on what they were doing. Corporal punishment and humiliation were the rule, and feelings of unworthiness and shame were passed along through generations.

When we hear the stories of our ancestors and learn their history, forgiveness is called for because they did their best, given their upbringing and what they knew. Now, fortunately, we know better and we can do better. We can change dysfunctional traditions and patterns, and transform our family relationships.

For example, we know that corporal punishment increases aggressiveness and lowers both IQ and academic performance. We know that it damages trust and relationships. Our parents and grandparents probably did not know that. They did not know a better way to interact with or discipline their children, and everyone suffered as a consequence.

We have all been wounded, and we want things to be better for our own children. We can stop the unintentional repetition of harmful patterns from one generation to the next by learning positive parenting.

Self-Understanding

Everyone has unresolved issues left over from childhood. Everyone has been wounded and wants to do better for his or her own children. Many people have made the solemn vow: "I'll never do that to my kids." Old childhood wounds can propel us to become more positive parents.

The process involves honestly assessing how we were raised, then learning better methods, and healing our wounds. It's the most important and exciting journey of our lives. (Recall the discussion on healing in chapter 3.)

Changing patterns is heroic work that requires parents to

- become more aware of how they manage their own emotions
- tune in and be responsive to their children's needs and feelings

- put themselves in their child's shoes
- take good care of themselves

Here's the good news: we can loosen the grip of old negative habits, "change our minds," retrain our brains, and operate at a deeper, more conscious, more gratifying level. As we wake up to what we are doing and why we are doing it, we can make a different choice. As we put new skills into practice, we can put the past where it belongs—behind us. Plasticity of the brain makes this possible. (See chapter 16 for more on the brain.) Positive parenting helps us transform damaging patterns and create a healthier and happier family for our children, our grandchildren, and ourselves.

When we learn better relationship skills, we discover new possibilities that can keep us from backsliding. We learn to rewrite the old fear-based "script," heal damage from our childhood, and become wonderful parents to our children. With more positive and encouraging interactions and an uplifting style, we can heal our hearts and souls while we rear our children.

Positive Parenting for the Long Run

Instead of starting from the assumption that you have to beat the badness out of a child, turn on that empathy and compassion switch.

— DACHER KELTNER, PROFESSOR OF PSYCHOLOGY AT THE UNIVERSITY OF CALIFORNIA, BERKELEY, AND AUTHOR OF *BORN TO BE GOOD: THE SCIENCE OF A MEANINGFUL LIFE*

It's not unusual for teens to resist their parents' questions: "Where are you going?" "Who is going with you?" "Will their parents be at home?" While parents may feel at times like they are nagging, their care and concern helps adolescents feel loved and secure, which in turn leads to their becoming a good parent later on in life.

A study that began in 1984 tracking three generations of males between the ages of eight and thirty-three found that positive parenting—with plenty of warmth, involvement, monitoring of children's activities, and consistent discipline—has a measurably positive impact on adolescents.[8] The study also found that positive parenting impacts the way adolescents eventually parent their own children. David Kerr, the psychology professor in charge of the study, said, "What surprised us is how strong positive parenting pathways are. Positive parenting is not just the absence of negative influences, but involves taking an active role in a child's life. We see now that changes in parenting can have an effect not just on children but even on grandchildren."

A closer look at positive parenting reveals the "positive" part of the equation—the place where you exhale and tell yourself

- I don't have to be perfect.
- My child doesn't have to be perfect.
- When we falter, we forgive.
- We are free to love without conditions.
- My child's behavior today does not define who he or she will be tomorrow.

. . .

9

• • • •

A Warm Family Climate

Happy families are all alike;
every unhappy family is unhappy in its own way.

— LEO TOLSTOY, FROM *ANNA KARENINA*

Did you ever watch an episode of the TV program *Supernanny*? In each episode, celebrity babysitter Jo Frost would go into a home with out-of-control kids and, in forty-two minutes of airtime, bring the chaotic climate under control! First she would observe how parents interacted with the kids. She would then help parents identify where children were insecure and empower them to set limits, which would allow better connections between family members.

Both Frost's approach and Tolstoy's quote imply that there is a "blueprint" or "pattern" for happy families. We know the characteristics of families that contribute to the bullying dynamic (identified and discussed in chapter 3). This raises a good question: *What do happy families know and do that unhappy families don't?*

It has been proven over and over again that a warm, caring, and positive emotional climate builds resilience and other strengths that help children avoid bullying dynamics. If you didn't grow up in a caring family climate, you have a lot to learn—and a lot to *un*learn. This process begins with awareness, followed by commitment, dedication, vision, and perseverance. In this chapter we provide ways to strengthen the relationships in your family, making this process easier.

Joy vs. Fear

You can't make joy or well-being happen, but you can create the conditions in which those states more naturally arise.

— JAMES BARAZ, *AWAKENING JOY*

When you reflect on your parenting style, perhaps you notice certain attitudes and practices that seem to contribute to problems. Awareness is the first step. Let your insights light the way and be a guide. One mother observed, "Society tried to teach me that children are by nature selfish, out-of-control, and demanding, that their goal is power and that they are always trying to see how much they can get away with, that you can't let children manipulate you or become too dependent, and that disobedience equals disrespect."[1] Society seems to teach us to be fearful.

All of the "red flag" thoughts in the previous chapter come from a position of fear: Perfectionism comes from fear; violence comes from fear. But what do we, as parents, have to fear? After all, we are the grown-ups. We have power, money, and logic on our side, as well as the keys to the car. Still, we fear losing things, like jobs, money, control, and the people we love.

These common fears are real, and they influence our thoughts, words, and actions—especially if we are unaware of them. Every person has his or her own fears, and every family has its own fears. When fears are unacknowledged, they can take the form of anger. When fears are unexpressed, they show up in the body as tightness, stress, pain, and even disease. Fear makes us rigid. In a pessimistic culture, suffering is often seen as the norm, while joy is seen as fleeting.

Kristen's grandmother, Nida, lived in a mobile home. She reveled in her raspberry patch and the peregrine falcons that perched on poles above the railroad tracks. In Al-Anon she had learned to find and guard her joy. She had many legitimate fears: whether the social security check would last to the end of the month, what she would do if the car broke down, or whether her husband's emphysema would put him in the hospital that winter. But she always found joy in little things that nourished her soul. Making her delicious chocolate cake (with sauerkraut!) for family, going fishing at the reservoir, and gathering wild asparagus brought joy to her, as well as to those around her. Parents who create warm family climates are parents who guard their joys. They create and cherish moments that make them feel close to each other and to their children. And these precious moments build resilience and good memories in their children.

Subconscious Programming

Subconscious programming takes over the moment
your conscious mind is not paying attention.

— BRUCE LIPTON, *THE BIOLOGY OF BELIEF*

Biologist Bruce Lipton explains how young children's brains operate primarily in a hypnogogic state (which adults experience just before sleep), passively absorbing millions of facts and experiences, accepting them all as "truths" about the way the world is.

If kids experience a reliable reality in their early years, between birth and six—informed by nature, complex language (communicating thoughts and feelings), physical experiences, and accurate information—they build a good "operating system." If, however, the information children receive consists of loud TV commercials, adrenaline-fueled video games, family chaos, and fearful messages, the information children store will not "run programs" reliably when they find themselves in social interactions later. This is another way of understanding how ACEs create patterns of disease later in life.

When the family climate is full of comfort, love, and attention, children conclude that they are loved and that the world is a friendly place. When they experience neglect, harshness, and pain, they conclude that they are not safe and cannot trust; they feel fear and distress. These cumulative experiences shape the development of children's brains. Underlying every experience are these central questions: Am I safe? Am I okay? Am I loved? Am I accepted? The answers become beliefs about who they are—their self-identity—and whether they are lovable, worthwhile, and good enough . . . or not. This is how children learn. This is how their life program develops.

When we as parents care for our children, our minds wander back to memories of our own childhood, like rewatching a movie. We become conscious of our own original programming: the behaviors, attitudes, habits, and routines that were uploaded to our own subconscious during childhood. It seems at first as if the easy road is doing what comes "naturally"—acting on autopilot. If, however, we find ourselves reliving the whole movie, we may regret it.

The harder and more exciting road starts with allowing those earliest memories to open the door to deeper self-understanding. If we are willing to take a closer look and consciously examine the programs, we empower ourselves to make better choices and change the course of our family history.

If our early years were short on nurturance and good memories, we are not doomed to repeat them. We can re-examine and rewrite the old program for our own children—and heal ourselves in the process. This is the journey of heroes. Today we are in charge of the home climate and can create the kind of family connections that we can enjoy forever.

Conscious Parenting

Creating a new reality takes shifting the way we look at our children and their behaviors, along with how we look at ourselves and interpret our own behaviors.

— REBECCA THOMPSON, *CONSCIOUSLY PARENTING*

Conscious parenting is a way of thinking about our role that acknowledges the power of awareness and intention. Consider the difference between this and mainstream parenting, which is characterized by

- an oppositional mindset: "us against them"
- having set formulas for trying to change behaviors
- operating from fear-based control
- being emotionally disconnected from children
- being emotionally disconnected from ourselves

- the idea that needs and feelings are inconvenient, and unrelated to behaviors

Conscious parenting, on the other hand, is characterized by

- the idea that needs and feelings are part of the experience and need to be discussed
- recognizing infinite possibilities and solutions to resolve challenges
- the pursuit of loving, relationship-focused attitudes
- intuition, which is sought and listened to
- the idea that harmony, peace, and joy are normal experiences[2]

Notice that one of the values of conscious parenting is intuition. To truly connect with our children, we need to be able to connect with ourselves—our feelings, our cares, our inner wisdom. Society's hype and spin can distract us from our intuition and make us distrust hunches and gut feelings. The impulses of old programming may masquerade as wisdom, insisting that we employ the old behavior-correcting strategies that cause disconnection. One way to turn off the autopilot that repeats the past is to learn to listen to the quiet voice of our intuition, which shows us where harm is being done and where balance can be found. As we find and learn to trust our inner compass, we can help our children find theirs.

One mother was upset about clashes with her nine-year-old daughter. In an attempt to reduce the tension, she made a conscious effort to keep the old voices quiet, deciding instead to simply do more touching. Over the next several months, she would pat her daughter on the shoulders and back, hug her more often, and hold her hand on walks. "As I increased the amount of physical contact, her acting out and resentment decreased," the mother said.

This parent's new approach—affection—soothed the tension and deepened her connection with her child. Her intuition guided her toward this win-win resolution. Conscious parents who tune in to their intuition have far fewer battles. (For more on this, see the *Locus of Control* section in chapter 10.)

What Kids Really Need

The same mother who talked about the negative societal perception of children earlier in this chapter realized that it was false. "My child's primary goals are having his needs met, feeling connected to others, and feeling self-worth. His misbehavior is an attempt to get a need met or to feel significance and connection . . . and my job as a parent is to help my child identify and meet those needs in appropriate ways."[3]

When children are cold, hungry, thirsty, frightened, or distressed, they need their caregivers to pay attention, meet their needs, and dissolve their distress. When children are soothed, calm, and content, they are wonderful to be around; they are happy and at peace, and life is good.

Over fifty years ago, Abraham Maslow identified specific human needs that must be met in order for children to be able to learn. Both brain research and educational experience confirm his theory. Maslow's hierarchy of needs is like a ladder. You can't get to the top rungs without firm footing on the bottom ones. These requirements are (starting from the bottom)

- physiological needs—nutrition, sleep, exercise, health

- safety needs—emotional and physical safety

- love and belonging needs—a home environment with affection, trust, respect, unconditional love, people who listen

- self-esteem needs—adult affirmation of child's worth; child has the opportunity to make choices in order to achieve and be successful

- self-actualization needs—abilities and strengths develop, problem-solving skills improve

As you can see, every need on the hierarchy is important. A child may have the love and support of a family, but if there is hunger in the family or if sleep is interrupted, learning will be more difficult. Or a child may be safe and have survival (physiological) needs met, but have the psychological or emotional insecurity of a stressed-out family. *We cannot blame children for what they do not have.* When basic needs are not met, destructive behaviors just "come naturally."

On the other hand, it's natural for children who feel included, cherished, and protected to become healthy adolescents and good citizens. By promoting mental, physical, and emotional health, we can prevent problems. Love helps keep kids' brains on track.

When a car is low on gas, there is a gauge that lets us know. Because kids don't have gauges, parents must decode cues and symptoms such as yawns, whining, and grumpiness to figure out when children are running on empty. But what part of them is empty? What are their needs?

When someone is "off," practical wisdom tells us to stop and figure out what's going on. When your kids are having a hard time, ask yourself if they are **h**ungry, **a**ngry, **l**onely, or **t**ired. These words spell "HALT" (a concept taken from *Alcoholics Anonymous*), and it's a great rule of thumb for figuring out anyone's needs.

Don't forget to also breathe deeply. When we are calm, we can choose the most appropriate response.

Now, we know we must fulfill the child's needs, but those needs must be met in the right way. For example, when a child is feeling lonely and grandma offers a cookie, this sends the misguided message to fill connection needs with sweets. A generation of children has been raised in this way, contributing to the devastating rates of obesity in our youth. Before you reach for sweets to fulfill children's needs, encourage them to talk about what's wrong, and then listen carefully and patiently to their words and try to sense emotions. Good listening can, in and of itself, unravel many problems.

There may be times, of course, when food *is* called for. If a child is actually hungry, he or she may say some terrible things, even rebuff offers of love and kindness. A young family friend would often get surly and unreasonable during after-school playtimes. Eventually one of his friends noticed he had a built-in fuel gauge: Andrew's ears turned red when he was hungry!

Ways to Engage

Researchers at Kansas State University studied ways to help single mothers improve their relationship with their children. To the researchers' surprise, they found that the more time, on a daily basis, that moms spend engaging with their child—for example, playing or reading stories—the more energy and less stress the moms had.

Everyone knows that mother-child engagement benefits children. Now we know that this is *mutually* beneficial. In other words, engaging is a win-win arrangement—good for babies *and* good for moms.[4] In fact, anyone can enjoy a fulfilling connection by engaging with children.

Connecting with a child is not always easy. There are many things, both inside of us and outside of us, that can get in the way. Sometimes we really have to work to carve out a moment, but a moment is all it takes to begin the process. Here are a few suggestions.

Build Connection Rituals

Family routines and rituals can build long-lasting connections. They can take the form of big things, such as a camping trip each summer, or little things, such as always greeting each other with hugs. Having dinner together is a classic and important family ritual that is proven to make a difference. Being together at dinnertime is one of the most important ways to maintain a continuity of connection, night after night. At dinner, people can look at each other's faces and talk. It's been proven that in families that eat together five or more times a week, kids are less likely to experiment with risky behaviors.

At any age, ritual conversations can build comfort, teaching, and connection into the routine. Following are a few examples:

- **Favorite part of the day.** Each person shares something good that happened that day. By telling what happened and remembering and integrating events, your child builds self-understanding. Rules can be added, such as "No talk about screens" (i.e., television programs, online social networking, or video games), "It's okay to pass and speak later," or "Everyone stays until everyone has shared a favorite part of the day."

- **Good news/bad news.** Each person tells a story of his or her day that goes something like this: "The good news is there were cupcakes at school. The bad news is I ate too many and I felt sick. The good news is, when I drank some milk I felt better." Sharing the highs and lows of a normal day can integrate them into a child's memory.

- **How I changed or will change for the better.** In this scenario, family members talk about something new that they tried, or plan to try, in order to get better at something or to give back to their school, community, or the world.

- **Goodnight kisses.** Regularly using words and touch to start and end the day creates bonds that are shared by all who participate—and a good way to work hugs and "I love yous" into the routine.

Tell Stories

Stories—be they personal memories, fairytales, anecdotes, or myths—help us make sense of change and find our connections to others, to the natural world, and to our past and future. In families we know that we are not alone; we are part of a unique pattern of the social fabric, a pattern that links generations together. Stories help us understand and make sense of the events of our lives. Child psychiatrist and author Daniel Siegel writes of the importance of stories: "Storytelling is fundamental to all human cultures, and our shared stories create a connection to others that builds a sense of belonging to a particular community. The stories . . . shape how its members perceive the world."[5]

Siegel discovered that the most powerful predictor of a strong bond between parent and child is the parent's willingness to speak openly about his or her own childhood. Teenagers like getting acquainted with the earlier version of their mother and father, and take comfort in knowing that their parents didn't always have it all figured out.

How we tell stories shapes how we perceive and feel about our problems, and our ability to solve them. Letting children tell their stories in a variety of ways can help them, too. When a child tells Mom and Dad and Teacher about an event, for example, each telling brings different aspects and feelings to light.

Take Care with Words

The words you use can attract people or repel them. When connections are strong, families can be more carefree with their language. But don't make assumptions; always verbalize the words that keep you connected to your family. For example:

- I love you.
- I care about you.
- I care what happens to you.
- We care about what happens to each other.
- You matter to me.
- We matter to each other.
- We work together to build this family.
- Family is important to us.
- We all try to do our best.
- We all make mistakes sometimes.
- We care for each other's feelings.
- We care about the world.
- What you feel is important.
- Keep us in the loop.
- I am here for you.

Touch

Touch is a vital part of life. Children need caresses and cuddles as much as they need food and water. Nothing else communicates like touch does.

Touch can be a sweet gift of love and pleasure, or it can be a cruel and damaging violation. What we learned about touch from our parents probably affects us to this day. If our parents cuddled and hugged us a lot, we savored their touch and our connection.

If they avoided touching us (neglect), we learned either to crave physical contact or to close ourselves off to it. If their touch was painful and punishing (physical abuse), we learned to fear and avoid touch, and/or to punish and abuse others. If our parents' touch was inappropriate (sexual abuse), we most likely suffer deep wounds that must be healed and never repeated. The types and amount of touch that mothers, fathers, and other caretakers provide can become a blueprint for future relationships. In our touch-hungry society, we may have lingering memories of bad touch, and a fear of violating boundaries—our own and those of others. Yet we still have a deep need for touch.

In Sweden, the Peaceful Touch program was introduced into kindergarten and elementary schools in order to curb violence. Because teachers are prohibited from touching students, children in this program are instructed how to tap, rub, pound, and pat each other's backs and bodies with appropriate boundaries and permission. This training helps kids relax, connect peacefully, and support one another. Since 1996, over 600,000 children have participated in this child-to-child massage on a regular basis. As a result, students report reduced levels of anxiety, stress, and aggression, and also increased self-esteem and ability to concentrate on academics.[6]

In the 1980s, futurist John Naisbitt envisioned the society of the twenty-first century that is our current reality. He anticipated the "megatrend" of engulfing technology. He cautioned readers that to cope with the technological tsunami, we need to increase the amount of touch in our lives. "The more high technology around us, the greater the need for human touch," he says.[7] In other words, with the astonishing increase in tech toys and tools, children need more cuddles and more hugs to become calm and balanced.

Nurturing touch gives a sense of safety that promotes growth during every stage of life.

Freewheeling Play

Creative, unstructured, freewheeling play is the real business of childhood. It can be the best remedy for overscheduled, overprogrammed, hurried, and stressful lives. Best of all, it reconnects children—and us—with nature and the magic of childhood.

Playing together is a powerful way to enhance family climate. Structured play—throwing a ball around, family game night—is a key component of many well-connected families. Equipment isn't necessary; fun can be created out of thin air from ordinary household items. The best kind of play costs nothing and has only one requirement: imagination.

Play is crucial to physical, intellectual, and social-emotional development at all ages, says author David Elkind. "This is especially true of the purest form of play," he says, "the unstructured, self-motivated, imaginative, independent kind, where children initiate their own games and even invent their own rules."[8] Make sure there is always time for play, since the family that plays together, as you know, stays together!

A Greater Culture

Families who bond together can support each other. Friendship with other mothers and fathers who have the same vision can provide mutual support. Many churches provide a larger culture that supports families. Some groups of mothers who met in birth classes build friendships and form support groups, and later play groups.

In the United States and the United Kingdom, where family structure is very nuclear—in that children live with only one mother and father—parents can tend to isolate from one another; but this is unnatural. In traditional life, a village is a place where many generations of families live together and belong together. Mothers and fathers, aunts and uncles naturally share best practices and support one another.

It is important to get support wherever you can find it. A healthy culture cannot be created in isolation. Find a community of positive parents to reinforce your family's values and vision. Talk about positive parenting with others. Commit to support each other in doing what's best for the children. Take parenting classes and exchange phone numbers. Ask for feedback from your friends, your spouse, and your kids . . . and you'll never need a supernanny.

• • •

10

. . . .

Your Most Important Relationship

*Setting an example is not the main means of
influencing another, it is the only means.*

— ALBERT EINSTEIN

In the bullying dynamic, bullies show little regard for the feelings of others, and victims have trouble standing up for their own needs. What is true of both extremes, and also of so many people in between, is that there is an "inner bully" who only makes things worse.

Sometimes we wish our kids could be all the things that we're not, but kids, like little mirrors, often reflect our emotional states. About half of the children with depressed mothers develop depression—three times more than normal. They are also more likely to be anxious, irritable, and disruptive than other youngsters. But when mothers get help for their depression and get better, so do their children. Depression in fathers also affects children.[1]

Who you are is what you teach. Children learn best through imitation; they learn how to live by watching how you live, and they learn to blossom by watching you blossom. This chapter is a guide to taking care of, and understanding, yourself . . . but it is also a lesson for your kids. All of the concepts in this chapter can and should be taught, as well as modeled.

Take Care of Yourself

Your relationship with yourself is the foundation
of your relationships with everyone else.

— RICK HANSON, *BUDDHA'S BRAIN*

When Louise was a teenager, the concept of "self-care" didn't exist; any woman who did something to take care of herself was put down in her family's hardworking immigrant culture for being "selfish." We now know that parents must take good care of themselves in order to take good care of their children. You cannot give what you don't have.

How your kids turn out depends to a large extent on the relationship you have with yourself. The way you treat yourself also sets the standard for how you expect to be treated.

When parents don't take care of their own needs, they may try to get their needs met through their kids; unfortunately, this is backward and unhealthy. If children feel pressured to live out their parents' aspirations, they may not be able to think for themselves, or to stand up to manipulation and pressure from peers. Conversely, they may rebel fiercely and break the relationship. Their search for their authentic selves may become a lifelong issue, and it most certainly affects the parent-child relationship. As Carl Jung said, "Nothing has a stronger influence on children than the unlived lives of their parents."

Parents can take care of themselves by

- recognizing and speaking up for their own feelings, needs, and wants
- taking time out to manage their stress
- surrounding themselves with family and friends who give practical and emotional support
- using their gifts both in and apart from the family
- having their own identities

Be For, Not Against, Yourself

Many people spend their lives searching for what is wrong with them—always focusing on faults, failings, and imperfections.

Such a negative focus blurs the self-image of many people. Blind to their own beauty and the good qualities their friends see, they hunt for what's wrong rather than what's right. Those who are hypercritical of themselves became this way by constantly being criticized in childhood. The critical remarks and put-downs they heard from their parents, siblings, and peers repeat over and over again in their self-talk—for decades or a lifetime—making them suspicious of praise and compliments.

A strange and common characteristic of people with a negative personal focus is that they can vividly imagine that others are disapproving and criticizing them, even when that is the farthest thing from reality.

A healthier and happier option is to be for, not against, yourself. Instead of focusing on what's wrong, make a concerted effort to focus on what's right. Old buildings must be retrofitted to make them earthquake-proof. Old computers need new operating systems to be able to run new programs. We, too, benefit by upgrading the beliefs that someone installed years ago. It is never too late to strengthen the foundations of our mental health and resilience.

Self-Talk: "How You Talk!"

One of the most significant findings in psychology in the last twenty years is that individuals can choose the way they think.

— MARTIN SELIGMAN

Ninety-five percent of your thoughts today will be a repetition of past thoughts. They may be last year's thoughts, or perhaps some very old thoughts from childhood. If these thoughts make you feel good, *great*! If not, you are likely to repeat this flow of negative thoughts—the "stinkin' thinkin'" of the "inner bully"—for another year, or another twenty years.

How you talk to yourself determines your self-esteem and the quality of your connection with others. The way you talk to yourself is probably the way your elders talked to you as a child, and probably how you talk to your children. If you were disrespected and rejected, blamed and shamed, put down and humiliated as a child, you may be recycling those cruel messages in your self-talk. But if you could choose to think differently, would you?

We can beat ourselves up—bully ourselves—or lift ourselves up. We can control our thoughts, or let our self-talk control us. And guess what? We get no bonus points for beating ourselves up.

Your computer has a spam filter, but you have to intentionally sort through what turns up in your mental inbox, and toss the junk into the trash. What else can you do with "junk thoughts"? Consider the following ideas:

- You can send them out to the trash can of the universe.
- You can replace them with positive thoughts, just like changing the TV channel.
- You can argue against negative thoughts, as recommended in chapter 7, and replace them with positive thoughts.

Just as an editor changes words in a manuscript before it becomes a book, we can edit our thoughts before we start believing them. When your inner bully says, "You're not ___ enough" or "I'm not ___ enough," dispute it, since it's only true if you are looking at things a certain way. Argue against that lie; then list the reasons that prove you *are* enough. You may surprise yourself.

You don't have to put up with put-downs, especially from yourself.

As you gradually stifle the inner bully, you will notice an increase in self-respect, self-esteem, and self-confidence.

Self-Respect, Self-Esteem

Positive self-esteem is the choice to respect, accept,
and love yourself fully. It is a commitment to yourself,
and the best gift that you can give and receive.

—LOUISE HART, *ON THE WINGS OF SELF-ESTEEM*

About sixty years ago, the head of a department store chain declared, "It's our job to make women unhappy with what they have." Since then, advertisers have targeted women's self-doubt and insecurities by promoting impossible ideals of feminine beauty and perfection for them to live up to.

The financial success of the beauty, fashion, and weight-loss industries demonstrates the advertisers' victory. Unfortunately, their success and profits have come at an immense cost—to our self-confidence, self-esteem, and pocketbooks.

This long-established tradition in our society, which also affects boys and men, convinces us that, for many reasons, we are not okay. Humiliation and shame are linked to who we are and how we are "different." In chapter 4, it was noted that those who appear to be "different" attract bullies. But with good self-esteem, we can love our differences as the unique qualities that make us who we are.

Every person wants and needs to feel important, capable, lovable, and worthy. In order to recover self-esteem, we must be willing to let go of self-rejection and affirm self-acceptance and self-love. We are lovable. We are valuable. We are and have always been okay. We have done our best given the information we had at the time. And as adults, we are in charge of our self-esteem.

Here are a couple of activities you can do to lift your self-esteem:

1. Write down your strengths, abilities, and positive qualities, plus the compliments and praise you have received from others over the years. When you feel your self-esteem sagging, pore over these notes. This list can help you see the truth about who you really are.

2. Look at yourself in the mirror. Instead of looking for your flaws, focus on a part that you love—perhaps a feature that makes you look unique, or a part of you that reminds you of a beloved parent. Then give yourself a compliment. If there is a part of your body you don't love, appreciate it for what it does. For example, "I love this soft belly for bringing me my children."

3. Make a list of twenty things you love to do either alone or with others. Put this list where you will see it often. Every day do at least one of these self-nurturing activities; if you are low,

or depressed, do more than one. Over time, these things may become self-care routines or rituals. This simple exercise can lift your spirits and feed your soul, perhaps inspiring others to do the same exercise.

People with high self-esteem have a high level of confidence. They tend to be assertive and speak with authority. High self-esteem is crucial for parents and children alike, and it is also an indicator of good mental health.

When parents have high self-esteem, children's self-esteem will also tend to be high. When moms and dads grow and become better parents, everyone benefits.

Self-esteem is not a silver bullet that solves every problem. Even bullies can have high self-esteem. A healthy sense of self-worth, however, is an essential ingredient for good mental health, well-being, and happiness.

Authenticity: Who Are You, Really . . . ?

Authentic means genuine and real, not false or copied. An authentic document is an original that has not been edited or falsified. Your Real Self is authentic—it is the core of who you really and truly are. This is not to be confused with who you think you "should" be.

Babies and small children are authentic beings, honestly in touch with their needs, their feelings, their curiosity, and the inner guidance system that directs their actions. As children grow and learn, they may or may not retain those qualities, depending on their personalities, their anxieties, and their experiences. But being a healthy adult means getting back in touch with, and operating from, that simple and pure essence we all had when we were born.

Authentic people consider the needs of others and seek win-win solutions without sacrificing their own needs. Authentic people are aware of the impact of their actions and behavior on others; they strive to take right actions that benefit—and are not harmful to—themselves or others. Authentic people accept themselves and others as worthy of attention and care.

Being authentic is paramount for good mental health and healthy relationships. Unfortunately, our culture tends to heartlessly thrust young people in the opposite direction, demanding that they be artificial and untrue to themselves, even put themselves at risk to fit in or "succeed." It's no wonder mental and physical disorders abound.

The Journey Back

According to author Brené Brown, "Authenticity is a collection of choices that we have to make every day. It's about the choice to show up and be real. The choice to be honest. The choice to let our true selves be seen."[2]

Animals have instincts to guide them. Humans also have intuition, a built-in guidance system installed deep in our souls—the source of our authenticity. In order to become who we really are, instead of a phony imitation, we need to tune out the noise of conflicting and overwhelming cultural and social messages and tune in to our inner voice, our intuition, our personal wisdom. We need to tune in to our own needs, emotions, and desires and define ourselves, instead of letting "them" define us by the needs, emotions, and desires they think we should have.

As we make more authentic choices, the pretense starts to crumble. We uncover the unique "original" we really are. When we admit we are not perfect, we are relieved to discover that we are still okay.

How we live our lives really matters. Living from inside out, we become a whole-hearted first-rate version of who we really are rather than a second-rate copy of someone else. James Baraz, author of *Awakening Joy,* says, "What is happening inside us is far more important than what is happening 'out there.' We can't control circumstances or other people, but we can train our minds to see clearly and our hearts to remain open, even in the face of pain."[3] What Baraz is referring to is the difficult task of feeling our own feelings. When we can do that, and face the painful stuff, we can separate ourselves from the situation without projecting our insecurities on others, including our children.

The journey toward authenticity is about releasing the fantasy of who you *think* you are *supposed* to be, and becoming the good, worthwhile person you really *are*.

Locus of Control

I am free because I know that I alone am
morally responsible for everything I do.

— ROBERT A. HEINLEIN

Good and bad things happen to all of us, regardless of what we believe about who or what caused them. But how we think about those things makes all the difference in our lives.

What is "locus of control" and why does it matter? Locus of control describes the degree to which people believe they can control the events in their lives. Every parent struggles with his or her personal locus of control, since from the moment that little baby arrives his or her needs become the top priority. Parents are faced with multiple responsibilities: kids, schools, jobs, and housework, to name a few. We are all beholden to outside forces. Those of us with a more external locus of control are attracted by trends and fashions; those of us with a more internal locus of control are guided by a moral compass and independent choices.

Do you tend to take responsibility for yourself, your thoughts, and your actions (internal locus of control), or do you tend to blame others or the situation (external locus of control)? This is similar to the explanatory styles discussed in chapter 7.

Children begin life with an external locus of control. They trust the adults around them to guide and teach them, clean up their messes, and tell them what to do. As they mature, they internalize their locus of control. This is a long, gradual process made of tiny steps in the right direction that is not complete until they reach their late teens, twenties, thirties, or even forties.

In the process of developing essential core strengths, adults encourage children to think for themselves, to have and express opinions, and to make decisions. Children gradually learn to trust themselves more—their inner "me" or authentic Real Self—and develop an internal locus of control. They learn cause-effect relationships, understanding that their behavior is directly related to outcomes and consequences—cleaning up their own messes, putting away their toys.

These youngsters are developing an inner locus of control characterized by the following:

- accepting personal responsibility
- being in touch with their Real Self, their intuition, and their moral compass
- finding their voices, speaking up, being able to eventually become upstanders
- doing the right thing, even when no one is watching
- having high self-confidence and self-esteem

Unfortunately, many people had childhood experiences that did not foster essential core strengths, characterized by the following:

- not being listened to
- not being encouraged to think for themselves
- not being able to express their thoughts and opinions
- not being allowed to develop their inner locus of control

Youngsters with an external locus of control tend to
- follow the crowd
- look to others for direction, becoming easy to manipulate
- be bystanders who don't speak up
- lack the fortitude to do the right thing unless someone is watching
- become bullies, victims, or bully-victims
- not take responsibility for their actions

Research offers even more insight on locus of control related to bullying:[4]

- Youngsters with an internal locus of control do not get involved in bullying; some have never been bullied by others.

- The bully-victims with the most external locus of control have the highest levels of aggression.
- The highest levels of external locus of control were reported by victims, followed by bully-victims, bullies, and no-status students.

An external locus of control is correlated with low self-esteem, learned helplessness, child abuse, and neglect. It is also linked with low self-efficacy, meaning one does not believe in one's own power or capacity to be effective.

This is a concept you can apply to yourself and to your children: Locus of control is absolutely essential to resilience and one of the major building blocks of increasing it. Although we all will experience disappointment, frustration, and personal pain at some point, an inner locus of control yields optimism and determination to move forward. The more internal your locus of control is, the more resilient you will be. Conversely, the more external your locus of control, the less resilient you will be.

Uncovering Beliefs and Assumptions

Children are exceptionally impressionable. Their brains upload everything they experience. In preparation for the rest of life, kids eagerly absorb everything they learn about the world, while looking to adults for caring, attention, guidance, and protection. If they don't find these things in their family, they will seek to fill their needs from other sources in order to survive—or to satisfy their curiosity.

Children don't realize that some folks cannot be trusted. Their underdeveloped brains cannot yet self-regulate, which puts them at great risk in this high-tech, materialistic, bully-filled culture. Preciously innocent and trusting, they do not realize that every TV program and every advertiser wants a piece of them. They do not realize they are being manipulated by digital media that care only about profits. They do not realize that they are vulnerable to the intentions of older siblings and playmates.

Kids observe everything. They notice when you touch them, and how you touch them. They notice if you're smiling or not smiling. They then draw conclusions—which become their "truths," their beliefs—regardless of whether they are true or not true. *They are doing their best with the brain they have.* One day they may realize that what was true for them when they were five is now only just one way of looking at it.

Countless adults in families suffer from the effects of adverse childhood experiences (ACEs), such as alcohol or drug abuse. Perhaps you grew up in a home where the grown-ups were not all that grown up. Maybe you had to figure out how to cope with emotional upheaval by hiding your feelings and needs, deferring to others and avoiding conflict, or becoming controlling or obsessive.

In truth, you were actually quite brilliant to figure out the strategies that helped you survive! You were doing the best you could with the brain you had and the parents you had, and you can be proud of yourself. You came up with creative ways to protect your sanity, your emotional safety, and your self-worth. Even if you came out a little battered and bruised trying to recover from your childhood, you survived. You earned and deserve to feel "survivors pride." The bad news is that what helped you survive in the war zone is now working against you during peacetime.[5]

Twelve Step groups such as Alcoholics Anonymous, Narcotics Anonymous, Al-Anon, and Overeaters Anonymous have helped countless people recover from old wounds, examine old beliefs, and unravel old patterns. Other resources include support and therapy groups, individual and family practitioners, community mental health centers, churches, hospitals, and crisis telephone lines.

Traps to Self-Understanding

Many forces keep us from understanding and becoming who we really are, or from grasping what is most important in life.

Substance Use

Some adults use substances such as alcohol, marijuana, and other recreational drugs to escape from the difficulties of reality.

But by using such substances we can hurt ourselves and those we love. Whether it's with our moods or our absence, we eventually either harm our relationships or let them wither from neglect. Our kids may seem fine, but when their attachment with us is broken, it's hard to repair. And our substance use can create danger. One dad stopped smoking marijuana forever one night when he had to take his son's friend who was sleeping over to the emergency room. "What if I had been high? I never want to be in that position," he declared.

A certain percentage of users are, for one reason or another, more susceptible to addiction. This means that the craving for the substance becomes a motivating factor in one's life, and using it again becomes necessary in order to feel "normal."

Does this have anything to do with bullying? You bet it does. Kids who are bullied—especially girls—are at risk for substance use, and those who use drugs are at risk of becoming victims of rape and violence. Parents who use substances are at greater risk of becoming or raising bullies.[6]

Codependence

Nearly one in five American adults lived with an alcoholic during childhood.[7] These adults are at greater risk for becoming alcoholic, for neglect or abuse, and for a variety of emotional problems. Everyone in an alcoholic's family is an actor in the complicated dynamics. Codependence is common in families and relationships where addiction and alcoholism are present. It is a condition where one's focus on the needs or control of another outweighs one's own needs.

However, codependence applies to anyone involved in any addictive behavior, not just alcoholics. In fact, the group Co-Dependents Anonymous welcomes "anyone who would like to have better relationships," since relating to others is difficult when expectations, responsibilities, and boundaries are misunderstood.

People with an external locus of control—those lacking in self-regulation, self-control, and sense of self—do as they are told. They are, therefore, vulnerable to manipulation, addictions, and codependency. They are more likely to be preyed upon and pressured by their peers. Like marionettes on strings, the more they are controlled by external forces, the more they lose touch with their authentic inner guidance system.

Codependent adults' external locus of control makes them rely on things and people outside of themselves for self-worth; thus, they are not in control of their own self-esteem, and neither are their children in control of theirs.

The good news is this: When people actively develop a dynamic sense of self, their mental health and well-being improves. Rebuilding a strong sense of self bolsters recovery from any mental disease. Starting to build a strong sense of self early in life, therefore, sets our kids on a path toward positive mental health and well-being.

When we take responsibility for our own emotional states, we find that happiness is a do-it-yourself job.

Ignorance

It is a sad fact that keeping people ignorant is a tried-and-true form of control.

There is a lot of subtle manipulation going on in the battle for people's minds, whether by the media or within relationships. A lot of untruths are being trumpeted as true, and many crucial truths are being forcefully denied by those who find them threatening.

Be critical when watching the news, when viewing commercials, when browsing the Internet, and when reading forwarded e-mails. Be on guard for messages that feel disingenuous. Be cautious of manipulation, and remember our brains are vulnerable to negativity. Pay attention to nonverbal cues, your feelings, and your intuition.

The culture of honor that we mentioned in part 1 is a commitment to ignorance, and to reacting without thinking. A strong force of anti-intellectualism in this country criticizes intelligent people as being "elites" and not to be trusted, even when using our minds is the only way to solve our problems.

Rampant negativity not only keeps us in the dark but also can stir up anxiety, fear, anger, depression, frustration, and low self-esteem, which can lead to bullying, aggression, and violence.

In other words, there are many forces that want you to keep a closed mindset. Be true to yourself. Keep an open mind, stay positive, and seek the truth.

Comparison

Do you compare yourself to friends, other parents, celebrities, and siblings? Do you judge others with thoughts like, "I would never treat my kids/wear my hair/drive my car like that"? Or do you find an enviable quality in someone else, compare yourself unfavorably, and then feel inadequate and inferior? Do you beat yourself up and put yourself and others down? Comparison sets us up for unhealthy competition. It drives wedges between people, creates separation, and enforces conformity.

Sadly, from an early age children are taught to compare themselves, rather than accept themselves and others. Attitudes of comparison are frequently in commercials: "Are you as good as *this*?" Comparison is also a factor in the power imbalance of the bully/victim dynamic, and something children can pick up on in their parents.

Consider those you admire to be models who can open you up to new possibilities. Instead of putting yourself down, use what you like in them to lift yourself up. Seeing with fresh eyes, you can find people everywhere who inspire you to new heights. Children can also be our models, inspire us, and teach us some of our most important lessons.

Perfectionism

"A perfectionist is someone who takes great pains," Louise says in her workshops, "and gives them to others." Perfectionists always look for something wrong, find it, and then are shocked and angry about it. They're constantly frustrated, disappointed, and seldom feel "good enough." Their thinking is distorted; they imagine or fantasize things are much worse than they really are—and are "always right," making everyone else wrong.

Being a perfectionist can be a wonderful thing on the job, if you are a copyeditor, a brain surgeon, a technician, or a conductor; performing a job to exacting standards can be exhilarating, satisfying, and meaningful. Striving for excellence is different, however, than perfectionism. Perfectionists tend to push people apart divisively rather than inspire them to work together toward the same goal.

When we harshly judge ourselves and each other, competition, disconnection, and bullying often follow. The feeling of never measuring up leads to terrible diseases such as eating disorders and personality disorders. A child is unaware that a perfectionist parent's remarks are erroneous, and the negative judgments are automatically internalized into the child's sense of who he or she is, like a virus or worm, damaging self-esteem.

What does a mistake mean to a perfectionist? Total failure! Yet mistakes are teachers. It is your privilege as a human being to make mistakes, and it is your challenge to learn from them—so you don't repeat them. Learn the wisdom each mistake offers you.

Then laugh at your bloopers. Your kids will laugh with you. They'll learn from your mistakes, and learn how to bounce back from their own. Being a "recovering perfectionist" is healthier and a lot more fun. Accept that you are a "good enough" parent who is getting better. Help your kids know that they are "good enough" and do not have to be perfect. *When you admit to your own imperfections, you take the pressure off your children—and yourself—and improve the connection between you.* Showing your children that you can make a mistake, own it, and learn from it will help them do the same.

Avenues to Healing

If you've been hurt, you need to heal. Creating an authentic relationship with yourself is an act of healing. The avenues to healing are unlimited, but here are a handful of possibilities:

- **Being honest and still being accepted.** Talk about your experiences with a trusted friend. Without the fear of being judged, knowing you'll be loved no matter what, you can find relief and gratitude when you're finally able to share what's bothering you.

- **Talking therapy.** Recounting the experience and expressing repressed feelings satisfies the need to articulate—to tell your story. Talk something through—over the course of days, weeks, months, or years—with a safe and supportive listener, such as a trained therapist. This promotes resolution and can release the grip of adverse childhood experiences (ACEs) on the psyche.

- **Autobiographical writing.** Writing about yourself in a journal can be remarkably beneficial. Journal writing gives you the opportunity to be totally honest in private while exploring and releasing whatever comes up. Writing and rewriting fosters clarity and integration. Sharing your writing with others may help them to heal as well.

- **Emotional Freedom Technique, or EFT.** This new "tapping" therapy is like acupuncture without needles. EFT is a modality that works with a person's subtle energies while he or she is talking about pain or trauma.

- **Bodywork.** ACEs contribute to disease, and because our emotions are stored in our bodies, it stands to reason that bodywork such as massage, Reiki, chiropractic, and acupuncture can help release stored emotion. One therapy called BodyMind integrates bodywork with talk therapy.

- **Meditation.** Quieting the mind each day and learning to separate ourselves from our thoughts helps us approach life's frustrations and annoyances with greater clarity and resolve. Moving meditations like yoga and t'ai chi build strength and insight as well.

- **Exercise.** Any form of exercise can help us get perspective on our problems and our lives. A daily run or dance class can help us sweat out tensions, focus on caring for ourselves, and foster vibrant health.

- **Mindfulness.** Mental health professionals rave about the benefits of a daily mindfulness practice. Research indicates that it produces cognitive and psychological improvements.

- **Psychotherapy.** There is no substitute for a good psychotherapist when overcoming serious trauma, any more than there is a substitute for a medical doctor when an arm or leg is broken.

Don't be afraid to seek healing if you've been hurt or if you've hurt someone. Past mistakes are meant to guide you, not define you.

The Positive Road of Parenting

Your relationship with yourself is the foundation of your relationships with everyone else. With commitment and a change of heart, you can give your children a much better start than you had. As you heal from the fear-based family of your past and create your own love-based family, you get to live in and enjoy a kinder, safer home.

An openness to learning and trusting leads to more positive emotions which, little by little, reshape who you are, beginning an upward spiral. New social and emotional skills such as assertive communication, nonviolent conflict resolution, and stress reduction can lessen or even eliminate drama and trauma, opening a world of positive experience. In sum, these skills can help fill in the developmental holes of parents and children alike—a step to becoming whole.

Positive parenting invites us to examine our own upbringing. It requires rewriting the old fear-based "script" we learned during our early years and developing a new love-based approach. This takes determination and patience. As we learn positive interaction tools and skills and develop a different parenting style, we can raise healthier children—while healing our hearts and souls.

• • •

11

· · · ·

Connection:
The "Super-Protective" Factor

Our effectiveness as parents is in direct proportion to the strength of the bond we have with our children.

— PAM LEO, *CONNECTION PARENTING*

We were at a busy restaurant the other day. On either side of our booth were parties of five, with kids about the same age. It was dinnertime, and all the kids were hungry and tired after a day of activity. Our ears perked up when we heard kids at both tables complain about their food! "I didn't want it with vegetables," one of them whined. "It's not what I thought it would be," said the other.

The mother at one table snapped. "It's what you ordered, so you have to eat it. I am so tired of this constant whining! You've been giving me the worst headache all day long, going against everything!" Soon everyone at the table was involved in the tension. Another child started acting out; a plate of food landed on the floor, and the whole family left in a bad mood, grumbling about never going to a restaurant again.

On the other side, the mother started talking to her son about the plate of strange food. She asked questions like "What part looks yummy and what part are you worried about?" The matter was resolved within a minute or two. The child ended up trying something new, eating the whole plate of food, and having dessert while the family enjoyed the time together.

One simple ingredient made the difference between things going right and things going wrong: one parent connected with her child, and the other parent didn't.

Anyone who has a computer knows that when you are having technical issues, you first check the connections: Is it plugged in? Has something disconnected? You don't need a repair person when it's just a matter of a cable coming loose. This also applies to children. When things are not right with children, the first thing to do is "check the connections." People with cell phones know how important good connections are. Without them, misunderstandings are inevitable.

The human need for connection is the most important emotional and social need of all, and a high quality of life is not possible without it. When the connection is disrupted or missing, it can cause a cascade of related problems. We talked about "connection deficit" in chapter 8; kids can act out, shut down, and get in trouble. Toddlers can have tantrums; teens can use drugs, skip school, or have sex before they're ready. Kids of all ages can bully or be bullied because they lack and long for a connection that grounds them.

Hardwired for Connection

Anything that promotes emotional connection has a healing effect on the brain and nervous system. Conversely, separation and isolation can lead to illness and dysfunction.

— THOMAS LEWIS, *A GENERAL THEORY OF LOVE*

Our brains and nerves operate from the firing of trillions of neurons (nerve cells) across synapses, which are nothing but little spaces where tiny signals, like sparks of electricity, jump from one side to the other. Electricity functions on circuits, which are circles that want to be closed, or connected.

Humans are hardwired for connection, which soothes and grounds our nervous systems. (Hugs are like emotional CPR. If the brain and nervous system are electrical systems, then touch is like grounding a live wire.) Our brains are built for making connections—this is how we learn. All of our senses are connected to memory and learning, and the more connections we build, the larger and more capable our brains are.

When we understand that our need for connection is just as important as our need for food or water, it is easier to understand bullying. Feeling they fundamentally lack a connection with others, bullies act out of a need for inclusion and acceptance.

Children with close connections to parents are social; they enjoy a sense of well-being, and they thrive. A child's primal connection with his or her mother, as well as deep emotional bonds with his or her father and siblings, determines and fixes a child's identity. A lack of these connections can trigger any number of behavior issues or disorders.

Mysteries of Attachment Parenting

First relationships set the tone for all future relationships.

— DR. BRUCE PERRY

The provocative cover of a 2012 issue of *Time* magazine showed a woman breastfeeding a child who appeared to be around six years old, calling attention to the "controversy" of attachment parenting. This style of parenting, based on a human infant's need to form a reliable emotional bond with his or her caregiver in order to survive and thrive, is as old as humanity, although it is often labeled as a "trend" in America.

The lifelong effects of a strong attachment have a more profound impact than most people understand. According to Attachment Parenting International (API), this parenting style is all about being prepared for parenting; feeding with love and respect; responding with sensitivity; providing nurturing touch, safe sleep, and consistent and loving care; and balancing family life with personal life. A secure attachment rests on the parent's ability to fulfill the child's need for trust, empathy, and affection by providing responsive care. Building healthy relationship skills, the parent provides critical emotional scaffolding for the child to learn essential self-regulatory skills.[1]

Whether or not a mother is able to breastfeed until her child is three years old (the actual age of the child on the *Time* cover), parental devotion creates an attachment bond that provides the infant with a sense of well-being, enhances healthy brain development, and brings pleasure to infant and parents alike. One recent study found that children who were raised with attachment parenting as infants have a larger hippocampus (a part of the brain involved in translating short-term memories into long-term memories) than children who were not.[2]

A person with a secure attachment style is generally able to respond to stress in healthy ways and establish meaningful and close relationships; a person with an insecure attachment style may be more susceptible to stress and less healthy relationships. Insecurely attached individuals are at greater risk for serious mental health concerns such as depression and anxiety.[3] And, as we know, depression and anxiety both factor into the bullying dynamic.

Attachment parenting is important for the child and for society. When a child does not develop a secure attachment with a mother or other primary caregiver in the first months and years of life, he or she is more likely to display aggressive and antisocial behaviors. An aversion to touch and physical affection, control issues, anger problems, difficulty showing genuine care and affection, and an underdeveloped conscience are medically recognized indications of attachment disorder, which is thought to affect 75 percent of prison inmates.[4]

The Secret to Attachment: Attunement

New mothers worry about not being able to attach to their child if the mothers are unconscious during birth, are unable to breastfeed, or have to work outside the home, but bonding happens in so many different ways: touch, spoken words and song, smiles, and eye contact, to name a few. Daniel Stern, who wrote *The Birth of a Mother,* says "Let the child know her emotions are being met with empathy, accepted and reciprocated."

With eye contact and close connection, parents can tune into their children's emotional states with such elegant accuracy that they know what their child needs before the child knows. Paying attention to attunement is essential.

Starved for Attention

When Kristen, as a teenage babysitter, first heard the term *attention deficit disorder,* she assumed it meant children did not have enough attention given to them. Later, as a work-at-home mother whose focus was directed in a dozen different directions—complicated by living in a neighborhood where kids were left on their own by single or otherwise overwhelmed parents, and being married to a teacher and sending her son to public schools at a time when staff was being cut and class sizes were growing—Kristen observed that *attention is the world's most precious resource.*

Best-selling author and physician Gabor Maté agrees that positive attention can change even the most difficult of situations. When parents contact him complaining about oppositional behavior, he gives them two weeks of homework before the first session. "View your child with *unconditional positive regard,*" he advises, using a term coined by author Carl Rogers that describes a warm, caring attitude. He tells parents to focus on attachment to the child—showing him or her with every action and word that the emotional bond is more important than anything else—and to never be the first to break the connection. For many families, this solves the oppositional behavior. Once parents build the habit of positive attention, the change in the child's behavior becomes permanent. (For more information on children's brains and nervous systems, see chapter 16.) Maté also believes that the rise in bullying, AD/HD, and other mental disorders in American children is the result of a disconnected and highly stressed society characterized by loss of nurturing from parents.[5]

Kids hunger for their parents' attention. And, like filling an empty cup, when you show interest in what your children are doing, feeling, and thinking, you are filling their need for attention. Undivided attention is also a good way to get to know your kids better. In fact, your attention may be the most important gift you have to give.

Study after study shows that children really do need the attention they crave. If that need is not fulfilled through positive attention, they will "act out," doing whatever it takes to get attention—whine, yell, or fight with siblings. Negative attention, after all, is better than no attention. Positive attention, on the other hand, results in better behavior with less need for acting out.

Sometimes busy parents don't have the time to be as attentive as they would like to be. But a pat on the arm, eye contact, or a smile are connections in and of themselves, and can help kids be patient until you can give them your undivided attention. Don't yell at a child who is bugging you; be kind, loving, and firm. Redirect his or her attention, perhaps to another activity, and then get back and attend to his or her needs.

A father and his pre-teen son sat across from each other at a Mexican restaurant. The dad was absorbed in a phone conversation, ignoring his son. The son's body language shouted his need for Dad to see him, to connect with him, to be there for him. Dad had picked him up at school and the child was probably eager to tell his father about his day. Unfortunately, without realizing it, the dad ignored the needs of his boy, potentially harming their relationship and most certainly missing an opportunity to engage and reconnect. If the father had known better, he would have done better. If he had looked at his son, he could have noticed his son's need; touched his hand across the table; whispered, "Sorry, this call is urgent—I'll be quick"; or told the person he was talking to, "This isn't a good time to talk. I am with my son now and will call you back." When parents listen, engage, and connect, they share with their children a sense of emotional well-being and good feelings that lead to positive memories. "Being there" for others affirms their inherent goodness and worth.

There are some children who get plenty of adult attention but still want more. A technique for making sure kids *know* they will get attention is to plan "special time" every day at a certain time. In some cases, you can talk about the special time beforehand, saying something like "I'm really looking forward to our special time." This helps your child remember that his or her needs are, indeed, on your radar. Then you can notice the time: "Our special time is in forty minutes." When the time finally arrives, your child is in control and has your undivided attention. You can say, "Five minutes until our special time is over—

anything else you want to do/tell me/talk about?" Toward the end of your time together, you can say something about looking forward to tomorrow's special time. Later on in the day, you can say to your child, "I really enjoyed our special time today." After a few days, this calms your child's insecurities noticeably, as your child begins to realize he or she is indeed part of your plan.

Adult responses reinforce and shape what children do and how they act. Positive attention is the best way to increase the behaviors you want more of. It is also the best reward for positive behavior.

Hungry for Affirmation

At the root of positive attention is love. Everyone has a deep and profound need for human love. Being loved is essential in order to feel valued and worthwhile, and it is also necessary in order to be able to love others. Feeling lovable and worthwhile creates in us an ability to give love. In other words, we must first be loved in order to love ourselves, and we must love ourselves in order to love others.

When children are provided unconditional love and emotional strengthening, their fundamental humanity is affirmed on a regular basis. Without affirmation, emotional growth is stunted, and a child can become anxious and depressed.

Love is communicated on an emotional level through the eyes, facial expression, and other nonverbal communication, as well as gentle words of acceptance and encouragement. As the child receives affirmation, emotional development naturally unfolds. One mother manages to give each of her eight children special attention each week with "sweetheart notes." She wrote each child's name on a paper heart and then laminated the hearts. She writes on them with a dry-erase marker, telling her children what she appreciates about them, what she notices about how they are growing and learning, or something good they did; sometimes she just tells them she loves them. She affirms their goodness, so they can share it with the world.

Teaching Attention

Some children have difficulty paying attention. Teachers are stressed by the neediness of these children, many of whom show up unprepared to learn. Basically, attention is like a bank account: if you don't have attention coming in, you can't pay it out to others.

The process of positive parenting passes on habits and thinking structures to children through attention, connection, and teaching. Children need to be led through life's simple procedures, step-by-step, until they are ready to do them on their own. They need to be taught how to buckle a seat belt, how to tie a shoe, and how to do homework and turn it in on time. It's harder for some children to learn habits, to be sure, but emotional connection helps in every case. (For more information about building "attention muscles," see chapter 16.)

In the restaurant story at the beginning of this chapter, the mother who connected with her child was also teaching her child. By giving him positive attention, and by breaking his food problem down into "bite-size" chunks, she was also teaching him how to slow down and pay attention. A good teacher, she knew that connecting with her child helped him build a bridge between what he knew and what he didn't know.

Repairing Broken Connections

There is a feeling people get in their gut, somewhere below the solar plexus, that indicates when a connection is broken. It is a feeling that happens when someone is mad at us, when we've made a mistake, or when something is wrong. Most of us learned somewhere along the way to ignore that feeling, to "suck it up," to "get over it," or to "deal with it." But our problems don't go away until we learn to listen to that feeling.

Sometimes when parents try to manage the demands of work, family, and money, the special bonds with their children can get shoved aside. When this happens, children's feelings can get hurt, perhaps without the parents realizing it. Unlike adults, children lack the ability to brush off hurt feelings. But stuffing these hurt feelings inside will only color a child's self-image, along with the relationship with his or her parents. It is possible, however, to repair broken connections, and it's up to the adults to take the lead. Remember the 3:1 ratio discussed in chapter 5 to help shift the energy and begin to reconnect.

Staying Connected in a Busy World

As we get busier and busier, the quality of the connection erodes between developing children and responsible adults. Regular, intimate face-to-face family interactions—that allow parents to model appropriate emotional and social behaviors, instill values, relate personal experiences, and deepen trust—disappear easily into other distractions. Yet what happens early on in a child's life impacts what happens later on. Violence, depression, behavior problems like bullying, and involvement with alcohol or drugs are all troubles that are connected to connection.

Attachment—bonding, touch, love, trust, and acceptance—is what "glues" children and parents to each other. These connections make it safe for children to be who they are and to make mistakes. When these connections are absent, children can develop a "false self," pretending to be who they're not. They seek approval and attempt to earn the love and acceptance for which they hunger. Look around and you'll see many examples of "connection deficit disorder."

For a teenager, nothing is more beneficial than a good relationship with his or her parents. Even when teens seem to be pushing you away, they yearn for more time and connection with you. Make a point to frequently spend loving quality time with them. Uphold your connection rituals (see chapter 9), or create new ones as life changes.

Perfectionism vs. Connection

In the previous chapter we talked about perfectionism, but let's look at it again as a roadblock to connection. If connection is like the glue that holds families together, perfectionism is a solvent.

Perfectionism can be very destructive in families, since a perfectionist mostly finds faults and failings and rarely says anything positive. Perfectionist parents may unintentionally contribute to bullying behavior in their families. Rampant negative emotions keep perfectionists—and the people around them—completely self-absorbed and engaged in perpetual self-evaluation, creating anger, anxiety, disappointment, frustration, low self-esteem, and depression. No one feels good enough. Perfectionism rigidifies behavior, making parents unable to respond spontaneously when flexibility is needed.

Perfectionism runs in families, and can be handed down from generation to generation unless someone along the way decides to make a choice to be different. Perfectionist parents have trouble connecting with their children because it's impossible for a child to trust, feel comfortable with, or feel close to someone who is continually judging him or her. Also, when a parent criticizes a child, both feel bad. It's impossible to be your authentic self around a perfectionist; therefore, a perfectionist rarely sees people for who they *really* are.

When you are truly connected to someone, when you accept all that that person is and love him or her unconditionally, you don't see imperfections; or, if you do see the imperfections, they appear as special qualities that make that loved one unique, with his or her own special challenges.

Perfectionists who take steps to be more connected to others, especially their children, find themselves becoming more forgiving. At the time Martin Seligman got angry with his daughter (see chapter 7), he was fixated on having a perfect garden. When he stopped to really connect with her, he saw her for who and what she really was: he saw her as perfect.

. . .

12

. . . .

Social and Emotional Learning

*Social and emotional learning is probably the most important
thing we can do right now for children.*

— DR. T. BERRY BRAZELTON, HARVARD SCHOOL OF MEDICINE
PROFESSOR EMERITUS AND NOTED AUTHOR

"There's nothing to do at this school," grumbled a substitute physical education teacher who was supervising the lunch period. "The kids all solve their own problems." The school secretary had to laugh. She told the poor substitute that before the staff had implemented their social and emotional learning (SEL) program, the office had been full of children in need of discipline after lunch.

"I'll have to forward your complaint to the PTA," she said. "They're the ones who did all the fundraising." SEL is a buzzword among today's teachers, but a culture of respectful and compassionate children largely depends on engaged and supportive parents.

Schools that focus on teaching social and emotional skills are the ideal; however, home is the first place to cultivate empathy and kindness, talk about feelings, and prevent bullying behaviors. Supporting one another, parents can reverse the widespread trends of disrespect and meanness. Kinder and more compassionate families always create kinder and more compassionate communities.

A child's developmental process is a wondrous transformation. Each stage builds on the previous one, and no stage can be missed. In the growth process, there are five different yet interdependent domains that every parent must help a child develop: *physical, intellectual, social, emotional,* and *creative.* All of these domains relate to bullying and other risky behaviors, but two do so more than others. The first domain seems obvious, since bullies dominate physically. Sometimes they dominate intellectually, but in terms of bullying, the third and fourth domains are actually key: social and emotional capability.

Educators now recognize that SEL is as important for success as the traditional three Rs. Brain expert Daniel Siegel suggests even more important "Rs": *respect, responsibility,* and *resilience.* We'll add three more: r*elationship, relationship,* and *relationship.* When children have learned social and emotional skills, they experience fewer negative emotions, are better behaved in school, can pay closer attention to academics and manage themselves better, have more quality friendships, and are happier.

Core Competencies

The Collaborative for Academic, Social, and Emotional Learning, or CASEL, is a leading force behind making social and emotional learning an essential part of education. In their report on bullying, they firmly establish that when homes and schools have a warm, respectful, and inclusive climate, youngsters are better equipped to manage their feelings, resolve conflict nonviolently, make smart decisions, and have healthy relationships. With social and emotional skills, behavior, relationships, and academic performance improve.[1] Because many of today's children are coming to school lacking social skills, however, schools everywhere are implementing more programs to pick up the slack. (You read about examples in chapter 6.)

Unlike the three Rs, however, there really is no standardized emotional curriculum. People pick up emotional skills inconsistently from family members, teachers, peers, clergy, and neighbors. Literature, movies, stories of all kinds give us guidance and clues to self-understanding, but other than traditions and taboos, we have no widely accepted social agreements for dealing with or understanding our emotions. Yet emotions are connected to everything we do.

Social and emotional learning is an educational movement gaining ground throughout the world. SEL focuses on the systematic development of these five core groups of social and emotional competencies:

1. **Self-awareness**—recognizing and naming our emotions, figuring out what triggers our stress reactions, seeing how our thoughts and feelings influence all of our actions and choices, and seeing how others are affected by our actions.

2. **Self-management**—learning how to handle challenging emotions (such as frustration, anger, and stress) in safe ways, being able to set goals, dealing with obstacles, expressing emotions appropriately, and recognizing and handling impulses.

3. **Responsible decision making**—being able to come up with smart and respectful solutions to problems, considering the consequences of actions to ourselves and others, and making ethical choices based on respect.

4. **Social awareness**—developing empathy for others, and noticing cues indicating how others feel; seeing things from another's perspective; appreciating differences.

5. **Relationship skills**—developing and maintaining positive relationships based on cooperation; having inner personal strength to be assertive; preventing and resolving conflicts respectfully; creating and maintaining friendships.[2]

These social and emotional competencies develop when

- children feel safe, respected, valued, and nurtured, and experience a structured and caring environment
- children have meaningful interactions with people who have social and emotional abilities
- children receive positive and specific guidance from caring adults

When these competencies occur both at home and at school, youngsters are doubly blessed with consistent messages from the most important adults in their lives.

Emotional Intelligence (EQ)

Emotions are one of humanity's most important survival mechanisms.

— ANTONIO DAMASIO

There are many types of intelligence—musical, mathematical, naturalist, body, etc. Daniel Goleman, author of *Emotional Intelligence,* argues that EQ may be even more important in creating a happy and successful life than IQ. Fortunately, as with IQ, you can learn many skills to increase your EQ and enhance all of your relationships.

Building emotional skills is a positive psychology technique. It involves identifying strengths and building upon them, rather than focusing on weaknesses and berating or excusing yourself. Just as musical skills allow people to express themselves in more complex ways on different instruments, and mathematical skills allow people to solve more complex problems and create elegant solutions, emotional skills help people manage feelings, cope with stress, understand others better, and have a more satisfying and gratifying personal life.

Researchers have identified four essential EQ skills:

1. The capacity to identify our emotional state and that of others.

2. The ability to grasp the natural course of emotions (understanding that fear and anger, for example, unfold differently and affect our behavior differently).

3. The ability to reason about our own emotions and those of others.

4. The ability to regulate our emotions and those of others.

People who have a high degree of emotional intelligence have the ability to identify, understand, and manage emotions in positive ways to relieve their stress, empathize with others, communicate effectively, diffuse conflict, and overcome challenges. They can build flourishing careers and have lasting, meaningful relationships. On the other hand, a lack of emotional intelligence can lead to widespread problems, such as bullying and other violent behavior.

Emotional Ignorance

The reasons youngsters bully are tied in with their emotional skills or lack thereof: without better ways to emotionally self-manage, bullies strike out aggressively in anger, or to relieve inner stress. Some students may be bullied because of their emotional outbursts and hyperactivity; also, those who have high levels of sadness and emotional instability are more likely to be bullied. Learning emotional skills can help all children develop emotional stability and can reduce the likelihood of being an aggressor or a victim.

Emotions can be viewed on a continuum. At one extreme is an emotional desert of numbness or apathy. When emotions are blocked, unprocessed, unheard, or stuffed inside, kids can lose their ability to be caring; yet those who don't care may become destructive—to themselves (e.g., cutting or suicide) and to others (violence). At the other extreme is emotional flooding, having tantrums and meltdowns. When people lack skills for managing emotions, they tend to hold them inside, trying to control them by not feeling or by "being cool," until one "final straw" pushes their buttons and releases a deluge of pent-up emotion.[3]

Self-Regulation

In the famous "Marshmallow Experiment" at Stanford University, conducted in 1972, four-year-olds were given one marshmallow. If they could wait for twenty minutes before they ate it, they would get an additional marshmallow. About a third of the children were able to wait to eat the marshmallow, and doubled their reward. Interestingly, it was found that the children who could wait and those who could not wait ended up living very different lives.

A follow-up study in 1988 showed that the ones who had controlled the impulse to gobble the treat down were able to benefit from the ability to delay gratification throughout their lives. They could focus better, screen out distractions, and persist in the face of frustration. They were more self-motivated, had on average a lower body mass index, and got into better colleges. In adulthood, they had higher incomes, greater career satisfaction, better health, and a higher rate of successful marriages. This is a great illustration of self-regulation.

Without self-regulation, children are reactive and impulsive, and may hurt others. They have difficulty managing emotions, handling stress, and expressing feelings constructively. They have little self-control. The children who could not resist the marshmallow treat were not as successful as their counterparts. Continually exhibiting little self-control, they tended to suffer from severe financial woes by the time they were in their thirties.[4]

Infants and toddlers cannot meet their own needs. They depend upon the care and stability that comes from adults, and they bond with those who meet their needs. Those adults help them establish regular patterns.

As babies develop, their brains require them to actively participate in their own regulation. Toddlers learn to understand and decipher their own body signals for thirst, hunger, fear, and using the toilet. As they grow, they are able to develop more thoughtful and creative solutions to more complex and challenging situations. If a child's capacity for self-regulation does not develop normally, however, he or she will be at risk for many problems, from persistent tantrums to impulsive behaviors, from difficulty regulating diet and sleep to an addiction to screens.

Self-regulation is a core strength that's essential for respectful and resilient kids. It is necessary for self-confidence and success, and for social and emotional health. According to child psychiatrist Dr. Bruce Perry, children struggling with this strength are impulsive and reactive; they hurt others and are easily overwhelmed by threats and violence. Although the first decade of life is the best time to develop an internal compass and learn self-control and self-regulation skills, with great effort, these things can be learned later.

This skill will pay off in many ways, such as knowing when enough is enough—enough food, enough sweets, and enough TV and video games—without being told. Self-regulation ability developed in childhood can set children on a positive trajectory for life.

Learning to Self-Regulate

Parents can help their kids develop self-regulation by

- giving them more attention, nurturing, and comfort when they are struggling
- providing more structure and predictability, with less freedom and flexibility
- modeling self-control with their words and actions
- redirecting the child's inappropriate words and actions toward more appropriate ones
- helping them feel safe
- preparing them for transitions (e.g., letting them know ahead of time about going to school, going to the dentist, etc.)
- modeling mindfulness
- providing emotional coaching
- keeping things simple

Mindfulness

Part of self-regulation involves paying attention. This can be difficult for children diagnosed with ADD or AD/HD, disorders that sometimes play a part in the bullying dynamic. People often complain when children aren't paying attention, but rarely does anyone teach kids how to do that. This section does.

A parent who leads mindfulness trainings tells this story about a child who was acting up in class: "A third-grade teacher asked me if I would take a kid out of class and speak to him, because his dad had been imprisoned the night before. This teacher was a good one; he had the kid draw all morning. I asked the boy if he would share his pictures with me. He did—cops handcuffing his dad, dad in a police car, dad behind bars. I asked him if he thought his dad would want him to worry about him or pay attention in class. 'Pay attention in class,' he replied. I asked him if he knew how to do this. 'Yes,' he replied, 'by breathing.' I asked him if he'd like to send his dad kind wishes and we did. He told me that everyone he lived with was sad. I showed him how you can hold hands with people and breathe together. He smiled and said he would like to teach them mindfulness. He returned to his classroom with a big smile on his face."[5]

The practice of mindfulness can improve attention and develop emotional regulation. Mindfulness slows down a knee-jerk reaction to a second-by-second awareness of what is going on, inserting a pause that changes impulsive reactions to thoughtful responses. This practice creates a peaceful moment that can expand.

Mindfulness has been used in hundreds of hospitals around the United States to treat stress, anxiety, depression, eating disorders, post-traumatic stress disorder, and AD/HD. It has been adapted to help schoolchildren reduce stress, make healthy choices, manage anger, study better, and resolve conflicts. Mindfulness teaches self-awareness, focus, impulse control, and empathy. There is currently a burgeoning movement to teach mindfulness to youth, although the practice is nothing new; mindful meditation is the foundation of some of the world's oldest religions and spiritual practices. People put their children into karate classes to learn discipline, but what they actually learn is mindfulness. Practices like aikido and yoga emphasize mindfulness and consciously teach peace.

The mind naturally wanders all over the place, through all kinds of thoughts and feelings. Most of these thoughts are about the past or the future, and most are automatic. Yet the past is memory, and the future is fantasy. The present moment is the one moment we can actually experience, and it's the one we most seem to miss. In a state of mindfulness, we notice what's going on *right now.*

By purposefully directing our awareness away from distracting thoughts and "anchoring" ourselves in this present moment, we create a space of calmness and contentment with mindfulness, or "sensing exercises."

Mindfulness is based on breathing—noticing the breath in and the breath out; feeling it inside your body; accepting each breath as it is, slow and deep or shallow and fast; opening up while breathing in; breathing out and letting go. Staying in the present. Sensing the body with no judgment.

Mindfulness techniques can help people to become aware in the moment, to relax, to manage strong reactions, and to rebalance the emotional brain. Mindfulness takes practice, and it is definitely worth the effort.

Mindfulness cultivates inner resources such as the following:

- self-awareness
- emotional navigation
- empathy
- compassion
- attention
- impulse control and self-regulation

According to Jon Kabat-Zinn, author of *Wherever You Go, There You Are*, "Mindfulness practice means that we commit fully in each moment to be present; inviting ourselves to interface with this moment in full awareness, with the intention to embody as best we can an orientation of calmness, mindfulness, and equanimity right here and right now."[6]

Researchers from Cambridge University found that mindfulness training improves mental health and well-being in teenage boys. The four-week training taught the boys to become more self-aware, especially of their bodies, their breathing, and other sensations. "Calming the mind and observing experiences with curiosity and acceptance not only reduces stress but helps with attention control and emotion regulation—skills which are valuable both inside and outside the classroom." Most significant, the adolescents who suffered from higher levels of anxiety were the ones who most benefitted from the training.[7]

Mindful Parenting

Mindfulness, obviously, is not just for kids. Practicing mindfulness can greatly benefit parents and children alike. Sit for a few minutes and simply pay attention to what is happening in the present moment. Focus on your breathing. Make this a daily habit and notice how it affects your parenting style.

As you gain awareness of the presence of your own mind and body, you'll develop a deeper consciousness about your own responses. You can notice the triggers or "red flags" that spike your stress level and get you into trouble. And with awareness comes choice. Once you identify what sets you off, mindfulness can help you breathe in and breathe out into relaxation, creating a space, a pause, that lets you deliberately choose the best response instead of automatically reacting. These practices can help you become a more mindful parent:

- Notice the trigger (for example: My kid slammed the door).

- Identify the red flags, your automatic reactions: physical, emotional, and behavioral.

- Look in your toolbox. Find strategies to help you rebalance your emotional brain and regain your composure and peacefulness/equilibrium. Examples of tools are deep breathing, meditation, writing in your journal, calling a friend, etc.

It sounds simple, but it is often difficult. Even when we think things are under control, we can find ourselves in moments of stress saying things we regret. But in moments of calm, we can teach ourselves and our kids how to handle even the worst moments. After making this a consistent habit, we begin to change the way our brains react to stressful situations. Being able to tolerate discomfort and self-soothe in times of trouble are skills that develop naturally from mindfulness training.

Mindfulness Helps Us Tolerate Distress

Bullying, conflicts, and accidents hurt. If you know how to deal with your feelings, you can change the experience from a nightmare to a manageable crisis. The following distress tolerance skills can help people manage anxiety, depression, and pain. When taught to kids, they can help slow down or stop situations where bullying might occur.

1. Accept yourself and the current situation. This does not mean you approve. It happened. Try to be nonjudgmental as you sort it out.

2. Focus on tolerating and surviving the crisis—accepting life as it is at the moment.

3. Then do the following:

   – Distract yourself. Do something to shift your attention to something else.

   – Soothe yourself. Self-soothing includes things like repeating song lyrics; stretching; rocking your body, head, or limbs a little; or doing self-massage.

   – Improve the moment. Do something you enjoy doing right now.

   – Think about the pros and the cons of a stressful decision. Think about yourself and the current situation—about the advantages and disadvantages of doing and not doing different actions.

Avoid judging yourself or others. Instead, come to matter-of-fact terms with the way things are, giving special attention to the present moment. Take care of your body's needs for comfort, and ease into recovery and healing.

Mindfulness helps us to develop inner resources associated with positive social and emotional experiences. Mindfulness is therefore highly preventative, addressing issues before they become deeply rooted problems.

Pro-social Skills and Social Intelligence

Pro-social skills refer to positive ways in which people interact with others. Children with pro-social skills—which translate into social intelligence—can make friends and maintain healthy relationships; they do not bully others. If everyone learned social and emotional skills and adopted pro-social values, there would be more respect and no bullying. While antisocial behaviors are characterized by separation and distance, pro-social behaviors invite positive interactions.

Here are some examples of what pro-social skills look like:

• making a gesture of friendship

- sharing and taking turns
- exhibiting self-calming skills
- being aware of one's own emotions
- recognizing and respecting the feelings of others
- impulse control
- ability to make eye contact
- problem-solving skills
- negotiation skills

Learning to share, taking turns, expressing kindness, and negotiating develop empathy and perspective-taking (being able to see another's point of view). Empathy and perspective-taking lay a foundation for all relationships in life. When reading books to children, adults can ask them how the characters feel, and teach them the names of emotions in the process. Puppets provide another way to help children learn different points of view. Parents and child-care providers, therefore, can help develop social skills by modeling perspective-taking, empathy, self-calming skills, etc. Positive social skills work to everyone's advantage.

As parents teach pro-social skills and help to develop a child's character, they in turn help to prevent bullying and other antisocial and risky behaviors. Their efforts put youngsters on a positive trajectory for success in school and in life. Parents do this by

- being interested and engaged; having warm involvement with children
- paying attention to feelings and behaviors; reinforcing positive behavior
- having proactive rather than reactive interactions
- establishing high and attainable expectations
- setting clear, firm limits
- consistently holding others accountable with nonpunitive discipline
- being positive role models who act with authority

One of these pro-social skills is assertiveness. Based on respect, responsibility, and rights, assertiveness cultivates the kind of relationships that can head off bullying before it develops. (We will explore assertiveness more in chapter 14.)

When parents hold respect, peace, and safety as basic family standards and expectations, families become an oasis in a sea of fear. They can counter rampant negativity by creating positive environments full of goodness and joy, using positive discipline and other concepts covered in this book.

Courage and confidence, assertiveness and resilience, faith and love can all trump fear. When we help children to be calm and peaceful, and when we encourage and uplift ourselves and those around us, we are part of the solution.

Empathy Is Elemental

As you may recall from part 2, building empathy is an essential aspect of halting the bullying dynamic.

Empathy allows us to realize that other people have feelings and struggles just as we do. With empathy we reach out to others—wanting to help, not hurt them. Youngsters who are able to recognize how others feel, who can put themselves in another person's shoes (perspective-taking), are more likely to help—and less likely to bully.

Give children lots of opportunities to help others. When kids realize they have something to contribute, they feel good about themselves, and they feel good about helping others. Children learn best by following your example and doing it with you. When children are exposed to people who are less fortunate, they learn compassion and gain a sense of perspective.

Do you know what empathic listening sounds like? Complete silence. But to show we are paying attention, the silence can be sprinkled with a few questions like, "How is that for you?" "I wonder what's coming up for you?" or "How are you doing?" Such expressions of authentic caring and support enhance trust in your relationship. When empathic listening occurs, a lot of things can shift. You do not have to agree with the other person; just be there and understand that individual in the moment. Empathy frees you from trying to fix people. Everyone needs to be listened to and to be heard. Being there for the other person and really listening is a huge gift.

Many parents try to teach empathy by demanding that kids say they are sorry when they've done something wrong. But putting words in a child's mouth and making him or her feel bad is not helpful. Talking to the child privately and asking a simple question ("How would you feel if that happened to you?") gets the message across more respectfully. As mentioned earlier, it is also helpful to prepare a child for upcoming situations. Here is a simple, assertive sentence you can use to teach your child how to behave appropriately and empathetically in various situations: *"When (this happens), people feel (describe it), so we/you should act like this (desired behavior)."* For example:

- "When someone is sick, people feel scared and sad, so we're going to be quiet while we're at the hospital. You can walk around, but no running or talking loud."
- "When someone invites you to dinner at their house, they really want you to like their food or hospitality, so make sure you say something nice."
- "On the first day of school, a teacher doesn't know everyone's name yet. Don't be offended if she calls you the wrong name."

Dealing with Feelings: An Emotional Handbook

Anything that's human is mentionable, and anything that is mentionable can be more manageable. When we can talk about our feelings, they become less overwhelming, less upsetting, and less scary. The people we trust with that important talk can help us know that we are not alone.

— FRED ROGERS

To be fully human, we need to experience a full range of feelings. As we grow and develop, we learn to identify the expanded range of emotions, what they mean, and how to manage them without causing harm. We need to learn to deal with all kinds of feelings in order to get along with others, since everyone is different. The possibilities are endless, but a solid emotional foundation is the best gift parents can give their children. This section is adapted from a chapter in our first book, *The Winning Family.*[8]

Healthy children emote all the time. They roar and cry and giggle and keep their emotions in motion—moving through them. Their words (and noises) and body language clearly let you (and everyone else!) know their emotional state. When children hurt themselves, they cry as though their whole world has fallen apart; a few minutes later, they're playing and laughing again. Like the weather, when an emotional storm has passed, the sun comes out, the tears dry up, and all is well with the world.

Feelings are energy in motion; they move through us on purpose, identifying needs, letting us know what is important, what is happening inside, and how to take care of ourselves and to grow. Feelings can be a roller coaster, stretching us until we feel we're tearing. They can be tremendously painful, but they tell us we are fully alive. Feelings are transient. Even though it may seem that they will never move through, they are temporary and always pass.

Feelings are our evolutionary and biological guides to action. Installed in the brain at birth, they let us know what is important, what is happening inside, and what we want. They tell us what we need to take care of ourselves. Our feelings tell us when we need food, water, shelter, and sleep. They tell us when we need to go out and find love. They tell us when we need to work harder or flee to safety. Feelings tell us when it's time to change. They move us to action. There is a continuum between our physical feelings and our emotional feelings, and sometimes it's hard to tell the difference. Emotions have countless benefits: they drive behavior, identify our needs, and connect us to our authenticity and internal guidance system. Emotions connect us to the special people in our lives.

Everyone wants to feel good, and those who feel good are less likely to get into bullying and other risky behaviors. Children (and adults) all need to learn to get past negative feelings and find good ones in healthy ways.

"Help, I'm Having a Feeling!"

One mother of two formerly troubled boys admitted that she used to smoke two packs a day. She simply didn't know what to do with certain emotions. Whenever she had a negative feeling, she lit up. So many people do this! They turn to an outside crutch to "calm their nerves" rather than turning inward and simply listening to themselves.

David Servan-Schreiber, M.D., Ph.D., says in *The Instinct to Heal* that "Poor mastery of emotions is one of the major causes of obesity in a society where stress is common and food is used abundantly to deal with it. People who have learned to handle stress generally do not have a weight problem. They have learned how to listen to their bodies, identify their feelings, and respond intelligently."[9]

Negative emotions feel bad, and when people experience them, they look for safety. If they cannot find a safe place to hide, they may freeze in place. People on this slippery downward slope can move from feeling unsafe, to fear, to contraction, to distrust, to disconnection, to looking out for Number One, to depression.

Parents who have trouble accepting their feelings can have a hard time accepting their children's feelings. The process of parenting awakens us to all of our lost feelings and gives us another chance. Getting comfortable with all of your feelings can help you re-parent yourself as you parent your child. What does this mean? When you accept your feelings—even if you don't fully understand them—and acknowledge they are yours, you can think about where they might have come from, what they might mean, and what they might be telling you.

Often as adults we realize there were stages of our development that, for some reason, we skipped over. If, for example, there was tumult in your family at a stage in your life when you were just learning to be independent, you might feel a lack of confidence or guilt about being independent. When you accept the fact that you have developmental holes, you can give yourself permission to learn new emotional skills to fill them.

In her book *Liking Myself*, Pat Palmer writes, "Let yourself feel even the hard feelings, because holding them back and pushing them down inside just makes them stay, and stay, and stay and keep hurting. Let out the hurt feelings as fast as you can. You don't need to hold on to them. Let go of them so that they can leave."[10]

Once emotions are acknowledged and released, they no longer control you. Managing emotions means listening to and understanding, accepting, and expressing them. This means having good communication within yourself, and having access to the right words.

Naming Is Taming

Talking about feelings does not come naturally to most people, for reasons discussed earlier; but talking about them, even the bad ones, actually shifts them. *Putting feelings into words puts brakes on upsetting feelings.*

It's hard to talk about anything without nouns, so the first thing we do with feelings is name them. Naming feelings weakens their power and keeps you from getting lost in them.

Feelings are very reliable in guiding us toward positive outcomes, because they are connected with our needs. Once the feeling is identified, it points to the action you need to take. When, for example, you're sad, what you would do is different from what you would do if you were feeling overwhelmed. Naming the feeling helps you know what to do to decrease the negative emotion and/or increase the positive emotion. In other words, *naming is taming.*

Strong emotions are experienced in the emotional part of our brains. Labeling the emotion is done in the thinking, logical part of the brain. Naming a problem helps us define it so we can figure out how to deal with it.

Talking It Out vs. Acting It Out

Because of how our brains are wired, putting feelings into words literally puts the brakes on powerful emotions. New studies that explain this process (which we'll discuss in greater depth in chapter 16) prove what intuitive people have always known: yelling at or punishing kids who are acting out may quiet them down, but it doesn't change their emotional state. The feelings get stuffed inside, but they will remain there until something triggers them to come out.

Giving kids a chance to talk about why they are tense and causing trouble helps end the trouble. It can be over in moments when they are given a chance to express their feelings, sort out their thoughts, and calm themselves down in the presence of another human being. They can find solutions on their own without being disciplined. They make amends.

Emotional Coaching Builds EQ

Everyone has bad moods and negative emotions. Kids need to learn how to find their way through them. Adults who are attuned to their children's feelings can help guide them back to stability when things are rough. In what ways do you handle bad moods and negative emotions? The happiest, most emotionally healthy young adults use these strategies:

1. They acknowledge their emotions.
2. They think about upsetting situations in a more constructive way.
3. After processing the upsetting stuff, they release it and let it go.

Parents can model these tactics for their kids.

The following are adapted from tips that Gwen Dewar, a biological anthropologist and parenting scientist, recommends to parents:

- **Seize opportunities to talk about feelings—especially with situations that provoke sadness or joy.** Young children develop better emotional self-regulation when they can talk about the causes and effects of emotions. "What happened before the incident? What happened after? How did you feel then?"

- **Do not dismiss your child's feelings.** Accept all feelings, especially the "bad" ones; take them seriously. If it's a very strong feeling—crying, a tantrum—calm and comfort first; wait thirty minutes to talk about it. (We will explore this more in chapter 16.)

- **Help kids explore the need behind the feeling.** "Maybe you did that because you needed to feel like you fit in. What do you think?" Ask kids what actions they can take to fill that need.

- **Teach kids a positive, "can-do" mindset.** Always counter feelings of hopelessness or helplessness by reminding kids how capable they are, and that tomorrow always brings another chance. Believe in them until they believe in themselves.

- **Avoid authoritarian parenting.** Punitive approaches to upset emotions are linked to emotional problems in children.[11]

Above all, just talking to an empathic listener helps children to connect with the sensations of their body, discharge their emotional energy, integrate the experiences in their brain, and release negative attitudes.

Being an empathic listener is a gift and a loving service. Therapists get paid a lot of money because they are very good listeners, and they have training and experience. If you or your child can't get through this process, or if you feel "stuck" in a certain emotion, consider finding a professional to help you resolve it so you can get to the bottom of the issue and come out the other side.

Putting the Brakes on Bullying

In bullying events, there's often a knee-jerk reaction to cry, to get even, or to retaliate. Reactions mostly make matters worse, however, especially when they are hijacked by strong feelings and become overreactions. Here's how social-emotional skills can help stop an escalating bullying dynamic in yourself and in children:

1. **Stop bully/victim feelings before they start.** Even before an event happens, you can prevent problems by keeping out of harm's way and trusting your gut feelings. Notice what your body is telling you. Are your fists clenched? Is your jaw tight? Is your heart beating fast?

2. **Recognize when you're getting mad.** Learn to walk away from trouble. Walk away with confidence and awareness, perhaps saying, "See you later!" or "Have a nice day."

3. **Calm yourself down.** Talk things over in your self-talk. "Is this worth getting upset about?" Remember that the brain tilts toward the negative, even imagining life-threatening dangers that don't exist.

4. **Pause to prevent yourself from doing something you'll regret.** Pauses can help calm the emotional brain so you can think straight. Breathe deeply five times. Cool down. Walk away. Take a time-out. Identify your feelings: "I'm mad because . . ."; "I'm scared . . ."; "I don't like it when . . . ." Ask: "What can I do to make things better?" But don't pause forever and stuff your problem away. Find someone to listen to you and help you make smart choices. Take a break to figure out what will bring a good outcome for both parties.

Even though many parents teach their kids to "hit them back" when they're being troubled, physical self-defense should be used only as a last resort. Parents can teach and rehearse bully-prevention skills with their children, such as walking assertively and confidently; saying things like, "None of your business!"; and thinking through whom to go to for help in different situations.

Social and emotional learning is as important as reading, science, and math, since we all have to learn how to get along with others in this world. The next two chapters, on communication and assertiveness, go into greater depth about some of the skills kids need to learn in order to avoid the bullying dynamic.

Practicing *Zorgos*

This book is full of strategies for raising kids with a strong and positive sense of self. Building confidence in connecting emotions with experience is a key to good social and emotional development. Psychologist and author Tammy Hughes puts the issue in a nutshell. "Start early. Does your child understand the difference between thinking, feeling, and action?" She suggests three questions that can build these skills starting as soon as the child has language abilities.

1. "Tell me three good things that happened to you today." This

helps your child separate the events and his or her feelings about them. When your child is older, you can add question 2.

2. "Tell me three good things that happened to someone else." This builds empathy and understanding. As your child grows, add the third question.

3. "Tell me something you did that worked out well. Now, tell me something that someone else did that worked out well for someone else." This helps build a sense of personal power.[12]

Separating events and feelings. Building empathy and understanding. Personal power. Do you know what these things are? The building blocks of *Zorgos!* Remember *Zorgos* from the introduction? It's the antidote to bullying, made up of many qualities that superpower our kids.

. . .

13

••••

Good Communication = Good Relationships

The single biggest problem in communication is the
illusion that it has taken place.

— GEORGE BERNARD SHAW

A Peace Corps volunteer arrived late to dinner with a family in Guatemala. "Perdoname," he said. "Yo estoy muy embarrasado." The women all burst into laughter; the men clapped him on the back and said something about a medical miracle. The young American man smiled blankly, wondering what he had actually said in his creative "Spanglish." He quickly learned that the Spanish word *embarazada* means "pregnant."

Most people, most of the time, think that what they say is pretty clear. Yet what you think you said may not be the same as what they heard! Just because you communicate something to a child or a partner doesn't mean that he or she understands. And in school hallways, in gym class, on telephones, when texting, and on Facebook, it's *very* easy for kids to miscommunicate . . . and for situations to escalate.

Miscommunication and misunderstandings happen all the time, mostly without us realizing it; they are the source of much frustration and conflict. The better the communication skills, the more likely there will be real understanding, and fewer problems and conflicts. Effective communication is key to healthy families and successful relationships at school and in life. When youngsters know how to communicate, they are able to express their feelings, get their needs met, and solve problems nonviolently.

Everyone has his or her own way of conversing. Family members have their "normal" ways of communicating with each other, of trying to get what they want and need, and a family's communication doesn't always make sense to outsiders. If parents lack good communication skills, kids have a harder time learning to communicate effectively. Children who cannot express their feelings and needs in a socially acceptable way may become bullies or targets of bullies.

Communication skills are learned day in and day out through interactions with mothers and fathers and siblings. A strong positive family bond helps children learn these skills and resolve problems early on.

In nature we learn that when you plant a carrot seed, you harvest a carrot; when you plant a marigold seed, you get a pretty yellow flower. You reap what you sow, and families that sow the seeds of respectful, positive interactions are likely to enjoy more positive interactions and outcomes. Families that use harsh language and only get through to each other in win-lose ways are fostering bullying dynamics.

The Power of Words—For Better or Worse

Think of how your parents communicated with you: their words and their tone of voice. Were they kind? Were they cold? Were they funny? Did they hurt your feelings? Did they inspire you? Now think about this: do you ever hear their words coming out of your mouth?

The language adults choose and the way they use it can determine or undermine a child's destiny. Words can harm, and words can heal. Words can empower—bolstering strength, courage, and confidence. Words can cripple—discouraging kids and reminding them of their weaknesses and faults. Adults have the power to either build or shred self-esteem and confidence. And, for better or worse, words grow into feelings and actions.

How children turn out depends on family communication skills. What people say to them and how they are treated at home shape what they think and feel about themselves and, consequently, their behaviors.

A graduate school friend said, "In my large Southern family, it was okay to say anything we wanted to each other, but we had to be careful about *how* we said it." Early in life her siblings learned to be open, honest, and authentic, while also being kind, compassionate, and tactful. This outcome is truly the ideal, and what this chapter hopes to inspire.

Words That Build Confidence and Self-Esteem

Many well-meaning parents believe that "said once is said enough," and if the listener does not get it, well, shame on them. Yet this is a set-up for criticism and failure. People don't work that way—we learn by repetition. When you were growing up, for example, how many times did you have to be reminded to wash your hands after going to the toilet before you developed the habit?

Effective, respectful communication between parents and children is essential to keeping kids bully-free. This communication must be practiced consciously and consistently by parents as they support and encourage children through their struggles. And the words they choose are very important. Confident kids with healthy self-esteem avoid the bullying dynamic because they trust in themselves and are not easily manipulated—and they feel good and have no reason to hurt others.

So it stands to reason that the underlying message behind all of our words must support children's healthy confidence and self-esteem. Here are some examples of encouraging phrases that reinforce self-esteem and build confidence:

1. "What can you do?"
2. "What would you like to do/make happen/see happen now?"
3. "I've seen you solve some tough problems. I know you can get through this one, too."

When kids are allowed to experience their own mistakes and failures, they can discover the satisfaction and power of overcoming obstacles. They will not be cowed, nor will they bully.

Words That Drag Us Downward

Our communication patterns are rooted in our childhoods. If blame and criticism hurt us long ago, those mean words may still echo in our self-talk years after we've grown up, and even explode into nasty outbursts and careless shots at our partners and children that seem to come out of nowhere. Blame and criticism feel like attacks, so we counterattack in self-defense. Back and forth, the trouble escalates and our self-esteem plummets into a downward spiral with a zero-sum result—there are no winners.

We don't need to list these words; you know what they are. They are bleeped from the TV because they are offensive and vulgar, but we say them thoughtlessly—to our partners, to our children, to strangers —and yes, these words can do more damage than sticks and stones.

There are other words that seem "perfectly normal," but the way they are spoken carries no warmth or caring. Condescending or cruel words that damage self-esteem and confidence are spoken in a cold or nasty tone of voice, uttered without respect for others. Sometimes as parents, when we feel we are not being heard, we "turn up the volume" in hopes of improving listening ability on the other end. We get louder, meaner, more sarcastic. More often than not, though, these strategies are counterproductive. One child observed, "It's hard to learn if someone is yelling at you."

A shift in focus can make a huge difference. Always, always focus on the positive, and express it, and you will never be a bully to your kids. To quote Peggy O'Mara, founder and editor of *Mothering* magazine, "Be careful how you speak to your children; one day it will become their inner voice."

Nonviolent Communication

Nonviolent communication (NVC) is studied in universities, couples therapy, study groups, and prisons in more than sixty-five countries around the globe. The principles of nonviolent communication are based on the natural state of compassion that exists when there is no violence in one's heart.

All people everywhere share the same basic needs, and each action a person takes is a strategy to meet one or more of these needs. NVC assumes that all people are doing their best at every moment: if they could do better, they would do better. In NVC, everyone learns compassion for themselves and for others.[1]

There are four basic principles of nonviolent communication:

1. Instead of criticizing or judging, objectively state the facts. Describe the situation beginning with "I" rather than "you."

2. Concentrate totally on what you are feeling. Feelings are neither good nor bad.

3. Feelings are tied to needs. When feelings are not heard, there is anger. When needs are met, people feel good. There is no need to hurt anyone. (Do not confuse needs with wants and desires.)

4. Find creative strategies to meet needs. Think of three ways to get your needs met that are not related to or dependent on any one person.

Then, make a request, not a demand. A request is specific and clear; it communicates feelings and needs. It is doable right now. With a request, there is a willingness to accept either "yes" or "no." With a demand, however, it is not okay to say no. If a demand is not granted, resentment and rejection follow, along with a fear of failure. Demands use pressure and can escalate into manipulation, threats, and violence. It's better, therefore, to state requests; there is no pressure since you have other options for getting your needs met.

At first glance, it may seem like NVC is a wimpy way to parent. Parents who only make respectful requests of their child, rather than demands, may find themselves in the "whatever" realm. Children still need to know who's in charge; they need limits and authoritative direction. It's just that with NVC we can tell our kids what they need to do without using fear, shame, guilt, and coercion. (We will talk more about assertive communication in the next chapter.)

A Good Listening To

People are in institutions because no one would listen to their stories.

— CARL JUNG

Most people think they are good listeners, yet few really are. Good listeners take the time to be fully present for family and friends. They set themselves aside and step into the other person's shoes. This quality of attention says to the other person, "You are important and interesting and worth listening to," boosting the other person's self-esteem. Good listening keeps people healthy and happy and helps us discover that we have stories to tell.

More than "a good talking to," children need "a good listening to." As kids hear themselves speak, they can reflect on what happened, and then understand and integrate their experiences. Talking helps kids gain perspective. You don't have to fix anything. Just be there and really listen.

Try to recall a time when you had something very important to say, and were not well listened to. What happened inside of you? Did you feel ignored? Rejected? Unvalued? Unimportant? Perhaps you felt that your words didn't really hit their mark; perhaps you felt that the person you told was not interested. Perhaps he or she seemed to listen but didn't inquire further or engage with you. When children are not well listened to, such feelings of rejection and being undervalued can be taken to heart and become their "truth": "I'm not important." "I have nothing important to say." "He's not interested in me." "She doesn't care."

Let's look at some ways for you to become a better listener, so these negative feelings in your child can be avoided.

Active Listening Techniques

Invite your child to tell you about something that happened, to tell you a "story." Then do the following:

- Look interested; be interested. Lean forward. Look into his or her eyes.

- Put aside judgment and criticism; it erodes communication. Remember what judgment has done to your own stories.

- Notice nonverbal cues, such as gulping, sighing, inflection, and posture. Are your child's eyes glazed or teary? All these things add information.

- Listen to the words, but not just the words; notice your child's face, hands, breathing, and posture. Catch the feelings beneath the words.

- Open up to understand your child's feelings. What would you have felt if this had happened to you? This ability to share the same feeling is the essence of empathy.

- Ask questions to draw your child out further: "And then what?" "What was that like?" "What were you feeling?" or say, "Tell me more."

- Let your child finish his or her story. Do not interrupt, except briefly to clarify if necessary. It may be hard to resist jumping in and telling your own stories, but hold off. Bite your tongue.

- Finally, reflect your child's feelings back to him or her: "You must have been excited about . . ." "I bet you were scared when . . ." Your child can correct you, if necessary, until you are on the same page.

If you listened well and reflected accurately, your child will probably breathe a sigh of relief at being understood. Good listening skills may feel awkward at first. But with practice they soon become second nature.

Make time every day to listen to your partner as well as your children. Ask: "What was the best part of your day?" "What's going on?" "What do you think about that?" "How are you feeling?" "Would you please tell me about . . . ?" Or be more specific, "Who did you have lunch with today?"

Then listen. Just listen, and notice what happens. Listening can improve behaviors and connections. Listening and understanding are keys to creating a peaceful family.

Meta-Communication

Kids communicate with much more than their words. *Meta-communication* refers to the rest of the communication that's going on beneath the surface. Children's nonverbal cues—tone of voice, facial expression, sighs, etc.—either enhance or contradict their words. When parents are able to read facial cues and body language, they gain helpful information about what's going on inside.

Children also benefit from this ability, because it gives them some degree of protection. They can pick up on unfriendly vibes, notice danger, and get out of harm's way if a bullying event is about to occur. They can pick up fearful vibes from those who are likely to be bullied, summon their own assertive posture and courage, and become protective upstanders.

If you ask your children, "How are you?" and they respond, "Fine, I guess," while sighing and shrugging shoulders, don't accept "fine" at face value. Respond to the nonverbal message by saying: "Tell me more." "What's going on?" "How are you, *really*?"

The way you listen, look, move, and react signals whether or not you care, if you're being truthful, and how well you're listening. If your nonverbal signals don't match up with the words you're saying, the mixed messages generate confusion, distrust, and tension. When your nonverbal signals are consistent with your words, however, they increase trust, clarity, and rapport. When adolescents and adults become aware of their own meta-communication, they can learn to project what they want to project.

Blocks to Listening

Unfortunately, many things get in the way of being a good listener. A backlog of anger can be a trap for a child or adult who is trying to open up to us. Sometimes we respond with the best intentions, but our responses stop the necessary flow of emotions. Here are a few examples of these unhelpful responses:

1. **Giving advice or direction.** Telling the speaker how to solve his or her problem seems helpful, but it is not always welcome.

Wait until the speaker is finished and then, if you have some advice, ask if he or she wants to hear it.

2. **Arguing.** Wait until the person is finished talking; then, if necessary, go back and clarify the facts.

3. **Lecturing.** Remember your job is to truly *listen.* People need to talk things out so they can figure them out. If you are doing the talking, you are not listening.

4. **Interrupting.** Don't finish the speaker's thoughts or intrude with your own comments or opinions.

5. **Interrogating.** Ask a question only to draw someone out or to clarify what was said. Otherwise, you are controlling the conversation.

6. **Distracting.** Making jokes or making light of the problem by trying to sidestep the issue or change the subject can give the message that the speaker is foolish, and that his or her feelings are not important.

7. **Checking out.** Answering the phone, checking your e-mail, or watching TV while you are supposedly listening sends a message that the person in front of you is a low priority.

Sometimes it's uncomfortable to listen to feelings, but it's important to hang in there (see distress tolerance in the previous chapter) for the sake of the relationship. Save feedback until after the speaker has expressed his or her feelings.

Good listening takes time and focus. Sometimes busy parents feel stretched and think they don't have time to listen. But if the relationship is important—and your family is—you need to *make* the time. Say, "I want to give you my full attention on this. Can you wait until after dinner?" Then keep your word, create a safe space, and make the time to be present.

Listening to Trouble

Sometimes we just don't want to hear it. We don't want to hear our baby crying or our kid whine and complain. We may be uncomfortable hearing about our child being bullied or causing trouble, and brush it off. We don't want to get into power struggles or arguments. Sometimes we don't know how to fix what's broken.

Crying is the only way an infant can communicate. An upset infant urgently needs soothing and comfort, even if it hurts our ears. It's the same with older infants, toddlers, children, and teens. As much as you might want to leave the room (or the house, or the country), move closer. Your children's psychic pain is hard for them. With a gentle voice you might say you are sorry for their pain, you know that it hurts, and it will soon go away.

Everyone knows what to do for a hurt finger or scraped knee. Yet few people know how to handle the emotional pain that accompanies trauma.

Encourage upset children to talk about what is happening. Their brain can then incorporate the experience and release the emotional charge, and healing and resolution can occur. Compassionate listening helps them integrate the experience, calm down, and begin to heal. Parents can direct and coach children toward self-regulation with words like the following:

- "This is hard, and I know you'll get through it."
- "I'm going to sit here and take some deep breaths. When you're able to, do that with me."
- "You need a little time to cool down. I'm here for you."

Children may need to repeat their troubling issues until these issues are integrated, sorted out, and resolved in their minds. Sometimes parents are afraid kids will relive trauma if they keep bringing it up, but that is not true. Your attentive listening helps them put the trauma into perspective and extract meaning from it. Encourage them to let it out, and not to hold it inside.

Caring adults who know how to manage emotional trauma when it happens—without overreacting—can likely prevent unresolved trauma from boiling over into aggression and violence later in life.

More Tips for Good Listening

Here are some more ideas to help become a better listener and improve communication:

- Ask open-ended questions; for example, "What was the best thing that happened to you today?" These bring more satisfying responses than closed questions (such as "How are you?") that can be answered with just one word ("Fine").

- Beware of using "but" in a sentence. For example, do not say, "I hear your pain, but . . ." Never say, "I love you, but . . ." The word *but* erases everything that precedes it.

- Help children build an inner locus of control by encouraging them to come up with their own solutions rather than telling them what to do. Instead of jumping in with "You should . . . ," ask them, "What can you do?" "Tell me why you think . . . is a good idea."

- End the conversation on a positive note. People tend to remember the last interaction.

- Get into the habit of expressing your own feelings. Practice makes perfect. Kids can read/sense your emotions, even though they may be unable to label them, or know the reason behind them; unfortunately, they might also draw the wrong conclusion. They might assume you're mad at them, when you're actually upset about something else. Try using "I feel . . . because . . ." statements, which can prevent misunderstandings and teach your children how to express their feelings in a healthy way.

Now let's talk about the next step: holding children accountable.

Damage Control

Parents sometimes say dumb things without thinking about them first. A kid climbing a tree hears his mom yell, "You're gonna fall!" A dad trying to get his daughter to brush her teeth predicts, "Your teeth will rot and fall out!" Or a mom trying to get a jacket on her child says, in exasperation, "You're gonna get sick!" Instead of talking about what they *do* want, parents can fall into the trap of focusing exclusively on what they *do not* want, striking fear and negativity into the child's developing heart and brain. Here's an example of this indirect and manipulative communication. A family was on the beach with a small child who was throwing sand. "If you don't stop throwing sand," the mom said, "I'm going to get that dog over there to come and bite you." How much simpler and kinder it would have been to redirect the child's behavior, saying, "Don't throw sand; pile it into a hill instead."

The things that we say to our children and how we say them can have a far-reaching impact on their feelings, assumptions about life, behaviors, and attitudes. Think before you speak.

Before you open your mouth, ask yourself these questions:

T — is it *True*?

H — is it *Helpful*?

I — is it *Inspiring*?

N — is it *Necessary*?

K — is it *Kind*?

Louise remembers saying something thoughtless at a picnic with her children in the mountains of Colorado. After finishing eating, twelve-year-old Damian asked, "Mom, can I climb that mountain?" Louise looked at the mountain, noticed a trail nearby, and said, "Okay." Soon after Damian left, Louise's seven-year-old son asked, "Mom, can I climb the mountain?" Thoughtlessly she replied, "No, Felix, you're too clumsy." Louise wanted to eat her words. Not only were they not true, but they weren't helpful, inspiring, necessary, or kind either. Unfortunately, she didn't know how to "undo" what she had done.

Back home in the days following the picnic, Felix became a walking disaster. He dropped, bumped into, and fell over everything. Whenever he poured milk, it spilled all over the counter. He was probably saying to himself, "If my mother thinks I'm clumsy, I must be clumsy." His mother's words had become a self-fulfilling prophecy.

Feeling guilty about and responsible for this problem, Louise made some big changes. She told Felix she had made a mistake, and she became more thoughtful about her words. After two weeks, Felix returned to his normal, not-so-clumsy self.

Careless Words

Every parent makes mistakes. All parents say things they later regret. Sadly, careless words can have unexpected, lasting consequences. Your little children believe everything you say. They think that you say what you mean and that you mean what you say. Hurtful words, therefore, can cut deeply.

Children take everything personally, internalizing your words and repeating the criticism to themselves over and over—possibly for the rest of their lives. The harsh words can go on and on, well after you said them, perhaps becoming their core beliefs—defining who they think they are.

Louise spent a lot of time "replaying" the picnic incident. She figured out things she could've said instead or just after to soften the emotional blow of her comment:

- "Felix, that was a clumsy thing for me to say. I'm sorry." Then she could have given him a hug and asked his brother to take him along.

- "I'm sorry, Felix, I didn't mean that. Kristen and I will do it with you! Let's try to catch up with Damian."

- "When you're twelve, you can climb a mountain by yourself. But look, there's a stream over there that looks full of things a seven-year-old could discover."

Encouraging Felix to talk about how he felt would also have helped him heal and integrate the experience into his brain.

Mistakes Are Teachers

Louise learned many lessons from this mistake that she is happy to share:

- **Never label children.** Labeling children (for example, "You're clumsy") hurts them and can have far-reaching consequences. They might believe the label, and they might become it. (Note: "Bully" and "victim" are also labels.)

- **Start sentences with "I"—not with "You."** If, instead of saying, "*You* are clumsy," Louise had said, "*I* don't think it's a good idea," or "*I* don't want you to do it," there might not have been a problem. "I" statements increase the likelihood of a positive response, while "You" statements frequently bring on a negative outcome.

- **Bite your tongue.** Sometimes we have to bite our tongues so that they don't get us into trouble. Scar tissue on the tip of the tongue means that you care enough to stop, cool off, and not inflict wounds on the child you love.

- **Speak and listen with respect—from your heart.** You'll worry less about damage control.

Feedback and Criticism: Positive and Negative

Recall the 3:1 ratio we discussed in chapter 5: we need three positive emotions to lift us up for every negative emotion that drags us down. Positive feedback can build positive emotions. It can halt a downward spiral and begin an upward spiral.

Positive feedback is validating. It encourages, acknowledges, appreciates, compliments, and supports. But it must be sincere and specific: for example, "I liked how you took out the trash without being told." Positive strokes build morale in the workplace and bolster warmth, safety, and friendliness at home.

Appreciation and encouragement can improve the emotional climate in your home. Here are samples:

- "Wow! Look how hard you worked."
- "That was a good try."
- "You put a lot of effort into it."
- "I appreciate . . ."

Remember to reward the effort children put into their endeavors. Little words of encouragement can make a huge difference in their lives.

Now let's look at negative feedback. Blame and criticism are common tactics to try to get kids to behave. These control strategies may have been in your family for generations. But blame and criticism feel like attacks and can actually hurt relationships.

Although initially these methods seem to work, in the long run blame and criticism can instill a sense of fear, self-protection, and defiance. Furthermore, they can damage self-esteem and even rupture the parent-child bond, leading to a downward spiral of bad things getting worse. Many people don't realize that there are better alternatives to managing behaviors.

Many years ago, Louise realized that when she criticized, blamed, or yelled at her kids, they felt bad and so did she. When she said mean things, everyone suffered. Then she learned some new skills. She listened more and became more understanding, and in turn the family felt more connected.

"No Fault" Feedback

All humans make mistakes. They do dumb things and make bad choices. Kids are no exception; they are just learning and often miss the mark. But there is no reason to add shame to their actions, or "insult to injury," as the cliché goes. "No fault" feedback is a strategy for dealing with dumb mistakes, while remembering that the person who made the mistake is still a good person. Based on mutual respect and kindness, "no fault" feedback values the relationship and does no harm. When it is well delivered, this feedback changes behavior and feels like a gift.

Let's look at the difference between "your fault" criticism and "no fault" feedback: (see chart).

"No fault" feedback is specific. It describes the behavior. For example, to say "You're lazy" is very different from saying "You're late." The former makes assumptions and attacks the character of the person, which is unfair; the latter describes a specific behavior that causes problems. Actually, it's better not to start with "You," but with "I." "*I* noticed that you were late for your piano lesson." Careful and caring speech reinforces boundaries and can build trust.

Criticism can have a long-term impact on a person's self-esteem and confidence. Criticism replays over and over as negative self-talk,

	"YOUR FAULT" CRITICISM	"NO FAULT" FEEDBACK
Based On	External pressure/force	Internal motivation
Language	"You" statements that may be global: • "You always . . ." • "You never . . ."	"I" statements that are descriptive, specific, and limited to the issue at hand: • "I need . . ." • "I think . . ." • "I feel . . ." • "I want . . ."
Strategies	The whole person is blamed, criticized, labeled, put down, rejected.	Deals with specific behavior delivered in a matter-of-fact, friendly, or stern manner.
Time Frame	May drag in old grievances and past events.	Deals with the present, and how to do better next time.

spreading the damage into the future, and possibly even inflicting the next generation.

In order to have healthy "win-win" families, it is extremely important to curb criticism and negative feedback. When you catch "your fault" words slipping out of your mouth, try to fix the damage and reframe your statement. Use words like

1. "I'm sorry!"

2. "I didn't want to say that!"

3. "Let me say that differently."

Problem Solving

Problems and conflicts are natural events in life. Everyone experiences them. We don't choose hassles, but we *can* choose how to deal with them. Some strategies—reacting and retaliating, for example—intensify problems and create distance, distress, and low self-esteem. Other strategies de-escalate the conflict and bring about resolution, closeness—maybe even triumph and relief!

Without skills and confidence, every problem can be a crisis. With skills and confidence, however, a problem becomes a challenge to take on, an event to deal with, and an opportunity to clear the air and develop stronger relationships.

It's not a parent's job to fix everyone's problems. Ask: Whose problem is this? That person is responsible for the solution. Parents help most by listening as youngsters talk about their troubles, think through the situation, and sort out the options. Ask, "What can you do?" Encourage children to solve problems for themselves. When children solve small problems, they are empowered to solve bigger problems. If, however, it is something a child cannot do, ask if he or she needs help.

When we solve problems for other people, we deprive them of the opportunity to gain competence, confidence, and personal power. In addition, our solutions may not be the best ones for them. If bullying is the problem, however, and if someone is in danger, it is our responsibility to step in and do something.

We need to encourage and support children through their struggles—and to believe in them, telling them, "I've seen you solve some tough problems; I know you can get through this one, too." We need to allow them to experience their own mistakes and failures while helping them discover the joy of overcoming their problems. Problems themselves don't necessarily overwhelm children; self-doubt and lack of experience and skills do.

Share some of your own struggles with your children, tailored to their ages. If we pretend to have it together all the time, they may conclude that something is wrong with them for having problems. When we share our mistakes, our losses, our failures, and how we dealt with them, they understand that we, too, have disappointments and that we, too, are human. And they can learn from our mistakes. (But don't burden or overwhelm kids with your adult problems.) Hold weekly family meetings where everyone has the opportunity to talk and listen and keep communication channels open. When dealing with family problems, start off with the belief that there is a solution; you just have to find it. Second, listen carefully to clearly understand the situation. Finally, have the willingness and courage to make necessary changes.

When all involved parties assume responsibility for the problem and the resolution, there's hope for a positive outcome.

The more our children learn to work out their conflicts, the less likely they are to withdraw, collapse, run away, or become aggressive.

Mediation and Conflict Resolution

Many schools teach conflict resolution through a peer-counseling program. When Kristen's son, Donald, entered sixth grade, the school used the first week of physical education class to train kids in problem solving. Children learned a simple format for resolving disputes, and mediation skills for helping their peers work through problems. Donald's parents were surprised a few months later when he walked into the living room while they were arguing and asked if they'd like a mediator! He had learned through role-playing and practice how simple it is to offer and deliver help during a conflict.

In his school's peer-counseling system, anyone could request a mediator. The mediator would sit down with a piece of blank paper, write the names of the people involved at the top, draw a line down the middle, set some ground rules, ask a question, listen, take notes, and then ask for solutions. The ground rules were: One person talks at a time, no interrupting, and no name-calling. The question was: "What do you think the problem is?" After each person had answered the question, the mediator would turn the paper over and ask for solutions, then write them down. Finally, he or she would ask if the people involved could agree on a solution or two, and have them sign and date the paper, thus making it "official." The official document helped the students keep their commitment.

Twelve Steps to Peacemaking

Here are some peacemaking steps developed by another school:

- Calm down. Take a deep breath. Count to ten.
- If you can't calm down, get help and put it off until later.
- Willingly agree to talk it out.
- Turn toward each other and make eye contact.
- Take turns talking about what the problem is.

- Use "I" statements.
- Listen to each other. Don't interrupt one another.
- Acknowledge that you heard and understood the other person.
- Suggest compromise and solutions.
- Agree to a solution and shake hands.
- Take responsibility. Apologize with sincerity, even if it was an accident.
- Work together to build trust.[2]

Communication Rituals

I've learned some of my most valuable lessons of leadership at the family dinner table.

— ANNE M. MULCAHY, FORMER CHAIRPERSON AND CEO OF XEROX

We've talked a lot in this book about family rituals that create bonds. In fact, one of the greatest protections against preventing bullying and other risky behaviors is making family dinner a regular ritual. For one thing, the food itself is important; many troublesome feelings and behaviors are connected to improper nutrition. One study found that malnourished children showed a 41 percent increase in aggression at age eight, a 10 percent increase in aggression and delinquency at age eleven, and a 51 percent increase in violent and antisocial behavior at age seventeen.[3]

Everyone needs to eat, and quality food satisfies that hunger. Yet everyone also has a deeper hunger—for quality connecting, for belonging, to be seen and heard, to be valued. Regularly sharing meals establishes that people and relationships are the highest priority, and that family members care about and center on one another.

A new report from the National Center on Addiction and Substance Abuse at Columbia University states: "Compared to teens who have frequent family dinners (five to seven per week), those who have infrequent family dinners (fewer than three per week) are almost four times likelier to use tobacco; more than twice as likely to use alcohol; two-and-a-half times likelier to use marijuana; and almost four times likelier to say they expect to try drugs in the future."[4] Three simple rules can "superpower" these family dinnertimes:

1. Turn off the TV.
2. Get kids to help prepare the meal.
3. Everyone at the table must share something about themselves.

The less time a child spends with a parent, the greater his or her risk for substance abuse. The more time kids spend with parents, the less likely they are to get into trouble. Built-in family time has a powerful and stabilizing impact.

Around the dinner table, people can practice communication skills that help them maneuver difficult social situations. They can learn how to start a conversation or participate in one, how to listen without interrupting, how to respect different opinions, and how to ask for what they need.

During dinner, family members can learn to be respectful of others, to think for themselves, to find their voices, and to get along with others. Frequent interactions with attentive parents keep the lines of communication open and establish a continuity of events. Youngsters learn social and emotional skills, such as empathy, assertiveness, and how to take turns. In setting and clearing the table, kids practice being responsible and accountable to their community.

So much happens when people sit around a table looking into each other's eyes: listening, connecting, being interested in others, and learning about others. When people are listened to, when they feel heard, they feel connected. Good listening creates safety, trust, and a willingness to continue sharing at a deeper level. With better listening, connection happens. If people don't feel heard, they are likely to disconnect and withdraw.

Children who are bullied often feel alone—that there is no one to talk to, and nowhere to turn. Dinnertime conversation and stories can prevent a cycle of silence and disconnection from happening in your family.

Inclusion at the dinner table can also prevent bullying behavior. Feeling safe and trusting others, kids can talk their problems out so that they don't have to act them out. Everyone belongs; everyone "has a place at the table."

Inviting people outside the family to share a meal expands everyone's experience and mixes things up. Frequently dining with other families, other family members, friends, and even strangers can open up new worlds of communication.

Keeping Parents Talking

In every relationship, the quality of interactions determines the quality of the relationship. Once two people have children together, they are in a forever relationship with one another. Whether—and how—they are in each other's lives depends largely on whether or not they can interact successfully with each other.

Functional parenting relationships require lots of effective communication, from "How are you?" to "The baby is sick." Every couple can benefit from establishing good communication habits with each other, and seeking help when they need it from a book, a class, or a counselor. Here are a few good habits that lead to good parental communication and, therefore, functional parental relationships:

- daily check-ins with nonjudgmental listening
- weekly planning meetings
- weekly hangouts (exercise, eating, or errands) with time to talk
- regular dates or special time for intimacy
- using "I" statements and other assertiveness skills
- understanding of backgrounds and family dynamics
- willingness to keep trying in good faith
- agreements about housework, money, and parenting
- agreements for fair fighting when times are tough
- daily expressions of love and appreciation

Clearly, it takes a lot to have a functional parenting relationship. But don't worry. No relationship is 100 percent functional at all times. Like everything else, they are works in progress. But paying special attention to good communication habits can pay off a thousandfold.

The challenge of parenting is enormous, and at certain ages our children's issues can really put a strain on relationships. Good communication can get us through the hard times and back to loving each other.

The next chapter covers some of the pitfalls of communication and subtleties of assertiveness.

. . .

14

. . . .

Assertive Communication = Effective Communication

To know oneself one should assert oneself.

— ALBERT CAMUS

Like a lot of short kids with glasses, Apple CEO Steve Jobs was bullied. A lot. But he didn't suffer in silence. In the middle of seventh grade, he insisted his parents put him in a different school because he couldn't learn properly "in such a torturous environment, day in and day out."

As a young boy, Steve Jobs changed the trajectory of his life by being assertive. He knew that he did not deserve bad treatment and was fed up with the bullying, so he spoke up and asked for what he wanted. Fortunately, his parents listened, took him seriously, and were able to arrange a better situation for him. Had young Steve not had the courage to stand up for himself again and again in life, there would be no Apple computers or iPhones. Thank goodness Steve Jobs had *Zorgos*!

There is a certain persistence and faith in oneself that all people with *Zorgos* have. Bruce Springsteen is another example. He was bullied by *adults* when he was young—the nuns at his school put him in a trash can! But his personality was unstoppable, and his unfailingly positive outlook brought him success as he shared his stories of resilience with all of his listeners. He found positive ways to get what he wanted.

Assertiveness skills help people get out of the bullying trap. Youngsters who are assertive do not bully, and they do not attract bullies. They get their needs met without being mean, bratty, coy, or manipulative. They find their voice and speak up; they stand up for themselves and for their friends. Assertive kids have the inner strength and moral compass to be upstanders when aggression and injustice occur.

The Gutsy Middle Road

In chapter 4, we explained a model of conflict styles that looks like a speedometer. The left side is Passive, and the right side is Aggressive. These are both ways of dealing with conflict that feel "natural" because they are modeled by our family members and in the media, and also because they are impulsive. A sensitive person might think it just *feels easier* to be passive about a problem, to just give up. A strong person might think it just *feels good* to be aggressive or dominating. But both of these approaches are unbalanced and create problems. Straight in the center is the Assertive path, which requires both sensitivity and strength. Assertiveness takes *guts.*

Assertiveness is also a win-win communication style, because it allows both people in a conflict to be right. In a conflict involving a passive person and an aggressive person, you know who is going to win and who is going to lose. The world is full of win-lose situations, especially on television, where win-lose situations are often dramatic. But in real life, no one needs that much drama. What people really *do* need is to learn how to get along. And getting along means *everyone* getting what they need.

Why is assertive communication so hard? Since it is the best solution, it seems like it should come easily to us. But so many people have been taught not to recognize their own needs, or to be careless about the feelings of others, that having a straight, effective discussion can seem impossible. Yet when people have the courage to use "I" statements, everyone involved can feel better in the end. Why? Because it *feels right* to be assertive.

What Is an "I" Statement?

"I" statements start with the personal pronoun "I," followed by words that express feelings or acknowledge needs. For example:

- "I need some time to think about what you said."
- "I feel frustrated, worried, and disrespected when you arrive late."
- "I feel good about what you did for me. It made me feel like we're on the same side."
- "I feel scared when you raise your voice."
- "I need help figuring out what to do."
- "I want to be better friends with you."

In true win-win communication, both parties make and hear "I" statements. Many people think (or joke) that "I" statements can sound like this:

- "I think you're wrong."
- "I feel like you are an idiot."
- "I hate that jacket; it's ugly. Never wear it again."

These "I" statements are clearly put-downs or complaints and lead to problems, not solutions. These kinds of statements can sound intimidating to listeners, especially if they are locked in a mindset that is passive, aggressive, or passive-aggressive.

Polishing an "I" Statement

Sometimes it takes a few tries to get your "I" statement right. In a recent argument, one mom said to her pre-teen daughter, "When you are short with me, it makes me worry that I raised a jerk." The daughter felt judged and hurt by her statement; it sounded like her mom was using an "I" statement to call her a name. She expressed that, and Mom tried again: "When you are short with me, I feel shut out and sad." That was something the daughter could relate to. Then Mom really got it right when she rephrased it slightly, with an important addition: "I feel distressed and sad when you are short with me, because I care about you." This statement broke down the barriers and allowed the daughter to express her own need for closeness.

Polishing an "I" statement takes practice and time. Learning how to do this with a family member or close friend can build trust and improve the connection in the relationship.

Communication Equality

The basic difference between being assertive and being aggressive is how our words and behavior affect the rights and well-being of others.

— SHARON ANTHONY BOWER

Assertiveness is based on respect, responsibility, and rights. People who are assertive express their opinions and listen to others. They talk out problems and are able to work through conflicts peacefully with negotiation and cooperation. Mutual respect paves the way to arriving at win-win solutions that meet the needs of both parties. In order to have successful, win-win relationships, people need skills to ask for what they want, and skills to say "no" to what they do not want.

Widespread Non-Assertive Interactions

The widespread interaction style in our society is: I win/you lose, I dominate/you submit. It feels so normal we don't even realize that's the game we play. There is nothing wrong with winning and losing—as long as everyone has agreed to play the game and has agreed on the rules. But when people use passive or aggressive ways to get what they want on a regular basis, relationships can suffer.

The truth is, everyone is important. Everyone's needs and feelings matter. Assertiveness skills can give men and women, boys and girls a common language and interaction style. Just as listening skills can help us understand others, assertiveness skills can assure that we are understood. Assertiveness skills lead to an inner restructuring that in turn leads to more effective lives. It can set children and their families on a positive trajectory that will benefit everyone throughout their lives.

Mice, Monsters, and Me

Recall that in the best-selling children's book *The Mouse, the Monster and Me: Assertiveness for Young People,* Pat Palmer describes the three basic communication styles of Passive, Aggressive, and Assertive with a clever metaphor. "When you use mouse or monster ways to get what you want, you feel bad, and so does everyone else around you," the author says. (See chapter 4.)

The Passive "Mouse" style includes crying, whining, begging, pouting, hinting, getting sick, and hoping someone can read your mind. Mice can be nice, but sometimes they get stepped on. Timid, unassertive mice are afraid to express their opinions or stand up for their rights. Passive people want to avoid conflict and may keep their feelings bottled up inside. It doesn't mean, however, that they don't get angry!

The Aggressive "Monster" style describes the reckless shouting, hitting, intimidating, and manipulating strategies that some people use to vent their anger. These "human bulldozers" are determined to win, often at the expense of the other person. And no, they're not happy inside.

The Assertive "Me" is about asking for what you need, saying "no" to what you don't want, and setting personal boundaries. "Being assertive means you are letting yourself and others know what you want, not in a pushy way like monsters do, or a scared way like mice do, but in an honest way by just being YOU," writes Dr. Palmer.[1] Assertiveness can head off bullying before it starts.

Palmer's empowering book, with charming illustrations by Sue Ramá, is written for youngsters ages eight and up—but people at every age can discover their aggressive inner "monster" and their passive inner "mouse," and can develop their assertive "me" self. Even children younger than eight can understand some of the concepts. When adults and children read together, both can learn and support each other in developing new skills.

With assertiveness training and practice, aggressive kids (and adults) can learn to get their needs met without being mean. Passive children can find their voice and learn to ask for what they want. When youngsters and grown-ups alike learn nonreactive, nonviolent interaction tools, they are released from the knee-jerk bully culture. They are superpowered with *Zorgos*!

All About Asking

Many things are lost for want of asking.

— ENGLISH PROVERB

It seems so simple: if you want something, you ask for it. But most of us try everything else first. There are two kinds of communication: direct and indirect. Let's explore both kinds, keeping in mind that a power transfer is always involved. The one who has what the other wants has the power.

Indirect Communication: Nice or Nasty

Indirect communication can be nice, respectful, and nonthreatening. It can be considerate of the relationship and is respectful of emotional subtleties. Hinting at what one wants, for example, is an example of indirect communication. Sometimes it works, and sometimes it doesn't. Indirect communication conceals what the asker really wants; it takes a very perceptive listener to figure out what that is.

With indirect communication there is an assumption of give-and-take, allowing room for the other person to make up his or her own mind or make the final choice. These sentences imply or suggest a desire without stating it obviously or directly.

- "Are you done with that?"
- "Hey, let's go to a movie."
- "Do you want to take a walk?"
- "Why don't you clean your room now?"

However, indirect communication can also be manipulative and controlling. Passive-aggressive people, for example, will never state their desires but will control others anyway. Here are some examples of indirect communication with an edge:

- "You're not wearing *that*, are you?"
- "If you give me that sticker, I'll be your best friend."
- "If you want people to like you, you'll drink this."
- "Don't mind me. I'll just sit here in the dark."

Indirect communication can be ineffective if it's too subtle or if it's clumsy, and can do some damage if bad feelings are behind the words, even if they are the kindest words. Indirect communication may get you what you want, but it can make everyone feel bad.

Direct Communication: Straight or Tough

Direct communication can be clear, respectful, and action-oriented, while respecting the boundaries of each person. It has a clear objective. Direct communication makes it obvious what the asker wants. Here are some examples:

- "Can I have that?"
- "I'd like to go to a movie."
- "I want to take a walk with you."
- "It's time to clean your room."

However, direct communication can also be insensitive or controlling. An aggressive person, for example, will act on his or her desires without consideration for the feelings, needs, or desires of others. Grabbing and taking are direct communication—but also quite rude. Here are some other examples of direct communication that is too tough:

- "You can't wear that; it looks terrible on you."
- "Give me that sticker, or I'll take it from you."
- "Shut up and drink this."
- "Turn on the damn lights!"

Direct communication can fail to be effective if it's unkind, and it can do some damage if it's too harsh. It can get you what you want, but can make everyone feel bad.

Assertive Communication: Nice and Straight

Hinting, manipulating, attacking, complaining, and grabbing are clearly unhealthy ways to get what you want. Asking assertively is direct communication that is also kind and respectful. A request, not a demand, allows the other person to say "no"; it does not use force to

241

get what you want. See how these sentences compare with the ones in the previous section.

- "If you're done with that, I'd love to have it."
- "Would you like to go to a movie with me?"
- "I want to take a walk. Will you join me?"
- "Will you please clean up your room before our guests arrive?"
- "I think you should wear something else."
- "Could I please have one of your stickers?"
- "Would you like a drink?"
- "Could you please turn on the lights?"

Alternatives to Asking

Becoming a Man (BAM)–Sports Edition is a nontraditional after-school program in Chicago that helps at-risk teens develop social-cognitive skills. Each of the boys in the original program had missed about forty days of school the previous year and had poor grades; one-third had been arrested. Jens Ludwig, the director of the University of Chicago Crime Lab, explains the "fist exercise" that the program had developed:

> Two boys were paired; one had to squeeze a rubber ball in his hand; the other boy had to get the ball within five minutes. The two boys generally would bite and punch and "beat the crap out of each other," yet few succeeded in getting the ball.

What is most astonishing is this: nobody thought to ask for the ball. Why not? The boys were afraid of being seen as weak. They assumed and feared the harsh judgments of others. They were used to aggression instead of acknowledging their fear, so they resorted to their fists. Says Ludwig, "The key idea behind BAM–Sports Edition is that correcting certain 'thinking errors' can help protect young people from becoming involved in impulsive behaviors, including violence."[2]

Children often learn that they don't always get what they ask for. But if the denial they receive is stated with respect, and if "no" is balanced with an occasional "yes," fewer problems arise.

Many of the boys in the BAM–Sports Edition program had had negative experiences with asking. When, as children, they had asked for something, many of their parents quickly denied the request. And some of these boys had parents who would deny the request, then *humiliate* their child for even asking ("Shame on you! You should know better than to ask for . . ."). The boys' pain was compounded when parents would bring up the request and the humiliation over and over again. ("I can't believe he asked for that!") Children treated this way can have great difficulty asking for what they need. They frequently resort to either attacking (using aggression and force) or withdrawing (giving up, giving in), and neither method is desirable and neither gets you what you really need.

Contrast this story about boys with anecdotes from Rosalind Wiseman's Empower Program. Wiseman, the author of *Queen Bees and Wannabes* (the basis for the film *Mean Girls*), asked groups of middle- and high-school girls how they get what they want, and this is what she learned: They cry to get sympathy. They gossip and spread rumors about each other to get power. They shun old friends and trick each other into hurting people. They put each other down in subtle ways. They steal each other's boyfriends and call each other devastating names. They use sex to manipulate the social atmosphere to their advantage. They poison one another emotionally, without even raising their voices. Fortunately, there are programs to help girls with relational aggression, such as the Ophelia Project, the Girls Empowerment Network, and Owning Up.

All children need to be taught the dynamics of asking, for their own sake and for the sake of others. When left to themselves, children tend to do what their peers do.

Asking, Not Whining

Before children are verbal, parents have to decode their crying, squirming, gestures, and grunts to understand what is wrong. Once children can talk and learn to ask, it gets easier. Teaching children to ask empowers them to get their needs met—and can make your life a heck of a lot easier! You don't have to try to read their minds.

Kristen's house is a "no-whining zone," and all children who visit are coached to lower their voices and ask politely and directly for what they want—and they get results! Young children who know how to ask don't have to whine or cry or act out in other undesirable ways to get their needs met. The beauty of this age is that children are infinitely teachable. Be clear and kind with them and let them know that asking gives people who care about them information so they can get their needs met.

Sometimes the hardest part of asking is not knowing what you want. A child may whine or cry because she feels bad and doesn't quite know why. Part of asking requires tuning in to identify and clarify the need yourself and figuring out what you want. An adult can help a child figure this out. This helps to foster children's emotional intelligence. Take an extra moment to help your child figure out what the need is, then teach and encourage him to ask for what he needs.

Effective Asking 101

Nobody likes being told what to do, but most people, deep down, want to help others. There is an art to asking for what we want that invites others to help without using force or obligation. Here is a simple example: "I'm hungry. May I have something to eat?" The asker starts by giving information about what he or she is feeling and needs (notice it's an "I" statement), and then makes the request.

An asking sentence typically starts with "May I . . . ?" "Could I . . . ?" "Would it be all right if I . . . ?" or "Do you mind if I . . . ?"

Kids learn by experience, however, that simply asking does not always get results. You might still get "no" for an answer, even if asking is hard to do. When you ask, you are likely to get what you want, but it's not guaranteed. But if you never ask, you are unlikely to get what you want, and have to settle for taking what you get.

What can children, or anyone, do to increase their chances of getting what they want if they aren't using force or manipulation? They can show kindness, respect, and caring.

There are reasons why etiquette columns are a mainstay in many newspapers. There are reasons why the families of diplomats go to special schools to learn cultural niceties. In previous generations, good manners were seen as an essential skill that parents were required to teach children. Recently, however, parents have been much more indulgent of their children's burps, running, colorful language, and loud voices. But when children are not taught otherwise, it's easy for them to grow up thinking they don't have to be considerate of others. Manners teach kids to be considerate of others.

Why Asking Is Difficult

According to Jack Canfield and Mark Victor Hansen, authors of *The Aladdin Factor,* these are the five reasons why people don't ask for what they want:

1. **Ignorance**—We don't know what we need or want, and/or we don't know how to ask.

2. **Limiting and inaccurate beliefs**—We were taught by our parents, schools, media, church, etc., not to question, not to ask; so we can only wait and hope. We might think things like, "If you really loved me, I wouldn't have to ask." Yet people cannot read our minds.

3. **Fear**—We worry about appearing weak, needy, stupid, or powerless; if we do ask, we might be humiliated or abandoned.

4. **Low self-esteem**—We feel unworthy, that our needs are not important.

5. **Pride**—We fear others' judgment and believe that we are supposed to be able to figure things out for ourselves.[3]

But asking is not a weakness; it's a strength. Asking for help can make you stronger and more capable—and build support. Borrowing something from a neighbor, for example, might open the door to a friendly connection. Asking kids "What do you want?" shifts the focus from what is not wanted to what *is* wanted. Asking helps children to get in touch with their needs and wants.

If you are a parent who hears a string of complaints from a child about how awful things are at school—"She promises she'll sit with me at lunch, but she doesn't"; "He pushes me and makes fun of me";

"He acts like he doesn't want to be my friend"; "She stole my friend and turned other kids against me"—ask these two empowering questions: "What do you want?" and "What can you do?"

Asking kids "What can you do?" moves them from complaining and feeling like a passive victim to a place of activation to do something. This question empowers them to imagine and explore possible solutions to their problem.

Sort out the problem in rational terms. What happened? How did you respond? What was the outcome? But imagine if the same thing happened and you responded like *this* . . . then what would the outcome be? Come up with some alternate ideas for responses. Do they involve asking? They probably do.

Asking may feel strange for children at first, but it gets easier with practice. You can also try letting kids role-play to help them build confidence.

Saying "No" and "Yes"

Saying no, like brakes on a bicycle or car, defines and upholds boundaries. Saying no defines how far others can go, how far we are willing to go, and where we draw the line. Saying no helps us be in the driver's seat of our lives. It can help us take care of ourselves and decrease stress. Saying no lets us stop what we don't want and get more of what we do want.

When we say yes to someone's request, we often feel good. But sometimes—many times—we actually need to say no. Saying yes when we mean no weakens all of us—adults and children alike. It weakens our fabric, our ability to rise to the occasion. And it is dishonest. So we need to learn how to say no, and do it well.

Why Saying No Is Hard

Saying no has many benefits. Yet people often have great difficulty saying no. Women may have trouble saying no to men, and vice versa. Adults may have difficulty saying no to children, and children may have trouble saying no to their parents. Employees may have difficulty saying no to their bosses. Kindhearted citizens may have a hard time saying no to requests for money from charities.

If saying no is a problem for you, pause and complete this sentence several times: "Saying no means . . ."

For many, saying no can mean rejection or abandonment, hurting someone's feelings, that you won't be liked, that you're being "selfish," which can result in anger, feeling guilty, or even having to admit weakness or failure (especially for men).

Some parents mistakenly think saying no will hurt children's self-esteem, or cause their children not to love them. That is a myth! It is a lie that has gotten many families into big trouble. Children need strong parents to protect them, set limits, and hold them accountable. Parents who believe the "they won't love me if I say no" myth are what we call permissive—and as you have learned from this book, permissive parenting is strongly correlated with bullying.

It's the job of parents to stop unacceptable behaviors by saying "No" and "Stop that." Practicing saying no builds power and gets easier the more you do it. You might even learn it from your two-year-old!

Sometimes hearing no frustrates children, and they might say they don't like you. That's okay. Setting limits teaches children to deal with frustration within the context of a loving relationship. Sometimes disappointment happens in life, and children need opportunities to learn to cope with it early on. Many parents who made the decision to be permissive did so as a reaction to their own parents being too strict. But these parents need to see that saying no does *not* mean being mean, cold, or distant. You can be stern and kind at the same time. A parent can say no and still be caring; in fact, caring parents *must* say no at times.

Setting firm and *loving* boundaries actually makes children feel safe. It can lessen aggressive behavior and help them make better choices. Youngsters also need to learn how to say no to negative peer pressure and bullying behavior.

What Good Is No?

Saying no has countless benefits. Saying no

- curbs aggression
- supports structure

- teaches self-regulation
- holds others accountable
- delays gratification
- reinforces your authority
- keeps you from having to yell or threaten
- means choice, power, freedom, honesty, confidence, relief, peace of mind
- keeps you from feeling used
- lets you stand up for your beliefs
- lets you set limits
- helps you take care of yourself
- helps you discover who you are
- gives you the power to be yourself
- means you don't have to do something you don't want to do
- gives the other person a chance to look elsewhere

You can probably bet the people in your life won't like it when you first start saying no, especially if you've never said no before. You might notify them (especially your partner) that you're learning new skills and you'd appreciate their support. You can even encourage them to say no as well.

Saying no, just like asking, can be direct or indirect. You can waffle around, not quite saying no, or you can be forceful and rude. Or you can mix the two styles by being compassionate but firm, saying "No, thank you," "I'm sorry, but I'll have to pass," or "Now is not a good time."

See? *You don't have to be mean to mean business.* You can probably think of many more examples.

Balance is very important. When you say no, remember to occasionally balance it with yes. Getting a yes response to a request rewards children's assertiveness and makes them feel capable. Both yes and no are essential for structure, flow, and effective communication.

Assertiveness Rules for Family Members

Families need to have clear standards and rules for communication. It's best if norms are discussed and agreed upon, and then posted for everyone to see. When rules are open to discussion and approved by everyone, you get "buy in" and cooperation. With young children, parents make the rules. Older children can discuss the rules at a family meeting.

Here are some suggested and tested house or family rules from parenting experts Jean Illsley Clarke and Connie Dawson:

"People Rules":

1. Think and feel for yourself.
2. Tell the truth. Say yes when you mean yes and no when you mean no.
3. Figure out what you need.
4. Ask clearly for what you need and want.
5. Respect and be helpful to yourself and others.
6. Affirm yourself and others.
7. Be responsible for your behavior.
8. Cooperate.
9. No put-downs.
10. No "dissing" by anyone at any time for any reason.[4]

Do you notice how most of their "people rules" are about assertive communication?

There are no national standards for teaching kids how to deal with emotions. But every family has the power. You, the reader, are learning. Teach your children what you're learning. Help them talk about and manage their feelings, to ask for what they want, and to say no to what they don't want. Ask your school counselor about how assertiveness training could be taught at your child's preschool or elementary, middle, or high school.

Preschoolers who have learned about assertive communication are less likely to bully or be bullied in elementary school. Elementary kids with assertiveness training are less likely to be bullies, victims, or passive bystanders when they enter middle school . . . and so forth. At each level, children have the opportunity to become better communicators. And at every level, youngsters need the support of adults.

· · ·

15

. . . .

Restructuring Family Power

The most important factor for the development of the individual is the structure and the values of the society into which he was born.

— ERICH FROMM

A distraught mother asked for advice on Facebook about dealing with unruly neighbor kids:

> My kids are 4 and 2 years old and they love to play with anyone. However we live next to the world's worst kids (a 5-year-old and two 3-year-olds). Their mother constantly yells at them but does not impose any consequences for naughty behavior. They tear my yard apart, push and pinch my kids (rather violently), try to push my kids off of their bikes, and just do plain mean things for no reason at all. My kids are genuinely nice and nonthreatening, and have never experienced this type of treatment before, so how do I keep them from picking up these bad behaviors? I don't want them growing up thinking that this is how you play with your friends.

The vast majority of parents who responded to the Facebook plea recommended structure for the out-of-control kids next door:

- "I would put my foot down and tell the neighbor children that this behavior is not welcome on your property or with your children."

- "If there is no mutual respect (on a preschool level, of course), there can be no playtime."

- "I would take each opportunity to tell your children that what these kids are doing is wrong. Be specific. 'When Suzie pinched you, that was wrong. Ouch! We don't pinch others.' You can correct her children in a nice way and tell them what they *can* do. If they keep doing it, I would ask them to leave, but be nice about it."

- "I would let the neighbor kids know your house rules and if they break your rules, send them home. This is what I do and it has worked well."

This mother was having problems coming into contact with a family that had few (if any) ground rules and very little structure. This chapter explains in detail the dynamics of families that support a culture of bullying, and shows how those families can be restructured so that all people who are involved are happier.

Raising Bullies Is a No-Brainer

In earlier chapters, we talked about common and widespread child-drearing practices that are directly linked to bullying dynamics and other antisocial behaviors in youngsters. We will recap and discuss these in greater depth here.

- **General permissiveness.** Caregivers may be emotionally or physically absent, too busy, or preoccupied. For whatever reason, they don't say no to their kids when they need to. Allowing youngsters to get away with aggressive behaviors contributes to an "aggressive reaction pattern," also known as bullying.

- **Lack of clear limits.** Rules are lacking, and chaos and confusion rule. Adults need to enforce rules and hold children accountable for violations. Without organization that promotes fairness and equality, personalities struggle to control one another.

- **Aggression and violent emotional outbursts.** Parents try to resolve conflict with threats, force, power, and sharp or heated outbursts that involve yelling and/or physical punishment. Children in these families are likely to become either bullies or victims.

- **Lack of self-regulation.** Parents have trouble managing their own stress and anger. Children live in fear of verbal outbursts, spanking, or other punishment.

- **Negativity of primary caretaker.** Nurturance and warmth are lacking, and therefore a positive connection is not possible. Children do not feel fundamentally safe.

Without knowing it, many adults support bad behavior with their everyday statements and responses to children. Often these statements are made with good intentions. Many parents have not learned how to speak and behave as an authority, and do not know how to create structure and encourage good behavior. Many do not know how to establish clear limits and develop positive communication in the home. When children exhibit rudeness, disrespect, and other unacceptable behaviors, the adults don't know what to do. Parents—who are all figuring things out as they go along—are oblivious to and unaware of the grim long-term consequences.

The Power of Patterns

We are all familiar with patterns—a flight pattern for an airplane, a dress pattern for a garment, a pass pattern in football. A *pattern* is defined as

- a model considered worthy of imitation
- a composite of traits, features, or behaviors characteristic of an individual or a group

The way our moms and dads raised us helps predict what kind of moms and dads we will probably be. Fortunately, we have options. Instead of repeating the old mistakes our parents made, we can learn from them. Instead of wounding our children, we can heal ourselves. By changing negative family patterns, we can not only prevent harm to our own children but also protect future generations from routine abuse. A new positive parenting pattern will benefit your children, your grandchildren, and yourself.

Here's how it works: The patterns of behavior and communication learned in childhood are programmed into our brains as our operating system. Generally we aren't aware of this programming; we don't think about it until we are in relationship with others who have a different way of doing things. Two everyday examples are the "right" way of putting on a roll of toilet paper, and the "right" way to manage a tube of toothpaste.

Although mostly out of our awareness, patterns affect us profoundly. Old family patterns feel "right"; they seem like the way we ought to or have to do things. When unexamined and unquestioned, old patterns get automatically passed on from one generation to the next.

Are our old habits and patterns, or programs, positive or negative? Are they worth passing on or not? That depends on the program. Evaluate each one, and then *repeat the good stuff, repair the bad stuff.* Compromise on the ones that don't matter (like toilet paper or toothpaste).

We need to be especially aware of, and willing to let go of, patterns that inflict pain and suffering, or later on we will experience regrets and remorse. The automatic intergenerational transmission of damaging patterns can cause enormous pain in families and problems in society.

All parents have the right—and the responsibility—to think about what they want from their kids and to find a way to make that happen. You might not know exactly how to get there, but if you make up your mind to find a way, and don't give up, you will figure it out.

Automatic Parenting Styles

Parents have been understandably confused when it comes to structure. Before the 1960s, the autocratic style was predominant. Parents laid down strict rules, and children lived in fear, either becoming compliant or defiant. Then there was a cultural shift away from this heavy-handed, autocratic parenting style of rigidity, threats, and punishment.

As the hippie movement spread during the 1960s, teens and young adults rebelled against authority. Their hunger for freedom evolved into the permissive leadership style, which has since become the mainstream norm.

These "whatever" parents have a hard time saying no and setting limits; they have trouble holding children accountable. With this leadership vacuum, children grow up thinking they have the right to do whatever they want, including being mean and cruel to others. Permissiveness is understandably linked to the bullying epidemic.

Autocratic parenting still exists in some families, however, and children in these households either comply with or defy rules. In the school environment, these children clash with permissively raised children in predictable and unpredictable ways. At the very best, children have difficulty relating to one another. At worst, they develop animosity toward each other, with some kids feeling they must prove their power by dominating other children.

Sometimes houses need retrofitting to fix or shore up structural weaknesses; sometimes they need a new foundation. Getting our collective house in order means putting more stability into the emotional foundation.

This section will illuminate some familiar parenting patterns that emerge when we are parenting on automatic. See if they sound familiar to you.

Autocratic Parenting Style

We talked in chapter 3 about a history of fear-based parenting. With or without the element of terror, an autocratic (or authoritarian) leadership style is characterized by one parent having control over all decisions, with little or no input from either the children or the spouse. Autocratic leaders (in families, businesses, or governments) typically make choices based on their own ideas and judgments, rarely accepting advice from others. Some of the primary characteristics of autocratic leaders include the following:

- Group leaders make all the decisions with little or no input from group members.
- Group leaders dictate all the work methods and processes.
- Group members are rarely trusted with decisions or important tasks.

There are certainly benefits to autocratic leadership. When conditions are dangerous, when experience is needed, or when a single vision is called for, rigid rules can keep people in harmony and out of harm's way.

When survival is a top priority, autocratic leadership in families may have been necessary. However, it has its downsides, especially when power is abused.

In an autocratic family, the "children should be seen and not heard" message makes kids passive. It kills their spirit, along with their willingness to contribute and take part. Silenced and tongue-tied, they swallow their voices and become non-assertive. They don't know what they want, and they accept what they can get. They are raised to be compliant victims who stuff their feelings. An unspoken family rule might be "Don't talk, don't trust, don't feel." Some autocratic mothers and fathers still believe that the will of the child must be broken, to ensure parental domination without back talk. In autocratic families, respect is confused with fear.

Counterwill

Children of autocratic parents often feel guilty, self-rejecting, powerless, angry, and out of control. They are either compliant ("I'll be good") or defiant ("No I won't!"). There is no room for middle ground.

Dr. Gabor Maté, who gave us so much insight for attachment in chapter 11, gives us a new understanding of defiance. "Counterwill is an instinctive, automatic resistance to any sense of being forced. It is triggered whenever a person feels controlled or pressured to do someone else's bidding."[1] In other words, when someone tries to coerce or force you into doing something, a natural instinct automatically states, "No!" This "counterwill" occurs in both children and adults. It occurs more in some people and some situations than others and is the underlying mechanism behind the common complaint "he (or she) has a problem with authority." Blogger Linda Harrison explains, "People who demonstrate a lot of counterwill are labeled 'resistant,' 'non-compliant,' 'difficult,' 'oppositional,' 'inflexible,' and many other negative terms."[2]

But counterwill also has an upside, which is why it is such a strong force in the brain. It can be a positive, protective response to keep children from danger. If they have a good attachment to their parents, children with a strong counterwill will not be manipulated by siblings, peers, or strangers. If this strong parental bond is absent, however, the opposite may be true. We are designed to comply with people to whom we feel connected, not to those from whom we feel disconnected.

Oppositional and noncompliant behaviors may, therefore, signal problems related to attachment, trust, and connection in the relationship. In an authoritarian family, you can see how using force, punishment, or coercion can drive a deep wedge between parent and child.

This brings us back to what is crucial: the mother/father bond with the child. As mentioned previously, a child's connection with family is the "super-protective factor" for survival and a healthy development. Building, repairing, and reconnecting family relationships should be a top priority. Every child, every being has at its core the purpose of building a will: a conscience, a sense of self, a place of dignity in the universe. With good support and connection, a child can build a will naturally and gracefully, without pushing hard against someone or something else to get there. An autocratic family is a difficult place in which to do that.

Roots of Violent Behavior
Unfortunately, sometimes violence occurs in autocratic families, with one parent—or both, sometimes even taking turns—ruling the children, without warmth or compassion. When spanking and other punishment is a normal part of achieving desired behavior, a problem

arises: children become confused, and come to believe that hitting and violence are part of being loved and cared for. Spanking has been banned in thirty-two countries, but is legal in the United States, where it is deeply defended by many in spite of mountains of studies proving the harmful consequences.[3] Spanking passes shame from one generation to the next.

In chapter 4, we mentioned prison psychiatrist James Gilligan, who searched for the roots of violence in the lives of criminals for thirty-five years. He reported that overwhelming feelings of disrespect, humiliation, and shame are at the root of all violent behavior.

Violence is very often a desperate and risky attempt to gain (or regain) respect, attention, and recognition for oneself or one's group. Revenge for perceived disrespect is one of the engines of the bully culture, and it is a solution that "makes sense at the time."

Any form of physical punishment increases a child's risk of mental illness. Researchers studied people who were shoved, slapped, grabbed, and hit as children—actions that were considered milder than "punching, burning, physical neglect, or sexual abuse"—and the results were shocking:

- The risk of anxiety and depression was 1.4 times greater for people who experienced "mild abuse" than for those who did not.

- The risk of alcoholism increased 1.6 times for those who experienced "mild abuse."

- Abuse of other drugs increased 1.5 times for people who experienced "mild abuse."[4]

Permissive Parenting Style

In stark contrast to autocratic parents who hoard power, permissive parents abdicate power. They may be absent from the home due to overwork, exhaustion, or substance abuse; they may be "too busy," alcoholic, ill, or simply disinterested. In a permissive home, kids are neglected and unsupervised, and often lost. If rules do exist, they are enforced unpredictably and haphazardly. Surrounded by uncertainty and inconsistency, confusion and chaos reign in the lives of these kids. In this leadership vacuum, children will step in to fill the void and struggle to parent themselves, or even take care of their own parents.

In some high schools, students joke about "McParents"—those who do as little as they can get away with. These students rely instead on one another for information, for guidance, for values. For better or worse, they center on their peers rather than on their families. Peers cannot provide them with the same resources as stable adults can, but sometimes they do a better job than the McParents. Children of permissive parents are fearful and stressed out. Because they have to grow up too soon, parts of their development may be skipped. As we connect the dots, again and again we run into a widespread deficit in self-regulation—the inability of youngsters to manage their thoughts, emotions, and impulses. This is a result of poor regulation and structure in the child's home, since external structures such as rules and boundaries help children create internal structures, building *self*-regulation.

When adults do not exert their parent-authority, when they are not "in charge," kids don't learn self-control and easily become out of control. Lacking empathy and the "super-protective factor" of a strong loving connection to family, children can harm others—and themselves.

Disrespectful, aggressive, rebellious kids who exhibit antisocial behaviors are pushing the envelope to see how much they can get away with. In return, society views them with distrust and disdain. A vicious cycle follows, as society becomes less tolerant of children's mistakes and less friendly to children in general. Furthermore, unregulated freedom also creates unlimited opportunity for those who might be bad influences on children.

Structure trumps chaos. To restructure their family, permissive parents need to learn to engage from the heart, to speak and act with authority, and to find their backbone. At the same time, they need to nurture empathy, compassion, and love, and to learn social and emotional skills.

Finding a Balance

How kids turn out depends on the leadership style of their parents. These two extreme styles—autocratic and permissive—lead to kids who feel disconnected, don't trust, feel unsafe, and are at risk.

A Pendulum Swing

When we recognize damaging patterns, we may be so intent on avoiding them that we do the opposite. But that can often send the pendulum in the opposite direction. This back-and-forth pattern can repeat for generations.

Here is an example. During Louise's workshop at Fort Richardson, Alaska, a young soldier shared his story: his grandfather had been a colonel who used the autocratic parenting style, his father was a hippie and had used a permissive style, and here he was back in uniform. His experience illustrates perfectly our country's major cultural shift, and the hidden power of patterns.

Like adjusting the temperature while taking a shower, we can swing back and forth from too hot to too cold, trying to get it just right. But once we understand this tendency to overreact, we can make smaller adjustments to gradually reach a happy medium.

When parents decide they no longer want to spank their kids, they probably don't know what else to do, so they do nothing. Flipping from one extreme to the opposite misses the wise middle road for one reason: people know what they *don't* want, but do not know what they *do* want, or how to create it!

These leadership styles, with their different use of power and control—from overpowering (an autocratic style) to abdicating (permissive)—greatly affect the character and life of children.

In our introduction to part 3, we discussed the tendency to oscillate from one extreme to the other extreme—sometimes going too far. This can be a decision made once or several times a day with "ping-pong parents."

Ping-Pong Parents

A husband and wife attending one of our workshops came to the realization that he was autocratic and she was permissive. The more he swung one way, the more she swung the other, confusing their children and causing trouble for the entire family. They labeled themselves "ping-pong parents."

With their new insight, both parents were able to work on improving communication and establishing mutually agreeable strategies. With more consistency, their children's behavior and the family climate improved. When partners have different leadership styles, the children are pulled in opposite directions. Confused, they may play one against the other. Swinging to and fro between extremes does not solve problems; it replaces one set of problems with another and can actually make matters worse.

Sometimes the ping-pong effect happens with only one parent, who will bounce back and forth from permissiveness ("Whatever you want, dear," which results in chaos and frustration) to emotional outbursts ("Stop that right now," which is followed by guilt). This pendulum swing is followed by a bounce back to "whatever."

Children need consistency in order to feel safe and to be able to trust others. Predictability helps them learn cause-and-effect thinking. Basically, a parent with a leadership style that is not working has the following options:

- repeat the pattern; stick with the problematic style
- swing to the opposite (which may be worse)
- ping-pong from one problematic extreme to the other, and back again
- learn the balanced middle way between the two extremes

Balance trumps extremes. The broad middle way is balanced—the stable road between the two extremes. This type of positive parenting is calm, connected, consistent, and comfortable—with much less stress. With conscious attention and commitment, parents can develop a balance between structure and freedom.

Think about how you were raised. Were your needs met? Were you attached to your parents? Did you feel safe and able to trust others? Did your parents accept you for being who you are? Do you want to parent differently? How?

Our parents did the best they could, given what they knew. They were probably repeating old patterns because they didn't know better. When you know better, you do better. And now we know better!

The Essential Dimensions of Balanced Parenting

There are many dimensions to raising healthy children: nurture and structure, proactive and reactive, negotiable and non-negotiable, in-bounds and out-of-bounds, flexing and yielding, rights and responsibility. Parents are the architects of their family infrastructure. On a daily basis, acts of parental leadership bring out the best—or the worst—in children. Here are some of the principles of creating a solid and balanced foundation.

Nurture and Structure

Nurture and structure are both important. Without structure, a nurtured child becomes self-centered. Without nurture, a structured child feels unloved. Both permissive and autocratic parents attempt to build these dimensions—but fail.

Nurture—caring, empathy, connection, and compassion—is essential for building emotional depth. Nurturing means giving daily attention to something with the best outcome in mind. We nurture ideas, plants, projects, and relationships until they are fully realized.

Nurturing happens naturally when a parent is warm and engaging. Nurturing relationship skills increase family effectiveness and satisfaction.

Some people are natural nurturers, and they are natural parents. Others are intimidated by the idea. These parents need to know: *You don't have to take care of everyone and everything all of the time!* You *do* have to take care of your loved ones—especially babies and young children—and be there for them as they grow, develop, and become more responsible. With good nurturing, children become fully realized. Little by little, they become able to fill their own needs, and their need for nurturing tapers off.

Structure trumps chaos. Children crave structure. Structure feeds the basic hunger for safety, certainty, and predictability. Structure can streamline family life. With no structure, there is no safety—only chaos, confusion, and fear. With structure, there is a flow to life.

Young children cannot provide structure for themselves. They must learn these things by taking turns, standing in line at school, etc. They need adult regulation, supervision, and guidance in order to develop *self*-regulation, impulse control, and (gradually) autonomy. The tools of structure are rules, schedules, routines, and expectations. And none of these tools are helpful without consistency.

People, especially children, thrive on routines. If children know when they can expect things to happen, they feel secure. Basic routines for breakfast, homework, and bedtime create more ease and flow during the day. Routines are comforting and can help calm and normalize children after an upsetting or traumatic event; they can also prevent reeling from one drama to another.

Early on, parents provide structure by consistently meeting the emotional and physical needs of children. As children grow, this structure expands to teaching them a wide range of information and life skills, which develop their competence and confidence. This helps build internal structures, safety, and self-esteem. Caring adults teach youngsters pro-social behaviors and thereby prevent and curb antisocial behaviors.

We all need just the right amount of structure in order to function effectively. When there is too much structure from adults, children don't develop their inner structure and responsibility, creativity and uniqueness. When there is not enough structure, there is confusion and chaos. In both instances, children's needs go unmet; they live in fear and are likely to become aggressive bullies or passive victims.

Parents who are comfortable with their authority are prudent in turning responsibility and power over to their children bit by bit, as they become ready for it.

Balance Strictness with Nurture
Sometimes parents, especially autocratic parents, confuse structure with strictness. Structure involves flexibility, while being strict can mean being non-negotiable. It's okay to be a strict leader with high,

attainable expectations, *if* the strictness is balanced with love and nurture, and is not punitive. Nurturance, empathy, and compassion are essential for health and well-being. Unfortunately, autocratic parents often don't possess these qualities.

Being strict, stern, and serious are important and effective stances to take, especially in our "whatever" society—as long as the nurture piece is in place. If the nurture piece is absent, strictness can turn into abuse. Autocratic parents need to remember: *You don't have to be mean to mean business.*

Reactive and Proactive Parenting

Reactive parents resort to threats, force, criticism, humiliation, ridicule, and punishment, all of which create negative feelings and stress in the whole family. Reactive language focuses on what was wrong: "You shouldn't have done that!" "Why did you do that?" Reactive leaders reinforce unwanted behavior by focusing on the past, which cannot be changed.

Parents who know what they want and clearly state their needs, expectations, and rules can prevent harmful knee-jerk reactions and bad feelings. They can turn hindsight into foresight and learn to become more proactive.

Proactive parents teach children to recognize unacceptable behavior: lying or being rude, inconsiderate, or inappropriate, for example. When necessary, parents deal with inappropriate behaviors as they happen, and then lead the child toward improving in the future: "That was bad. I know you can do better." "Next time, please . . ." "Why don't you try . . . ?" Proactive leaders give kids another chance, while guiding them toward a better outcome.

In addition, proactive parents teach the difference between private and public; some behaviors, words, and dress are acceptable at home, but not away from home. They also know that regular attention to relationships is as important as regular maintenance to an automobile.

Proactive leadership identifies dangers lurking in the world and gives kids permission, encouragement, and support to resist risky pressures. When Louise's younger son was a freshman in high school, for example, he noticed lots of billboards advertising alcohol. It started a discussion in the family about how advertising links drugs and alcohol with fun and success, and how we might feel manipulated to want to use drugs as a way of life. Louise's son entered adolescence with open eyes, and didn't feel compelled to take risks involving substances. An ounce of prevention is worth a pound of cure, right? In other words, an ounce of foresight is worth a pound of hindsight.

Positive parenting uses this proactive, uplifting approach to bring out the best in families. It can prevent dysfunctional behavior, addictions, diseases, and painful drama.

Think for a moment about the leadership style of your parents. Was it proactive or reactive? How did it make you feel? How did it affect your self-esteem? What do you want for your own children? Being reactive is a habit, and with better awareness, proactive habits can be learned.

Personal Boundaries and Responsibilities

Healthy boundaries need to be taught and modeled in families. This may be as simple as knocking on a closed bathroom door instead of just opening it. Everyone has the right to privacy and to have personal boundaries respected. Such rights are at the heart of assertiveness.

Healthy boundaries within a family life might sound like the following:

- "I can't start the car until seat belts are on."
- "Stop eating when you're full, but try something before you say you don't like it."
- "Can you say that in a low voice without whining?"
- "I need some private time."

Another dimension of healthy boundaries is modeling to kids the interplay of rights and responsibility. Children with rights but no responsibilities feel entitled to do whatever they want, and consequently can become unbalanced bullies who victimize others. Children with responsibilities but no rights (think Cinderella before the magic) live in mental and emotional poverty.

At the end of his powerful book *Man's Search for Meaning* (composed in the author's mind while he was captive in a WWII concentration camp), Viktor Frankl proposed that "the Statue of Liberty on the East Coast should be supplemented by a Statue of Responsibility on the West Coast." His point is that one cannot exist without the other.

Parents need to talk to their children about this balance between rights and responsibility as a matter of course: with every new right a child gains comes responsibility. A library card, a lunchbox, and a wallet are all big responsibilities that come at different ages. Discuss how or whether walking across the street alone, getting good grades, and driving are rights or responsibilities.

A Balanced, Democratic Parenting Style

Supporting autonomy is not the same as permissiveness.

— GABOR MATÉ, *SCATTERED*

Because Louise grew up in an autocratic family, that style of parenting was all she knew. She had a vague vision, however, of what a "good family" looked like, and gradually invented and groped her way. As her three children grew in their ability to think, communicate, and be more responsible, she slowly turned over control and responsibility, learning how to be a power-sharing parent. In the grocery store, for example, she would pick out three boxes of acceptable cereals, and let her children make the final selection. When they were older, she had them read the labels and select the healthiest items. The more she trusted them, the more trustworthy they became. She developed her own internal locus of control and skills, while helping her children do the same, and a democratic leadership style that allowed the family to become a resourceful and cooperative team.

How kids turn out depends greatly on the leadership style of their parents. While autocratic and permissive styles leave children feeling fearful and unsure of themselves, the middle road is a democratic style that gives children confidence to be who they are. Parents who use the democratic style prepare their children to flourish in a world that requires critical thinking skills at every turn. Parents who move toward the center are more successful at bully-proofing their kids. Everything in this book supports this democratic leadership style.

Develop Your Authority

It's best to work *with,* not against, the inner nature and developmental needs of children. The right leadership helps bring forth a child's goodness, and helps him or her to blossom and flourish. Abraham Maslow said, "The fact is that people are good. Give people affection and security, and they will give affection and be secure in their feelings and their behavior."

In the democratic (or authoritative) style, everyone's needs and emotions are important. Parents treat children as capable, worthwhile human beings who can think for themselves and make good decisions for their developmental stage. Parents allow freedom but teach responsibility, offer choices but have veto power. Family meetings involve everyone in making decisions, rules, and plans. There is also a balance of power between spouses; neither is solely "the boss." Democratic parents are proactive rather than reactive; using foresight, they prevent problems before they happen.

Raised in a democratic family system characterized by connection, communication, and cooperation, kids feel safe, respected, accepted, and free to be who they are. The Golden Rule is at the top of their rule list: *Do unto others as you wish be done unto you.* No one bullies, and no one is bullied.

Don't get us wrong—a democratically led family is not all sweetness and peace. People have different needs, and sometimes these needs conflict with each other. Sometimes democratic parents might raise their voices, but when they do, it is to deliberately command attention. Mindlessly losing control or being out of control is uncharacteristic. And it goes without saying that if alcohol is used, it is used responsibly.

Democratic parents function as counselors and coaches; they set boundaries and teach right from wrong—what is acceptable and what is not. Their positive focus encourages and rewards appropriate behavior, leading and nudging kids toward good choices and setting the framework for a win-win family.

Positive parenting, which is based on the democratic leadership style, embraces an open mindset and seeks out fresh, research-based tools, techniques, and attitudes that support the healthy development of wholesome, confident, and resilient kids. There is no place for bullying and other risky behaviors in this uplifting, optimistic win-win model.

Positive Discipline

As pointed out earlier, the word *discipline* has the same root as the word *disciple,* meaning pupil or learner. The purpose of discipline is to teach children acceptable behavior, and to help them develop inner structure—self-control, self-regulation, self-discipline. The short-term goal of discipline is to protect children from hurting themselves and others, and to guide behavior. The long-term goal is to instill self-discipline. This is at first done with little things in order to practice and develop strength to deal with bigger issues later on.

As parents, we often look at our children's behavior and ask ourselves, "Do we like this or not?" If we don't like it, we naturally try to change the behavior. Before we do that, however, it's better to ask, "What's *really* going on?" "Why is she (or he) behaving this way?" The truth is that behavior is a symptom. Our task as parents is to decode the behavior to determine what is bothering the child, and what the root of the problem is. Use your curiosity and deepest insights to discover these hidden needs and feelings.

Everyone who has a dog knows how to decode behavior. Barking at the door means it's time to go out. If we ignore the dog and the need is not met, there's a mess to clean up. Our dog is not a "bad dog," but a dog with needs that were not met. When children "act out" to communicate a need, they are not "bad kids"; they are just trying to get their needs met. Let's change our language and how we think about behavior.

In autocratic homes, discipline often means harsh punishment, for example, "Wait till your father gets home!" Respect means fear. In hands-off or permissive homes, parents do not know what to do, and they sometimes medicate themselves to solve their problem. Positive discipline is a kind and firm approach that develops inner control—*self*-discipline, *self*-regulation—so kids do the right thing even when no one is watching.

For the last three decades, Jane Nelsen has been writing books about positive discipline, a concept based on research that dates back to the 1920s. The goal of positive discipline is "to help parents understand that nonpunitive parenting is the most respectful and encouraging way to help children learn the valuable social and life skills of mutual respect, self-discipline, responsibility, problem-solving skills and social interest."[5]

If discipline is a problem in your family, then solutions to your challenges are sure to be addressed in one of her many books. Positive-discipline educators can be found in many towns and cities, offering classes where parents can systematically learn principles and techniques to gain skills. (For more information, see www.positivediscipline.org.)

The Soul of Discipline

One more important finding: studies show that how parents discipline children correlates to their own locus of control. Parents who look to outsource their discipline problems to teachers, doctors, therapists, and police officers should work on developing their own internal locus of control, which may not have developed properly because of how they were raised.[6] (See chapter 10 for a review on locus of control.)

Author and school consultant Kim John Payne offers an online course for parents called *The Soul of Discipline* that coaches them in the discipline process.[7] Stating that parenting and discipline change and evolve as our children mature, Payne addresses the three stages of child development and provides a guiding image for each phase:

- **The Governor**—early childhood through age seven or so—when we are a child's "benevolent dictator."

- **The Gardener**—middle childhood, ages eight to twelve or so—when we observe and cultivate a child's growing sense of autonomy.

- **The Guide**—tweens and teenage years—when we do our best by asking the right questions, helping children develop their own moral compass.

Set the Direction

Vision trumps all other senses.

— JOHN MEDINA, *BRAIN RULES*

Think about your optimistic, big-picture vision for your children— the vision that your ideal family structure supports. What do you want for your children's lives?

When your vision is clear, it plays into everything else. Having an optimistic big picture has many benefits. It can

- give meaning and purpose to your life
- uplift you and those around you
- sustain you through the hard times
- help you make smart decisions and solve problems
- guide you toward bringing out the best in your children

List your vision and goals, or perhaps create a vision board with pictures of your family. Post it where you will see it daily to remind you where you are headed, and talk to your family about it. Be specific and clear in the images you project. A family trip every summer? Good relationships between each pairing of family members? Special dinners every Sunday? Knowing what you want is the first step to getting it. Let the vision guide you gently, and don't worry if you waver or change direction.

Veering Off Course

Throughout life everyone makes mistakes; everyone veers off course. Mistakes are teachers that we can learn from. Forgive yourself, and ask yourself: "What is the lesson here?" "How can I correct the course?" As you know better, you will do better.

It is a sad fact that our permissive, materialistic society has veered off course and swept most parents and kids along with it. To save our children and ourselves, we need to pay attention to our inner locus of control and carve out our own way, refusing to follow the crowd and the media. When enough good people become "counter-culture"—especially those in positions of power—we can correct the course. Steve Andreas, author of *Transforming Your Self,* says, "It has often been said that 'A culture is the accumulated wisdom of a group of people.' But culture also contains the accumulated stupidity of a group of people, and our own culture is no exception."[8]

Flying an airplane requires constant correction of the flight direction. The plane's computer repeatedly takes in data and automatically adjusts the controls. Airplanes are constantly "off track" and "correcting the course." Therefore, pilots use compasses and screens in the cockpit and information from the ground crews in order to avoid any major deviation from the course. The constant auto-correction and the co-pilots get the planes safely to their destination.

Auto-correction also helps us self-regulate and live better lives. The first step to changing patterns is awareness—becoming mindful, becoming conscious, waking up. Speaking of auto-correction, Dr. Spock says, "In automobile terms, the child supplies the power but the parents have to do the steering." With this awareness comes choice. Then, bit by bit, step by step, we make new choices and move toward our desired destination.

Set Your Moral Compass

Children are great imitators. We have to give them something great to imitate.

Parents tend to lead more with their values and actions than with their words. This calls for integrity—walking our talk—doing what's right and saying what's right. "Do as I say, not as I do" confuses children. And it does not work.

Our deepest, most abiding values are a source of strength and power—and they are what our children imitate. We find and create meaning through clarifying our values; our values then create the quality of our lives.

What values are your children learning from peers, from the

media, from movies and pop culture? There is a lot of fun to be had in the world, but parents need to keep an eye on their moral compass. Like magnetic north, values are something to point to, even when you're traveling in the wrong direction. Without personal values, we have no choice but to go along with our permissive "whatever" society. We have no idea where we are in relation to where we want to be.

Here are some good questions to help you clarify your personal values:

- Do you want to raise children to be good citizens, or good consumers?
- Do you want to raise "me-me-me" children, or kids who care about and help others?
- Do you want to raise children who will dominate and bully others, or who will be friends and partners with others?
- Do you want to raise children who "never have enough," or kids who are satisfied and grateful for what they have?
- Do you want to raise children who have personal responsibility, or kids who blame everyone else for their problems?
- Do you want to raise children who have dignity and high self-esteem, or who go through life feeling there's something wrong with them?
- Do you want to raise children who play by the rules, or kids who are always trying to push the envelope and get around the rules?
- Do you want to raise children who are bonded to parents and family, or who are bonded to their peers and technology?

Think about your own childhood. What were the important values in your family? Are you still modeling the values you held most dear back then?

These questions would make a powerful discussion with your partner, as well as with other parents. Once you are clear what your values are, you know what to say when you see your children heading over the hills: "Is that where you want to go?" Your children will eventually define their own values, but your bond with them will determine whether you are going in the same direction.

Morality is part of our nature. Normal, healthy human development means growing an internal compass to guide you through life.

A Structure for Power Sharing

Structure is believable and acceptable to a child when the child feels loved. Structure without love and nurture is harsh and constitutes only half of what children and adults need.

— JEAN ILLSLEY CLARKE AND CONNIE DAWSON, *GROWING UP AGAIN*

More than anything else, bullying is about power. Whatever the specifics, every bully acts out with the conscious or unconscious goal of having power over someone else. Children are involved in power dynamics from the moment they share an environment with other children. Life is full of power dynamics. Power means *getting your way, accomplishing your goals*—in other words, *making a difference.* The more children understand about power, the more accessible it is to them.

Power comes from the Latin word *poder,* meaning "to be able." Everyone needs to be capable, to be competent, to have a sense of personal power. But power comes with a price. Super hero Spider-Man said it best: *With great power comes great responsibility.* A family structure that models good power sharing can help immunize children against bullying.

Much of what we have discussed in this chapter has been about power in the family. In autocratic families, the parents are powerful and the children are powerless. In permissive families, parents are powerless, and the children are sometimes powerful and sometimes powerless. In a democratic family, everyone has power.

Dimensions of Power

The family unit is the basic building block of society. It is a source of identity, strength, and stability for its members and the community at large. It is also where we first learn about power. To be healthy and effective, everyone needs a sense of personal power, and healthy parenting is nothing if not a process of empowerment. When we encourage our kids to be confident, self-reliant, self-directed, and responsible, we are giving them power. There are two kinds of power. "One is obtained by the fear of punishment and the other by acts of love," Gandhi explains. "Power based on love is a thousand times more effective and permanent than the one derived from fear of punishment." For better or worse, the patterns of power by which we live, and that our children copy, will profoundly affect their entire lives. When the family is a battleground for personal power struggles, kids either learn how to bully others or they learn how to be victims.

Power Taking

Many people confuse strength with overpowering others, as in "Might makes right." Their words or actions are used to gain power over, or dominate, another person. This is the source of win-lose conflicts, and it occurs everywhere: from playground struggles to the boardroom. For many people, violence and bullying are seen as a solution, rather than as a problem.

People who lack a sense of personal power may try to get it at another's expense. They dominate and disempower others, using any means—even violence—to gain control. Using "me vs. you" thinking, they put others down in order to feel one-up.

Yet we cannot have healthy relationships if people are always on guard or attacking and counterattacking. We cannot have a win-win family if we constantly make others wrong so that we can be right. And we cannot have healthy children if they get unhealthy messages and operate from a distorted value system that they consider to be "normal."

Power Sharing

When all family members enjoy a sense of personal power and uphold one another's right to have personal power, no one has to fight for it. Parents can begin to create a balanced power dynamic by stating out loud that everyone has power and needs to learn to use it well. When power is shared, it increases.

Another word for power sharing is cooperation. When people

work together to get what they want, the odds of achieving success increase. When parents accept more responsibility for their own behaviors, they gain personal power. By connecting and collaborating with others, they expand that power and create win-win relationships.

Power sharing in a family is important because it immunizes kids against the bullying dynamic. When kids know they have power, they don't have to prove it by bullying at school, and they don't give off a victim vibe. Having a strong family that's got your back is a deep source of power for all.

Power sharing is challenging, since children's capabilities change as they grow, and roles change as people's needs change. It requires a great deal of communication, flexibility, and assertiveness, but it's worth the effort.

With win-win values, people share power. They are for, not against, each other, and everyone enjoys respect and dignity. This approach underpins caring families, healthy partnerships, and all democratic organizations. Youngsters who are raised with these values—compassion, self-worth, and belonging—won't bully or be bullied.

. . .

16

· · · ·

Brain Science: Cultivate the Positive

The brain is wider than the sky.

— EMILY DICKINSON

Louise always told her kids, "Protect your brain!" One day she got a call from the school telling her that Felix had fallen off the jungle gym. Rushing to the school, then the hospital, she found her eight-year-old with a broken arm. He looked up at her smiling. "Well, Mom," he reported, "I didn't fall on my head!"

The human brain is the center of the nervous system. Although our brains are no larger than melons, our minds are infinite. Brain research over the past fifty years has increased our understanding of the mind by leaps and bounds. And it is interesting to note that much of what we are learning about our brains is supported by a lot of traditional wisdom.

A great deal of the psychology and parenting wisdom in this book, which at one time would have been dismissed as "soft" or "wishful thinking" by the medical world, is now being proven as fact, simply through an understanding of how the brain functions. All of our moods, memories, and motivations exist in our brains. In this chapter, we provide a guide to the brain with basic concepts that every parent should know.

In short: Day-to-day interactions shape the child's brain for better or worse. Love shapes the brain positively, while fear shapes it negatively. Children whose needs are not met, or who experience early neglect or abuse, are more likely to become aggressive than children whose needs are fulfilled.

This chapter is intended to be just the beginning. The more you learn about your child's brain development, the better you will understand its capabilities.

Brain Basics

The brain is an organic structure that is designed to grow in a certain way, and every part of it has a job to do. Just as a tree's roots draw water, and leaves turn sunlight into new cells, there are parts of the brain dedicated to processing language, memory, feelings, and thoughts. Like a tree, the brain needs the right nourishment to grow in a healthy way; and like a tree, it needs room to grow and spread out its branches. Just as trees adapt to different environments—growing out of rocks, growing around corners to reach the sunlight, growing sideways where there are constant winds—brains grow according to their environment.

Our brains are built to care, connect, and cooperate. As the social organ of the body where relationships are managed, the brain requires certain kinds of attention, such as smiling and engaging conversation. Like a muscle, it gets stronger with use and repetition—or in the case of neural connections, smarter. And like muscles, you have to use it or you lose it.

The brain goes through different stages of growth over a lifetime, like a tree in different seasons. The growth right after birth is considerable, and huge growth spurts occur when speech and reading begin, as well as just before the teen years. After age fourteen or so, the twigs, or neurons, are literally pruned back so stronger branches of thought, habit, interest, and ability can form as a young person's personality becomes more directed.

The brain is the body's historical organ. Everything is observed, and everything is recorded. The brain also is the primary organ for directing one's quality of life. For better or worse, the cumulative experiences during the early years of a child's life shape the development of his or her brain and future life experiences.

Revolutionary Findings of Neuroscience

Neuroscience is the study of the brain, from behavior to emotion to thought. The recent global explosion of neuroscience research can help parents improve their relationships with their children. When moms and dads (and other caregivers) understand the very different functions of the brain, they can be more understanding, compassionate, and—most importantly—effective.

The evolution of the brain is coded into its design.[1] The deepest part, like a bud emerging from the top of the brain stem, is the oldest part, and its functions are shared with every creature that has a spinal cord. This "lizard brain" is in charge of survival emotions. This is where our most primal sensations of "safe" or "not safe" register.

In the beginning of life, when the neural networks of the brain are young and most impressionable, the patterns start to form. Like footprints in wet cement, primal bonding in this early stage sets the moorings for the emotional backdrop that endures forever. Love—or the lack of it—changes the young brain forever. The brain decides early on whether life is safe or not safe.

Just up from the lizard brain is the mammalian or limbic brain. This brain is hardwired for connection. Think of mothers and cubs of all species when you think of this brain—the playing, the licking, the nursing, the carrying, the purring. All of these physical interactions create a bond and stimulate the right kind of brain growth for mammals. In humans, childhood is a time in which all of these mammalian connections—hugging, kissing, cuddling, tickling, chasing, playing peek-a-boo, and being carried—create attachments that can endure for a lifetime, connections that glue people at a soul level. But attachment is not just for babies. *All* kids need love to keep their brains on track. Attachment provides the foundation for the growing child to learn emotional intelligence, empathy, and responsibility while mastering his or her environment.

Over the mammalian brain, where our memories and emotional value judgments are made, is the neocortex, the part that separates us from other animals. This is where we think, imagine, and make rational decisions.

Sight, hearing, touch, smell, and taste are sensed with the eyes, ears, skin, nose, and tongue, and are registered and processed in the brain. The more parents do to build a child's senses, the more they help the child's brain grow. Senses close down in situations of chronic stress and fear. A child in a state of anxiety cannot absorb as much information through the senses. It is a fact that children who are exposed to severe trauma can have reduced brain sizes.[2]

One of the most fascinating recent discoveries of brain science is how mirror neurons respond to the emotions of others, and how this phenomenon, which we describe in detail later, connects us to others. Mirror neurons are at the roots of empathy. But first, let's look at the big picture.

The Architecture of the Brain: Horizontal Harmony and Integration

The brain is made up of two hemispheres that have very different functions. You've heard people talk about artists being "right brained" and mathematicians being "left brained." As we grow, we use and develop different parts of our brains.

Young children, especially during the first three years, are right-hemisphere dominant. That means that they are mostly nonverbal, emotional, and intuitive. The right brain is more directly connected to bodily sensations and "gut feelings." Kids live completely in the now, feeling their feelings in the present moment.

Many people are uncomfortable with their feelings because they have been taught to devalue and hide their emotions, that they should instead be rational. This has caused much confusion, shame, and harm, with a corresponding disdain of or at least discomfort around children who cry, put things in their mouth, kiss and slobber, scream, laugh, and stare. Yet emotions are absolutely crucial in order to live a meaningful and full life. Being around emotional children is the perfect opportunity for parents to learn about and get comfortable with their own neglected right hemisphere of the brain, and to understand and accept their own emotional brain.

Daniel Siegel, coauthor of *Parenting from the Inside Out*, says, "Someone has got to stick up for the right hemisphere! Remember, the right-hemisphere brain processes are important for self-regulation, a sense of self, and empathic connections to others. Finding ways to encourage your child's right-hemisphere development and its integration with the left may be crucial for developing a sense of resilience and well-being."[3]

When kids start asking "Why?" all the time, their left hemisphere is starting to kick in, along with their abilities for language, logic, and putting things in sequence and order. The left brain turns feelings into statements, "I feel . . . happy . . . sad . . . mad." Labeling, therefore, calms big emotions. The left brain, however, is not fully developed until the mid-twenties, so children and teens are not yet capable of integrating the two hemispheres. They do the best they can with the brain they have.

In *The Whole-Brain Child,* Daniel Siegel and Tina Payne Bryson write, "By helping our kids connect left and right, we give them a better chance of avoiding the banks of chaos and rigidity, and of living in the flexible current of mental health and happiness."[4] The way we do this is by letting them talk, letting them ask questions, giving them a lot of experiences, and then discussing those experiences with them. Using all of the senses, self-expression, reasoning, imagination, and relating build circuits all over the place.

The brain works best when the left and right hemispheres are in harmony. The right brain is like a floodlight; it gathers big-picture information using intuition, sensations, memories, and nonverbal cues. The logical left brain is like a spotlight; it gives perspective and logic so that good decisions can be made. In a balanced, well-developed brain, they complement and enhance each other.

Sometimes, at certain ages and stages, the left and right brain get out of balance. As a result, there is either an "emotional flooding" or an "emotional desert," which we discussed in chapter 12. A child who is experiencing an emotional flood cannot hear you, and cannot be reasonable. Don't waste your breath trying to use logic during a tantrum or meltdown! Be patient. Calm the child and attend to the emotional needs of the right brain—connection and being present.

Later, after the storm passes, you'll be able to talk about what happened; then the left brain will be able to reflect on and integrate the experience.

Children who are told to "get over it," "stop crying right now," or control their feelings will teach their left brain to dominate the right, suppressing their feelings. Later on, these people may find themselves in an emotional desert, unable to tap their conscience and their passions, and having difficulty with relationships.

The Architecture of the Brain: The Upstairs-Downstairs View
In addition to the right and left parts of the brain, there are also vertical parts, like a mental staircase—the upstairs and downstairs of the brain.

The cognitive brain—the prefrontal cortex behind the forehead—deals with thought and language, understanding, and problem solving. When you read to children, explaining things and teaching them, you are developing their thinking brain, which helps them do well in academics. To some degree, the thinking brain can operate separately from the emotional brain.

Parents need to remember that the prefrontal cortex is under construction and does not mature until a person is in his or her mid-twenties. Do not expect preschoolers to act reasonably, and prepare for your teens to have lapses in judgment. Again, you will have to remind yourself, but saying "you know better" and "act your age" doesn't improve the situation. As we've said before, your children are doing the best they can with the brain they've got.

The limbic brain is responsible for instincts and emotions. It governs a large part of the physiology of the body, as well as one's psychological well-being.

As we mentioned earlier, the emotional brain records everything that is experienced. Babies and little children take in every experience and then draw conclusions: "I can trust" or "I cannot trust." "I am safe" or "I am in danger." "My needs are met" or "I am alone." These conclusions become core beliefs ("truths") about the way the world is and about who they are. For example, "I don't deserve love" may become a core belief with a lifelong effect.

Deep inside the limbic brain is the mechanism that regulates our deepest emotions. The amygdala is like a guard dog, always watching for danger. Like the alarm bell of the brain, its job is to ensure survival. The amygdala is hardwired to focus on negative information and react immediately and intensely. When there are no dangers triggering the amygdala, both the emotional brain and the thinking brain work together in harmony.

Fear is our most primal emotion. Once triggered, our emotional brain floods our bodies with hormones and chemicals that compel us to fight, flee, or freeze. The amygdala hijacks the thinking part of the brain and packs an emotional—and physical—wallop! Our stress system goes haywire on red alert. Unable to think straight, we may quite literally be "out of our minds," as stress hormones and chemicals gush through our bodies.

Louise recalls a time she was biking down a twisty, windy mountain path and suddenly heard someone screaming. Along with some others, she went to investigate and found a little girl on the ground next to her bike. The gathering crowd tried to figure out how seriously the girl was hurt, and whether she might have broken something. Soon the girl's mother arrived on the scene, examined the girl's arms and legs, and announced, "Honey, it's okay, that's just road rash!" The crying stopped abruptly: the little girl's amygdala calmed down, and she switched gears from her emotional to her rational brain. Once she realized her legs weren't broken, and that someone she trusted knew what the problem was, the girl stopped feeling scared. She brushed herself off and got back on her bike, her thinking brain back in charge.

The leadership style of parents influences the activity and reactivity of the amygdala. Positive parents calm the agitated amygdala as soon as possible, and proactively engage the thinking brain by guiding and teaching. Autocratic parents who use threats and punishment to control children keep them in a constant state of stress and fear. Permissive parents who are disengaged do damage by abandoning their kids. When fear, threat, or stress is ongoing, the brain's ability to understand, remember, grasp meaning, and think clearly is undermined. Kids cannot think straight or hear reasoning or logic. Many bullies live in this constant state of tension.

With awareness and skills, however, all parents can learn to prevent a volley of volatile reactions, apply the brakes, and stop being sucked into a downward spiral.

Upshifting and Downshifting

We talk about "putting on the brakes." But the brain can be better compared to the automatic transmission of a car as it moves through the continuum of emotions. As a car shifts up or shifts down to deal with road conditions and speed, the brain also shifts gears. When you feel safe, secure, and protected, you upshift into your cognitive thinking brain; in this gear you can learn, and be rational and creative. Security, praise, and encouragement promote upshifting.

On the other hand, when the going gets tough (e.g., bullying situations, fear, crisis, or trauma), the brain automatically downshifts. The amygdala perceives danger, thinks survival is threatened, and takes over. Bullying, trauma, crises, fear, and criticism cause this downshift in the brain. If the brain is mostly concerned with survival, the person, family, or organization gets stuck in first (survival) gear, and reason cannot grow and flourish.

When people are not hungry, upset, in pain, or chemically disturbed, they usually default to feeling the five Cs: *Conscious, Calm, Contented, Caring,* and *Creative.* As humans evolved, however, the necessary alertness of the amygdala played out its downside, and we developed the capacity to be easily driven from home base by mistrust, inadequacy, and anxiety.

The negativity bias, which we discussed in chapter 5, automatically tilts the brain toward anxiety, anger, depression, and conflicts. Without our conscious intervention, the bad thoughts stick as if our brains were Velcro, and the good feelings can simply slip off as if our brains were coated with Teflon. This tilt toward the negative makes people underestimate opportunities and overestimate threats; they also underestimate their internal and external resources. How do we right this neurological imbalance? To level the playing field, we need to deliberately lean toward positivity. There's a great bumper sticker that reads: "Don't believe everything you think." When we see the world more clearly, we can wake up from the paranoid, fearful trance.

Positive parents may not understand the evolution of the brain, but they do understand the importance of uplifting themselves and their children. Instead of always looking for what's wrong, they focus on strengths; they help kids notice successes, and they celebrate with them. Neuroscientific studies are pointing to what many parents have been doing all along.

Positive feelings have far-reaching effects. They increase optimism, resourcefulness, and resilience, and can counter pain and trauma. When bad things happen, they are dealt with and resolved so that life can return to the positive. Good feelings increase the likelihood of other good feelings, so much so that good days can become the expected standard.

Flipping Your Lid

Developmentally, your children are exactly where they need to be at this moment. But even though they are doing the best they can with the brain they have, some moments can be very challenging! When you understand and nurture your child's developing mind, you can maneuver meltdowns and other difficult moments toward positive outcomes. By understanding how the brain works, you can engage cooperation more quickly and prevent drama.

People who lack skills for managing emotions tend to ignore or suppress feelings, be "cool," and be in control, until the "last straw" that triggers and "pushes their buttons." They then "flip their lid" with aggressive and violent emotional flooding. We call these dangerous, perilous, hazardous outbursts tantrums or meltdowns. (Recall the *Emotional Ignorance* section in chapter 12.)

When trauma and painful experiences occur, the amygdala opens the floodgates and the thinking part of the brain is overwhelmed with strong feelings. This is an electrochemical process. During this deluge, people cannot think straight. It takes time for the flood to subside, and any attempt at rationalization is like throwing fuel on a fire. This is the scientific foundation for the motto "Connect before you correct." Do not try to use reason for at least thirty minutes when people are out of their (thinking) minds.

Meltdown Management

By now you realize that the root cause of explosive outbursts is the emotional brain hijacking the thinking brain. You also realize that children's brains are "under construction" and mostly operating in the emotional right hemisphere; they are doing the best they can with the brain they have. When a child has a tantrum, this knowledge (along with deep breathing) can help you calm yourself and shift into your own thinking brain for a better outcome for all.

The following tips can help you respond positively with compassion, comfort, and caring, instead of reacting with anger:

1. **Forget logic.** It's useless during a meltdown. *When the brain is flooded with emotion, logic gets washed away.* Arguing about what happened is like throwing gasoline on a fire.

2. **Calm yourself first.** Emotions are contagious. Do not "catch" the child's distressful emotions; it just makes matters worse.

3. **"HALT." What else is going on?** Is one of you **h**ungry, **a**ngry, **l**onely, or **t**ired? Look for the source of the problem.

4. **Calm a child down as quickly as possible before the situation escalates.** Express comfort nonverbally with empathic facial expressions (a smile), a touch, a nurturing tone of voice, and understanding words. Your goal at this point is attunement, so tune in to feelings. Try to determine the child's emotions. *We want children to be calm.* Set aside judgment.

5. **Name it to tame it.** *Put feelings into words to put the brakes on upsetting emotions.* Get the child to talk about it by asking "What happened?" and "Tell me more." If necessary, help the child retell the story several times. Telling the story engages the child's left brain and calms big emotions. It also helps him or her make sense of and integrate the experience.

6. **Identify the feeling.** Reflect it back to the child. "You're mad because . . ."

7. **Talk about the problem—afterward.** Remember, it takes thirty minutes for the flood to subside. Calmly discuss what happened. Ask, "What did you learn?"

8. **Normalize.** Physical movement affects brain chemistry. To change the emotional state, get moving: go outdoors, play. Movement helps shift gears and produce good feelings. Feel the relief as the storm passes. After you are calm and balanced, search for solutions that lead to a positive outcome—feeling good again.

Triggers and Hot Buttons

Do you recall the high school principal in chapter 6 who figured out that kids with discipline problems were troubled and needed listening? The principal quoted John Medina: "Severe and chronic trauma—such as living with an alcoholic parent, or watching in terror as your mom gets beat up—causes toxic stress in kids. Toxic stress damages kids' brains. When trauma launches kids into flight, fight or fright mode, they cannot learn. It is physiologically impossible."[5] So when a troubled kid is sent to the principal's office, the principal says quietly: "Wow. Are you okay? This doesn't sound like you. What's going on?" And he gets even more specific: "You really look stressed. On a scale of 1 to 10, where are you with your anger?"

Sometimes youngsters are not able to manage the flood of floating fear and anxiety because they aren't able to identify it. They may not have the language to talk about what's going on and release the feelings, or they may feel they can't honestly talk about such real stuff with anyone. The trouble they feel inside becomes trouble on the outside.

Trauma and painful experiences are stored in the body; if they have not been processed, integrated, and resolved, they may continue to cause trouble. Painful issues from your own past that weren't resolved, integrated, and healed can trigger outbursts. You now have the opportunity to apply what you know to handle the situation: calm the emotional brain, engage with deeper parts of yourself (through journaling, therapy, or yoga), and learn more about yourself. The sensitive, touchy, emotional loop in your brain reacts with a powerful charge carried over from an old traumatic event. You now have the opportunity to defuse the hot buttons, so they no longer blindside you.

Psychological healing and spiritual growth are related to each other. Individuals searching for resolution of trauma can benefit from integrating their emotions through both talk therapy and body work.

Healing calls for huge changes in the way we see ourselves, and a shift in our beliefs and mindset. It requires supportive people along with new skills, so that we can regain health, personal power, and sovereignty over our lives.

Red Light, Green Light

Becky Eanes, the founder of a popular blog about positive parenting, decided to put up a picture of a stoplight to help her children learn anger management. They discussed it together: *Red Light* means Stop (walk away, breathe deeply, sit down); *Yellow Light* means Calm Down (talk it over, hug, do something to take your mind off things); *Green Light* means Go (the matter is over, the child is calm). The stoplight picture hung on the refrigerator for a few weeks and was referred to occasionally when someone got angry. It evolved into a tool that became helpful for children and adults alike.

Anger has many sources. When children express their feelings ("I feel . . ."), the feeling is named and tamed. Intense anger can be harmlessly released by pounding on pillows or using a punching bag. Remember that emotions are temporary, and can move through us quickly when they are verbally or physically released.

Sometimes children's actions are related to unspoken tensions in the household. If parents are undergoing a separation or divorce, for example, children may act out as a "cry for help." Children of depressed parents may also act out, and bullying may become an outlet for the unexpressed emotions these children sense in their loved ones. If they feel powerless against a parent or a sibling, they are likely to harbor resentment. Children who are bullied by their parents may seek revenge on someone they can control.

So many of our regrettable choices are made in anger, when the amygdala is flipped and we can't think straight. Anger can make us thoughtless and out of control, even taking the form of abuse, violence, and bullying. On the other hand, anger that is swallowed turns into depression, physical ailments, and other symptoms. The healthy middle way between these two harmful extremes lies in knowing how to work with your amygdala.

Plasticity of the Brain

Scientists used to believe that by the time people were young adults, their brains were done growing. Now we know that this is not true. Every experience in life shifts, shapes, and sculpts our ever-renewing brain. The connections (synapses) between brain cells (neurons) continually realign and renew themselves as we go about our daily lives.

New information, experiences, and behaviors grow new neural connections, which strengthen with repetition. Doing simple things repeatedly gradually changes the brain.

Our brains are changing all the time. Like riding a horse, we can let our brains take us for a ride, or we can take the reins and take charge. As adults, we can submit to a haphazard "whatever" brain, or we can take charge of our brains on purpose. We can learn to rein in the willy-nilly barrage of negative thoughts ("stinkin' thinkin'") and thoughtless actions, and design and create a better life.

The brain's plasticity also helps explain "post-traumatic growth." People everywhere go through traumatic times, and yet a year later, many of these victims are stronger than ever. Trauma causes some people to break down while others experience a breakthrough.

Self-Directed Neuroplasticity

The plasticity of the brain makes it possible for us to not pass on old hang-ups and traumas to our children, but actually change the wiring of our brains in a positive way. Doing this requires the hard work of rewriting the brain's "script" or pattern; learning new attitudes, skills, and strategies; making positive changes in interactions; and asking for help when needed. With determination and new skills, we can create a love-based family and heal ourselves in the process. We can retrain our brains and "get over" negative patterns and wounds.

We can transform our family life if we

- have a vision and good intentions
- avoid at all cost the mistakes that our parents made
- re-examine what comes "naturally"
- acknowledge mistakes and repair them
- learn from mistakes—our own and those of our parents and friends
- heal our emotional wounds
- support and encourage ourselves during this heroic process

The plasticity of our adult brains makes it possible for us to keep from passing on disorders and dysfunction from one generation to the next. With intention and support, we truly can change the negative patterns of childhood and develop new love-based habits to replace the fear-based practices of the past.

Kind, compassionate, positive parenting supports the well-being of your children and can also heal your own inner child, or rather, the thought patterns you learned as a child. Changing family patterns is heroic work.

Mindfulness, meditation, physical exercise, and other practices can help you sort out where you're at and what you really want from what was automatically downloaded years ago, or what you have been talked into doing. Author and therapist Robert Rosenbaum, in his book *Zen and the Heart of Psychotherapy,* wrote: "When we are lost and confused, psychotherapy can help by giving us time out from the swirl of daily life and a chance to step back and get some new perspective." Consider therapy or counseling to help with healing and transforming your parenting approach. Take parenting classes to build new skills.

The Mechanics of Empathy

Empathy is the ability to understand another's behaviors and motivations. Empathy can be calming and soothing, building bridges between people. It allows us to glean useful information about what's going on inside another person, to get a sense of what the person is feeling. Being empathetic is one of the greatest predictors of future happiness, and is a sure antidote to bullying. We are designed to be empathetic!

Did you ever notice that when someone yawns, you suddenly feel the need to yawn? Just like yawning, emotions are contagious. When one person in a group is angry, the other group members can get irritated. When a loved one's eyes tear up at a concert or a movie, we might also blink back tears. The same cells are activated in both people.

In Italy more than two decades ago, a team of researchers studied monkeys' brains. When one monkey ate a peanut, certain brain cells in the animal lit up. What astonished the researchers was that in another monkey who simply observed, the very same brain cells were also activated. "Mirror neurons" were discovered![6]

When a child is happy and having fun, so are you. When a child is having a tantrum, you might want to scream, too; not only does the sound hurt your ears, but also the mirror neurons in your brain are lighting up. Mirror neurons are what make it so much more exciting to watch a live performance or a football game in a crowd of fans, rather than on TV.

Consider what happens in a fight. One child feels irritated and confronts another, who mirrors his or her anger. A conflict erupts. A crowd gathers and, feeding on everyone else's fear and excitement, becomes agitated. Emotions escalate by mirroring and amplifying one another. When fights are recorded on cell phones and posted on social media, the escalating emotions can unbalance a community (see chapter 18). Soon there's chaos and violence. Tweens and teens are easily sucked into crowd-thinking because of the enormous expansion of emotional growth happening in their brains.

But imagine if kids knew and understood that empathy can go

both ways. Would they have better peacemaking skills? Of course they would—and of course some of them already do. Kids can build their social skills by reading another person's emotions, guessing the cause, forecasting behavior, and predicting what a person is likely to do next. The same applies to you. After reading this chapter, you will find yourself mysteriously more aware and self-regulated. Knowledge is power, and as an adult, you have both. If you take care of yourself first—just like the oxygen-mask instructions on an airplane—your calm and centered mirror neurons set the tone and give your child the opportunity to mirror you.

Develop an Empathy Reflex

On TV shows and news channels, in movies and politics and on the street, the predictable first response to strong emotions is to get angry, to "get your back up." Preferable to this reaction would be the mindful response of turning to empathy. Here's how to do that:

1. Describe the emotion you think you see.
2. Guess what's going on behind it, where it came from.
3. Tune in to the upset person and imagine what the situation is like for him or her.

Empathy is not agreement, or approval, or solving another's problems; it's just noticing and letting the problem be. When you model this process for your kids, they see empathy in action.

In chapter 6, we told you about the unique bullying prevention program in schools called Roots of Empathy. Regular interactions with a baby help students connect with their innate empathy and develop the empathic part of their brain. This empathy-in-action program increases kindness and other pro-social behaviors, and significantly decreases aggression.

Setting Your Mind Right

The mind, which is mysteriously stored in our brains, is our most powerful source of energy. Energy in motion, or e-motion, guides our lives. We've talked about mindset throughout the book as being a person's set of beliefs that affects the outcome of all of his or her undertakings. Our mindset creates our entire mental world; it determines whether we see the glass as half empty or half full, how we raise our children, whether we believe we can or believe we can't. Our mindset predetermines our reactions and responses to situations, as well as our interpretations. Though we may not even be aware or conscious of our mindset, it affects the trajectory of our lives—and our children's lives.

When you change your mind, you change your behaviors. And when you change your behaviors, you change your life.

When you attempt to change your mind and thoughts, you are taking advantage of the brain's plasticity. While there are many older adults who think, "I'll never change—I'm too old," there are also many who believe they can do whatever they set their mind to, and their brains literally change as these people grow wiser and healthier. This is great news for grandparents—and everyone else—who want to learn "new tricks" and better ways to raise healthy children. Think you can't change? *Of course you can!*

Open vs. Closed Mindset

Of the many choices we make in life, the most basic and important is our choice of mindset. A mindset can be like a concrete wall—solid and impenetrable. Yet new insights, questions, and choices can chip away at this wall, making it porous and open to sunlight and a better way.

With a **closed or fixed mindset,** beliefs seem to be unchangeable, as though carved in stone: "I've always been a . . ." "That's the way I am." Over and over again, you prove this is so. This protective stance keeps people from taking in any new information or learning better ways. For example: "I don't mix well" or "Real dads don't need classes." Negative emotions and distrust limit your learning and new experiences, and reinforce this locked-down, narrow mindset . . . until life forces you to change.

With an **open or growth mindset,** people are receptive to learning and developing, changing and growing. They believe that they can cultivate positive emotions, qualities, and experiences through effort.

Positive emotions expand people's mindsets and social openness, which in turn can increase and expand positive emotions, reshaping who they are. An open mindset allows us to learn to use new tools for a richer and fuller life; it helps us move from being victims to designing and creating a better life. A solid feeling of empowerment can begin an upward spiral that allows the innate pleasure of being alive to burst from its shackles. With an open mindset, people become aware of the vast field of possibilities.

At any stage of life, it is possible to change one's mindset, opening the way to greater opportunities, fulfillment, and success. As we learn new information, we know better and can do better.

Reset Your Mindset to Raise Better Kids

There are so many ways to perceive experiences, and so many ways to interpret them. When we are connected with our children, our interpretations of their words and behaviors tend to be more compassionate and understanding; when we are disconnected, our interpretations tend to be more judgmental, blaming, and critical. How we perceive our children's behavior determines how we feel about it and the eventual outcome.

It starts with noticing what you're telling yourself—listening to your inner dialogue. Are your words compassionate, or are they critical?

When we change the way we look at things, the things we look at change. When we change the way we perceive our children—and change what we're telling ourselves about their behaviors—the outcome can improve. We start by changing our minds in little ways, with little shifts that can make a big difference. For example:

- Instead of thinking "My child is crying to get attention," tell yourself: "My child is crying because she needs me. I'll get closer and hold her hand."
- Instead of thinking "My child cries just to get what he wants," tell yourself: "My child cries because he has no other way of expressing himself; I'll figure out what he needs, and meet his need."

- Instead of thinking "My child is manipulating me," tell yourself: "My child is doing the best she can; I'll help her be more direct about getting her needs met."
- Instead of thinking "My child is a hitter," tell yourself: "My child is still learning appropriate ways to express himself. I can redirect his behavior and teach him a better way to get what he wants."
- Instead of thinking "My child is really misbehaving," tell yourself: "My daughter needs to learn some new skills."
- Instead of thinking "My child is acting like a baby," tell yourself: "My child actually is a baby! I don't expect him to behave as an adult."[7]

Watch what you say out loud, too. Sometimes we parents speak casually to our children, using metaphors or colloquialisms that they don't understand. Your children may believe that you literally mean what you say, and be harmed. Our language can be full of violence, as if we are coding all our messages as threats.

- Instead of saying "You are such a pain," say out loud: "You are having a hard time right now, and so am I."
- Instead of saying "You're lazy," say out loud: "You seem to need help getting motivated."
- Instead of saying "I want to kill you right now," say out loud: "I'm upset with what you did."
- Instead of saying "You're going to get it," say out loud, "You're acting out, and I need to find out what help and support you need."
- Instead of saying "You need to be disciplined," say out loud, "You need to do this better; I will help you identify the problem and focus on finding a solution."

From the Fear-Based Mindset to the Love-Based Mindset

Many parents have exclaimed, "I knew I didn't want to spank, but I didn't know what else to do!" The truth is, in order to shift out of the punish-and-control approach, you need to reset your mindset and learn positive parenting attitudes and skills. In order to make positive parenting work, you need to switch from the common fear-based mindset to the love-based mindset.

The fear-based mindset says:

1. I have to control my child's behavior.
2. My child learns to be good through consequences and/or punishment.
3. I am the dominant figure; my child is "under" me.

The love-based mindset says:

1. There is nothing more powerful than the love between parents and children. Our loving connection is the most important ingredient to achieving good behavior and cooperation.
2. I assume that my child is doing the best he or she can at any given time; I expect this of him or her.
3. My job is to guide and teach appropriate behavior, and grow a healthy human being.
4. My child learns through example, and through limits that are set and respectfully enforced.
5. I am the leader; at the same time, my child's needs, feelings, and rights are very important, including the right to be respected and to be heard.
6. When emotions flare, I will hold off trying to reason; instead I'll be patient, listen, and comfort.
7. My goal is to have a calm and peaceful home.[8]

Differently Designed Brains

Children with developmental differences are frequently involved in the bullying dynamic. It is natural for children to compare themselves to others, and some are very perceptive in noticing the slightest differences. When there is any sort of insecurity or fear, differences are often focused on and attacked. Yet the human brain can see beyond differences, and even recognize them as strengths.

Kids whose brains don't develop in exactly the same way as others may have different needs in terms of eye contact, touch, space, and language, but they still need the same love, attachment, respect, and empathy as anyone else. Assertiveness training is especially important for kids who have special needs, since—whether their behavior is calm and quiet or loud and rambunctious—they are often expected to go through life passively. Autonomy is always the goal, or at least as much autonomy as possible.

It is essential for you to understand the particularities of your child's brain. Many kids get teased for things they have no control over—or they can lash out for the same reason. Just like "normal" children, children with special needs can become aggressive because they do not have the skills necessary to resolve disagreements peaceably. Unless your child is severely developmentally disabled, there is every reason to expect children to learn to express their needs while being respectful and assertive, respecting their own boundaries and those of others.

AD/HD

Children with ADD or AD/HD (one version is inattentive, one version is hyperactive) have trouble filtering the information that floods into their brains. They can be very smart, but their brains don't always prioritize what to pay attention to, resulting in absentmindedness or forgetfulness. Children with these issues tend to be both intensely focused and distractible, which is a conundrum in itself.

Some kids with ADD have more trouble self-regulating than other kids, even when they are given the right support by their parents. "It's like I know what the rules are, I just forget them," a child might say. Children with AD/HD experience a higher level of frustration than most kids. Parents and children both benefit greatly from understanding how the brain works.

Dr. Anna Wong, who runs social skills groups for children and teens with AD/HD at Kaiser Permanente in Oakland, says kids with AD/HD get bullied more than they bully. "Since they seem to always be in trouble for something anyway, they tend to get blamed—and since they're highly reactive, they make the perfect target. They don't see it coming. They're not very good at self-advocating or self-observation, so they often take the blame as well."[9]

Parents with children whose brains develop differently need to stay positive and informed, keeping their expectations high but realistic. Albert Einstein couldn't tie his shoes until he was seven, as the legend goes. If his parents had criticized and belittled him for being slow or impatient, think of what the world would have lost; instead they focused on the positive and fed his hungry mind. Anyone who works with children or has kids with ADD or AD/HD should keep the positive side in focus—and there are a lot of positive sides.[10]

Mental Illness

Just as many people are now speaking out against bullying, many are also speaking up to destigmatize mental illness. Many social problems are connected to undiagnosed mental illnesses that need medical attention. The world now accommodates physical diseases, injuries, and disorders with dignity, for example, with kneeling buses and Special Olympics. But when the issue is a brain disorder, the handicap is not visible, and victims themselves are often blamed.

While meeting children's basic needs through positive parenting and preventing ACEs is critical, we need to recognize that many mental illnesses are hereditary and may be triggered by unpreventable stress. If you have a hunch that this describes your child, get professional help early. By the time the brain is mostly developed in the late teens and early twenties, mental illness becomes much harder to treat.

Protect Your Brain!

Louise's warning to her young children—"Protect your brain!"—needs to become the motto of parents everywhere. As children's brains grow, they need to be around caring and attentive adults, period. The rise in social disorders in American children is linked to overstressed, undersupported, undermined, and disempowered parents who are not there for their kids. This loss of nurturing is taking its toll. We need to find ways to slow down, to care for ourselves and keep our brains healthy—so that we can do the same for our children.

Several studies involving head injuries show that many people who exhibit violent behavior have injured brains.[11] Clearly, we need to protect our brains and those of our children. Teach them to wear seat belts and helmets and to protect their heads if they fall.

Children who consume a lot of junk food are likely to have a lower intake of vitamins, minerals, and essential fatty acids, all of which are vital building blocks for the brain. Making sure your kids eat right can help immunize their brains against bullying behaviors. Be sure they get enough exercise, sleep, and rest, as these are all essential for healthy brains.

What happens to a child's brain early on has an enormous effect throughout life. Our future depends on the healthy development of all of our children's precious brains.

• • •

·

17

••••

Hardwired for Resilience

Fall down seven times, stand up eight.

— JAPANESE PROVERB

As a homecoming queen and cheerleader, Jessica seemed to be popular in school. Still, she was on the receiving end of some mean pranks: "I had girls egging my home, writing curse words on the sidewalk in paint—just saying really nasty things about me."

Another Jessica spent her lunches in the nurses' office for solitude and safety, and her dad had to walk her to school so that she wouldn't be provoked.

Kate was bullied and teased for being chubby. She was nicknamed "Blubber," and was once locked in the art cupboard.

Eva was "a gawky, skinny girl with big teeth" who was tortured by two bullies all through junior high school.

Michael was taunted for his long arms, lisp, and "sticky-out ears."

Ranulph's classmates treated him with such "remorseless nastiness" that he was nearly driven to suicide.

As a junior high schooler, Bill was picked on relentlessly for being a "fat band boy" with bad taste in clothes. At a school dance one weekend, an older student teased him about his clothes and hit him in the jaw.

As the only black student in a private New York City school, Chris was frequently bullied and beaten up. "I got beat up just about every day. I got called n— every single day."

Winona recalls, "I was wearing an old Salvation Army shop boy's suit. As I went to the bathroom I heard people saying, 'Hey, faggot.' They slammed my head into a locker. I fell to the ground and they started to kick the s— out of me. I had to have stitches. The school kicked *me* out, not the bullies."

Day in and day out, kids everywhere are pushed into water fountains, spit on, tripped, shoved, kicked, and called some of the vilest names imaginable. They are slandered online, glared at, sneered at, teased, knocked down, whispered about, beaten up, and even killed—just for being gay (or perceived as such), female, short, brown, red-headed, shy, or otherwise "different."

For many people, bullying is the start of other problems. Many find themselves depressed or developing physical or mental disorders years down the road. People attribute the onset of panic attacks, eczema, OCD, asthma, and alcoholism to incidents of being bullied. Bullying can get under a person's skin and into his or her brain, and can erode self-esteem for a lifetime. Some people make choices to isolate themselves, hurt themselves, or even kill themselves because of what bullies do. Bullying can create ripples of pain throughout families and communities.

For every story of someone whose life was ruined by bullying, however, there is a story about someone who was bullied and came through it stronger. And just as Martin Seligman shifted his attention from the dogs who did not give up (see chapter 7), we now look at the resilient survivors.

All of the kids at the beginning of this chapter went on to become international celebrities. The first Jessica performed at the Super Bowl; the second one saved the universe in a blockbuster movie. Kate and Eva went on to become two of Hollywood's most ravishing beauties. Michael won more Olympic medals than anyone, ever. Ranulph became the world's greatest living explorer and was knighted by Queen Elizabeth. Bill grew up to be president of the United States. Chris became one of the world's most famous comedians. Winona was twice nominated for an Oscar. In this chapter, we talk about the strengths and skills that help people overcome hardship.

From Risk to Resilience

Life is not about how fast you run, or how high you climb,
but how well you bounce.

— ANONYMOUS

"At risk." We hear these words so often that we hardly know what they mean. Our only hope is that they don't apply to our own kids.

Children can be at risk of various things: for example, homelessness, drug use, joining a gang, or dropping out of school. The arts organization Americans for the Arts defines at-risk kids as "youth who are exposed to factors that may increase their tendency to engage in problem or delinquent behaviors."[1] The law in one Northwest town defines an at-risk youth as an individual under the age of eighteen years who

- is absent from home for more than 72 consecutive hours without parental consent;
- is beyond the control of his/her parent, and whose behavior substantially endangers his/her own or another's health, safety, or welfare; or
- has a serious substance abuse problem.[2]

The United Nations' Urban Youth At Risk conference defines at-risk youth as "young people whose background places them 'at risk' of future offending or victimization due to environmental, social, and family conditions that hinder their personal development and successful integration into the economy and society."[3] This definition would definitely include both bullies and victims of bullying.

The Opposite of Risk

Bullying is an unwelcome part of our lives, and it feels, at times, to be more than we can handle. We want to protect and remove children from the dangers of bullies everywhere, but since we cannot control all circumstances, preparing our children to be resilient is our best hope. Knowing we can recover from bullying can save us from feeling like victims forever.

It can be difficult to feel resilient when you are surrounded by worried and doubtful friends, doctors, and parents. Personal resilience is often overlooked or dismissed because of our preoccupation with problems and pathology. When people are so focused on what's wrong, it's difficult to discover what's right—and to connect with our resilient natures.

Yet resilience *is* a fact of nature. Weeds break through asphalt. Seeds sprout after a fire. Spiders rebuild their webs over and over and over again. Our hearts are built for resilience as well.

When life knocks us down, resilience is what helps us get back up. Resilience is the ability to rebound, to withstand hardship, to repair oneself. Resilience refers to the clusters of strengths that help us build or rebuild a good life, in spite of all the bad stuff.

Fortunately, we are in the midst of a major shift in thinking about youth development—reframing our focus from fixing their flaws to building their strengths. Over and over again we see research that shows us it's time to set aside the old, negative "deficit" model, and instead find the strengths in ourselves and in our children. The resilience model can transform negativity into optimism and hope.

The negative view of people is unbalanced and unfair—especially when the range of what is considered "normal" is so wide. Being engulfed in negativity, we have been seeing only half the picture—the faults, the shortcomings, the deficits. The negative emphasis reinforces negative self-image, damages self-esteem, and stifles resilience.

Additionally, with this model the very qualities that can help us bounce back are often put down, dismissed, or belittled. For example, persistent people are labeled "stubborn" or "thick-headed"; compassionate people are written off as "rescuers"; and those who express positivity are characterized as "attention seekers" or just "weirdos." Anyone who's been called any of these names either has brought or has yet to bring gifts to the world.

A Growth Mindset Builds Resilience

One of Louise's former bosses described to her that as a child his mother told him he would never amount to anything. He spent his entire life struggling to "become somebody" and prove his mother wrong. Another man told Louise a very different story. When he was eight years old, his grandmother put her hands on his shoulders, looked him in the eyes, and said, "You're going to be somebody!" Her strong belief in him set him on his life path to be a devoted teacher for inner city high school youth. Her inspiration fueled his life.

Sincerely stated sentences such as the following reinforce a positive explanatory style, and can motivate and bolster resilience:

- "What is right with you is more powerful than anything that is wrong with you."
- "You have what it takes to get through this!"
- "Practice makes difficult things easy."
- "At first it's hard, then it gets easy."
- "God helps those who help themselves."
- "When one door closes, another opens."
- "Make your own luck."
- "If at first you don't succeed, try, try again."
- "If plan A doesn't work, there are twenty-five more letters in the alphabet!"

Parents, grandparents, and teachers who believe in kids have great power to build their confidence and resilience from the inside out.

When kids have no one to believe in them, however, they may develop a closed, hopeless, fixed, pessimistic mindset with a negative explanatory style. But it takes just one person to instill positive beliefs and attitudes that can shift an "I can't" mindset to a "Yes, I can" mindset. One person can put a child on track for a better future and start an upward spiral. One powerful experience can shift a mindset—and change a life.

Children with a growth mindset look for opportunities and find second chances to do better. They do better academically and socially, and these benefits continue into adult life.

A Resilient Mindset Promotes Growth

An attitude of resilience can help a person deal with great adversity as well as with daily stress. A resilient mindset has special characteristics that include specific skills, knowledge, and dispositions. A person with a resilient mindset sees mistakes as opportunities to learn, has empathy, is flexible, and has an inner locus of control. These qualities buffer a person against bullying, by providing an internal infrastructure for good mental health, emotional fitness, and win-win relationships.

The following goals can help a person develop a flexible mindset:

- Change repetitive behaviors that have negative outcomes.
- Develop empathy.
- Communicate more effectively.
- Accept yourself and others.
- Develop self-discipline.
- Take responsibility for your actions and their effect on others.
- Set realistic short- and long-term goals.
- Adopt an optimistic "can-do" attitude.

Mindshift to Resilience

Here are some useful ways to look at building more resilient thought patterns:

- E+R=O. The **e**vent plus the **r**esponse determines the **o**utcome. Our response is the most important thing, and the thing we have the most control over.

- A+B=C. **A**dversity plus **b**eliefs creates **c**onsequences. What we believe about a problem determines its impact on our emotions and behavior.

- First and second "darts." This is from Buddhist philosophy. The first "dart to the heart" is pain; it is a fact. The second dart is suffering—our reaction to the pain. How we explain it—"you meant to do that; you wanted to hurt me" vs. "it was an accident"—can cause or avoid long-term suffering.

Persistent negative thoughts keep us stuck in three ways: negative responses create negative outcomes; negative beliefs cause negative consequences; and "second darts" cause us emotional pain and suffering. Brain expert Daniel Amen defines nine types of automatic negative thoughts (ANTs): Always-or-never thinking, focusing on the negative, fortune-telling, mind reading, thinking with your feelings, guilt beatings, labeling, personalization, and blame.

We have to notice, call out, and challenge our ANTs. They're rarely true, yet they often determine our level of happiness. Ask yourself: Do the facts support your negative thought? Does that thought do you any good? Does it get you to where you want to be?

Saving Graces Help Us Survive

Those who develop a resilient mindset do so by depending on saving graces outside the struggles life puts in front of them. These include sports, religion, music and art, friendships, meaningful work or volunteerism, reading books, and a sense of humor.[4] Many people find a relationship between their personal saving graces and their present life and work. Perhaps your childhood resiliencies have in some way shaped the quality of your adult life. All of the kids you met at the beginning of the chapter are examples of how saving graces can give you power:[5]

- **Spirituality.** Jessica Simpson credits her unfortunate youthful experiences with helping her as a high-profile celebrity—recording artist, actress, television personality, and fashion designer—learn how to deal with constant scrutiny from the media. "I grew up in that fishbowl of always being judged and watched. I really do believe that was God preparing me for the life I'm living now."

- **Art.** Jessica Alba never fought back, not wanting to lower herself to the level of her bullies. Instead she found an outlet for her frustration and fear: acting classes. Alba recalls, "The idea that for an hour I could be someone different was amazing. I was determined that this was something I was going to be good at. This was a part of my life no bully could ruin."

- **Assertiveness.** Although her bullies made her miserable at school, Eva Mendes eventually found the courage she needed to push back against them. "Only later could I see that I was showing them my fear and that's what they were pouncing on." Now an actress, model, singer, designer, and "Sexiest Woman Alive," Mendes recalls, "When I finally stood up to my bully, that's when things changed for me."

- **Sports.** Michael Phelps, the most decorated Olympian of all time, found an outlet for his anger in sports. His coach says, "Michael is the motivation machine—bad moods, good moods, he channels everything for gain."

- **Humor.** Chris Rock's sense of humor prepared him to be a comedian. After watching his TV sitcom *Everybody Hates Chris,* one of his teachers wrote to him: "I knew it was hard on you, but I had no idea. If anything happened to you because of me, please forgive me."

- **Principles.** Bill Clinton did not give the bully what he wanted; he chose to stand his ground rather than fight back or back down. "I learned that I could take a hit and that there's more than one way to stand against aggression." (Talk about *Zorgos!*)

Always encourage your children to nurture their interests and talents, be they artistic or athletic or intellectual. These saving graces will nourish them throughout their lives and help them build inner strength.

Internal Resources: Strength from Inside

According to Dr. Bruce Perry, the idea that children are naturally resilient is a myth. Children are, in fact, more vulnerable to trauma than adults. They are more fragile and therefore need more protection and care.

What makes children resilient are the inner resources consistently nurtured by moms, dads, grandparents, and other adults who comfort, teach, and play with them. Those fortunate children raised with positive parenting have a reservoir of self-worth to steady and sustain them. They have the internal scaffolding for resilience.

Emotional resilience is an inner strength and fitness developed in children by caring adults. This fitness starts with attention, connection, and routines, all of which build love, respect, and deep trust. Children develop a sense of self along with an awareness of their needs, wants, and desires, because it's safe to express who they really are. This evolves into a positive self-concept, built from self-worth, self-esteem, self-expression and mastery, and self-advocacy: being on their own side. In the day-to-day process of respectfully living together in a family, children gradually build other strengths: self-direction, self-reliance, self-regulation, being able to get along with others, and eventually an inner locus of control and autonomy.

We often don't know we are resilient until we are tested. Not making the team, not being invited to a party, or getting a bad grade are typical childhood hardships; children can either give up or find the inner strength to practice more, reach out to others, or push themselves harder to get a better grade. Sometimes life brings greater difficulties: death, divorce, even natural disasters. In surviving these things, children are tested to the breaking point, but over time they can get stronger and build inner resilience.

People don't build this resilience alone. Gabor Maté explains what helped him survive the horrors of war in Budapest: "Resilience doesn't come from adversity; it comes from love. . . . For what resilience I do have, I credit my mother. Despite all those terrible circumstances, she did her powerful best to love me and get me through."[6]

It Takes a Village: Strength from Outside

In his heartbreaking book *A Long Way Gone: Memoirs of a Boy Soldier*,[7] Ishmael Beah describes in detail how he was swept into the front lines of revolution at age thirteen. The soldiers all took drugs to numb their feelings, watched *Rambo* and other violent movies daily, and gave in to a culture where horrifying violence felt normal. Beah was one of the lucky ones plucked out of that world by the United Nations, but it took months and years of rehabilitation before he returned, mentally, to humanity.

Beah describes the steps he took with each person on his way back to a new life he could never have imagined on the day the war arrived at his doorstep. Throughout the book he relives the memories of his village—the people, the faces, the rituals, and the stories told during normal life—that had built his inner structure. All the people he once knew are now gone—his entire family and all of his friends. Those who remain in his country all share his horrifying memories of war. The reader can see the greater structure of a world coming to his aid and nurturing his resilience—a larger village made of caring individuals and refugees from all nations.

Resistance, Retaliation, and Revenge

Martin Luther King Jr. said, "Man must evolve for all human conflict a method which rejects revenge, aggression and retaliation." Being assertive means using your voice, your words, and your intentions to set boundaries, communicate your needs, and get what you want. But saying no with your body is a powerful form of resistance.

Tom's family moved around a lot when he was young. "I was always the new kid with the wrong shoes, the wrong accent," he said. "I didn't have a friend to share things with and confide in." And at each school, he faced the fresh experience over and over again. He was small for his age and easily pushed around. Eventually, he learned to stand up for himself, but at every new school, he had to fight again. "Your heart's pounding, you sweat, and you feel like you're going to vomit. I'm not the biggest guy; I never liked hitting someone, but I knew if I didn't hit that guy hard he was going to pick on me all year. I'd go, 'You better fight.' I just laid it down. I don't like bullies."

Learning to physically fight takes a lot of the fear out of confrontation, and for this reason many adults enroll their children in karate classes. The ideal of martial arts training is to "learn to use your fists . . . so that you never have to." Self-defense classes have been especially empowering for women and girls, because they don't just teach fighting. They teach how to communicate power with both body and voice. Some classes, like Model Mugging, even give women the opportunity to hit, kick, and struggle in a controlled environment so they can experience their own strength in safety.

There are problems with teaching kids to fight for themselves, however. The top three problems are the following:

1. The child can escalate a fight and get hurt.

2. He or she can be mistaken as the bully.

3. The child may try to solve problems with fighting that should be solved in other ways.

Some parents encourage their children to "hit him back"—or even to "hit him before he hits you." It sounds funny, but it is such common advice that some parents don't even realize what they're doing—that they are teaching their children the bullying dynamic. This is a mainstream parenting practice that we all need to reject.

Retaliation is a huge part of the bullying dynamic. Typically, a target gets goaded into retaliating, and the bully gets what he or she wants: to appear innocent. One viral video shows a young boy in an Australian school hitting a very passive big kid in the face seven times, until the bigger kid finally picks up the smaller bully and throws him on the ground, clearly hurting his ankle.

The urge to get back at a bully is strong—and a healthy expression of self-preservation, as well. Acting on this urge is confusing, however, because it breaks the Golden Rule of treating others as you wish to be treated. This is one of humankind's deepest moral conflicts. Ancient religious texts and laws, from the Old Testament to the Koran, call for an "eye for an eye." The moral problem with the law of retaliation is thus: although violence to the perpetrator may provide a feeling of justice, it also makes the punisher into a perpetrator of violence. Mahatma Gandhi addressed the consequences of retaliation with his memorable quote, "An eye for an eye leaves the whole world blind." There are other options to consider: compensation in some other way, for example, or simply forgiveness.

Movies are full of violent vengeful acts that mistakenly model revenge as a healthy choice without negative consequences. Feelings of revenge are natural and gratifying, but these emotions can become dangerous when acted upon. Verbalizing plans for revenge can help keep you from acting them out. At the same time, we need to make sure we imagine nonviolent ways to "teach someone a lesson" or resolve the issue in a positive way.

Here are three healthy steps for "getting back" at a bully, according to the Workplace Bullying Institute website. Although directed toward adults, these could be applied to children as well:[8]

1. Name the problem.

2. Take care of yourself.

3. Expose the bully.

There is enormous power in naming the issue. Call it what it is: bullying, harassment, verbal abuse, emotional abuse. Then do your homework and get the support you need. Getting even through proper channels is truly the best revenge, with justice on your side. But the most important thing to remember is to take care of yourself.

Children who have been bullied can take care of themselves by having some time away from school, staying close to parents or other caring adults. Like adults, they can also get a massage or other pampering, talk with friends, and create some pleasant experiences to buffer their feelings of vulnerability.

Education and Awareness

For eons, bullying has been accepted as "normal." Dan Olweus, the visionary psychologist we mentioned earlier, debunked these old myths with his studies, just as numerous mothers and fathers over the ages have done in their families. Bullying is a pressing social issue that must be taken seriously and systematically addressed. British anti-bullying activist Tim Field says, "Being bullied by a serial bully is equivalent to being stalked or being battered by a partner or being abused as a child, and should be accorded the same gravity."

Education plays a vital role in addressing the bullying dynamic. Many societal issues have been dealt with through education, including the following:

- **Smoking.** Fifty years ago, smoking was an accepted social norm. People smoked in the bathroom, in bed, at the table, at meetings, on airplanes, and even in baby nurseries, causing epidemics of lung cancer and emphysema. A massive educational campaign has made smoking the exception, not the rule.

- **Sexual harassment.** For years, women had to put up with inappropriate comments and innuendos about their looks and sexual relationships at work. When they would ask men to stop, they often heard, "Where's your sense of humor?" When companies finally began to train employees about sexual harassment, men's eyes were opened. Armed with a new understanding of their rights, today's women no longer have to tolerate demeaning and insulting behavior at work or in public.

- **Date rape.** Date rape has been a serious issue for a long time. Two-thirds of teens in one 1991 survey said it was okay for a boy to force sex on a girl if the couple had been dating for more than six months. A large number said it was okay if the boy/man had spent a lot of money on her. One in three said it was okay if the girl had been sexually active previously. Furthermore, boys often did not know when they were behaving illegally in sexual situations.[9] But there is good news: the incidence of sexual assault in the United States has fallen by 60 percent since that survey was done, thanks to education.[10]

Today the spotlight is on bullying. Fifty years from now, it will hopefully be seen as the crime that it is, and every child will be taught from a young age not to do it, supported by social structures that build *Zorgos*!

Resilience Training

Many anti-bullying programs are available. But since resilience is the antidote to risk, what if we taught children resilience first? There is substantial evidence that skills that increase resilience and positive emotion can be taught to schoolchildren. Resilience can also be taught to adults who want to turn their lives around. Let's look at a couple examples of resiliency training and how we can apply these principles in our families.

The Comprehensive Soldier Fitness Program (CSF)

In America, the military has traditionally been a stronghold of authoritarian leadership where bullying is normalized. Unfortunately, the classic military image of leadership—a verbally abusive drill sergeant—is what people turn to again and again when looking for solutions to the bullying problem.

However, the psychology of this leadership method does not translate well outside of the military environment. Re-entry into society and family life continues to be a problem for many soldiers. "Soldiers have experiences they can't really relate to others and that puts them at risk for a variety of physical and mental problems. If we can improve their ability to work together and trust others, they'll be in a better position to sustain effective well-being, and they'll return to civilian life as more complete individuals," says psychologist John Cacioppo, who helped design the Comprehensive Soldier Fitness program (CSF) for the U.S. Army. The focus of CSF includes building mental toughness, identifying signature strengths, and building meaning, purpose, and positive relationships.

The goal of the program is to strengthen a soldier's resilience using positive psychology, with a focus on five specific dimensions: emotional fitness, social fitness, family fitness, spiritual fitness, and physical fitness. This resilience training aims to increase the psychological fitness that helps soldiers and their spouses grow and thrive in the face of challenges, and bounce back from adversity.

Here are a few of the resilience skills the CSF program teaches soldiers and their families:

- **Hunt for the good stuff.** The common tendency to always look for the bad stuff magnifies the negatives and overlooks the positives. "Hunting for the good stuff" helps people notice the good things in their lives and change their thinking style. Finding the good leads to optimism and gratitude.

- **Don't catastrophize.** One of the central components of CSF training is to teach soldiers to identify and avoid catastrophic thinking. If, for example, a soldier you know is late returning from a tour of duty, instead of thinking of the worst scenario (he has been killed), think of a more positive scenario (he's probably hitchhiking and couldn't get a ride); then arrive at the most likely scenario (he's just lost and is probably safe). This skill helps to calm the amygdala and aid the thinking brain to regain balance.

- **Communicate more expressively.** Soldiers are taught how to actively and constructively respond to another person. For example, when a friend or partner gets a promotion, it's best to express sincere interest, enthusiasm, and happiness ("Good for you!"). A positive empathic response sets aside competitive win-lose thinking and acknowledges the emotions behind the other's words. The ability to be in tune with another is the essence of empathy, and is essential for good relationships.[11]

The Penn Resiliency Program (PRP)

The Penn Resiliency Program, which inspired the CSF program, teaches three essential cognitive skills: generating alternatives, producing counter-evidence, and putting it in perspective. Then it builds on these skills to teach assertiveness, coping skills, social skills, decision making, and problem solving. Here is a look at the very thorough twelve-week lesson plan:

Week 1: Link between thoughts and feelings—The first lesson looks at automatic thoughts or "self talk." Students deconstruct recent personal events and explore the link between their beliefs and the ensuing consequences.

Week 2: Thinking styles—This lesson looks at explanatory style, particularly the stable-unstable dimension, and optimistic and pessimistic "thinking styles."

Week 3: Challenging beliefs: alternatives and evidence—By now, students are able to identify their pessimistic automatic thoughts and have come to understand that they accept many thoughts and beliefs without question or evaluation. Students play games to practice coming up with alternate ideas.

Week 4: Evaluating thoughts and putting them in perspective— Using the classic story of Chicken Little as an example, students examine how negative events can affect their thoughts about the future.

Week 5: Practice—Students practice applying these new cognitive skills to inaccurate beliefs and catastrophic thoughts.

Week 6: Assertiveness and negotiation—The new skills are applied to interpersonal relationships, highlighting interaction style, social skills, and problem solving. Skits are used to illustrate aggression, passivity, and assertiveness communication.

Week 7: Coping strategies—Students are taught techniques to help them cope with difficult emotions or stressful situations, such as controlled breathing, muscle relaxation, and positive imagery. They are also encouraged to seek support from family members and friends.

Week 8: Graded task and social skills training—As students apply their new skills to projects and chores, they see how procrastination is a consequence of all-or-nothing thinking. Students learn to break large projects into smaller, more manageable steps.

Week 9: Decision making—Practicing everything they've learned, students realize that the same thoughts that lead to procrastination can make decision making difficult, and that indecisiveness is linked to depression. They examine the pros and cons of actions they've taken personally.

Week 10: Social problem solving—Students learn a five-step approach to problem solving:

1. Stop and think about problems before reacting impulsively. (Gather evidence for and against their initial beliefs, consider alternative interpretations, and get perspective.)
2. Determine what their goal is in the situation.
3. Generate a variety of possible solutions.
4. Use decision-making techniques to choose a course of action, and enact it.

5. Evaluate the outcome; if they haven't reached their goal, they try again.

Weeks 11 and 12: Application and integration—During the last two weeks of classes, students practice applying all of their new skills and integrating them into their new behavior. They have a party, of course! And they talk about the importance of booster sessions and supporting one another in their new good habits of thought.[12]

Beyond Bullying

The bullying dynamic is, unsurprisingly, linked to depression. Why unsurprising? Because bullying is a win-lose dynamic. It *never* feels good to lose, and it often doesn't feel good to win at another's expense. One study made it clear that many children, especially children at risk for depression and conduct disorder, "selectively attend to hostile cues and attribute the ambiguous behavior of others to hostile intent";[13] in other words, they're always on the lookout for hostility, and can mistakenly imagine others' intentions as cruel when they're in fact not.

Feeling good is an essential part of the bullying antidote! And resilience is an essential part of feeling good.

The Recipe for "Bounce-Back Kids"

Bonnie Benard, author of *Resiliency: What We Have Learned*, is a pioneer in defining the concept of resilience. She has noted that for children to become healthy, happy, and successful, three fundamental needs must be met: (1) they must have caring relationships; (2) these relationships must convey positive and high expectations; and (3) children must be given opportunities for meaningful participation. When these three fundamental conditions are not met, there will be problems. These three positive "ingredients," when they exist, lead directly to positive outcomes—good kids who are caring, competent, and confident.

1. Caring Relationships

What happens when kids are not bonded to a loving adult? Kids in this situation don't learn to trust and aren't taught to care; they feel worthless. They don't develop a conscience and can become violent. Kids who don't care about anything pose a great risk to themselves and to society; they have nothing to lose.

A healthy, caring adult is the first and most important ingredient in turning this situation around. Connection is the keystone for healthy development, strong mental health, and resilience. Positive regard and simple, sustained kindness attaches people at a soul level that can endure forever.

2. High and Attainable Expectations

What happens when positive expectations are lacking? Children in this situation experience prejudice (low expectations) and/or perfectionism (impossibly high expectations), which in turn cause disappointment and discouragement, and set kids up to fail. These children don't develop self-confidence.

"Just right" expectations—high, attainable, and age-appropriate—are essential. When you believe in kids, they rise to the expectations set for them, because they don't want to disappoint you!

3. Meaningful Participation

What happens when kids are not given opportunities to participate in a meaningful way? These children feel disconnected and isolated, and are unable to trust. They develop antisocial behaviors and can be attracted to gangs. Kids need to feel like they belong to their family, school, and community. They need to feel included and valued, to contribute in meaningful ways, and to be able to demonstrate their competence.[14]

Humans are hardwired for real, healthy connections to others. When kids feel deeply connected to family, friends, and organizations that are meaningful to them, they won't be tempted to get into gangs or exhibit other risky behaviors.

Kids become resilient by participating in things like after-school programs, music and sports programs, martial arts, theater, dance, gymnastics, Scouts, etc. Interacting with others teaches and strengthens pro-social skills. Having enriching experiences with peers and people of different ages can be especially good for kids who come from smaller families, or whose parents have to work long hours. Such resources can be saving graces during times of adversity.

The Core of Resilience: Inner Motivation

Jonathan Cohen, president of the National School Climate Center, wrote that there is "an important and growing body of empirical research that supports the notion that when we teach children to become more (intrinsically) motivated and promote engagement, we are also promoting resilience."[15] In other words, an internal locus of control (inner motivation) and participation (engagement) are deeply intertwined with resilience.

Early on, parents are in control of their children's experiences; they make the decisions, and clean up the spilled milk. In the process of development and maturation, children learn to clean up their own spilled milk, become more responsible, and learn to make good decisions.

As we've discussed before, there's a continuum from external control (in childhood) to internal control (in adulthood). What determines your own life experiences? Are they mostly the outcome of your own choices and behaviors (inner motivation/control)? Or are they from forces beyond your control (external motivation/control)?

When children are being bullied, it sure feels like forces beyond their control are running their lives. Children need to know that it's not their fault. Shoring up their inner strengths and resilience can help them start taking steps to move away from a bad situation and move toward the lives they want. However, a child may still need the help of an adult to stop the bullying behavior.

· · ·

18

. . . .

Swept Away by Technology

The Internet is just a world passing around notes in a classroom.

— JON STEWART

Millions of people visit the Amish country in Pennsylvania. One man taking a bus tour asked the Amish guide, "What's the difference between you and us?" The guide, turning to the group, responded with this question: "How many of you have televisions?" All the hands went up. "How many of you with a family think you'd be better off without a television?" Practically all the hands went up. "How many of you are going to go home and get rid of it?" Not one hand went up. "That's the difference between you and the Amish. . . . If it's bad for the family, we will not have it."[1]

Mr. Flenderson, a fourth-grade teacher, was having trouble with a student in his classroom. Mark didn't do his homework, didn't do his classwork, and spent every possible moment in school trying to get a rise out of the kids around him. Finally, Mr. Flenderson paid a visit to the boy's home. A seventy-two-inch TV filled up one end of the living room, where several adults sat staring at a game show. Not one of them stood up to greet him. Mark's mother came out of the kitchen to talk to him without turning down the TV. She blamed Mr. Flenderson and "all the teachers" for Mark's problems. Mr. Flenderson left feeling hopeless; the conversation had gone nowhere.

The contrast between the two all-or-nothing cultures is clear. One is authoritarian. One is permissive. Most of the parents reading this book will be somewhere in the middle. Most are familiar with the power struggles families have with technology today—and not just over who's got the remote.

Technology enriches our lives, but it also impoverishes our lives. Humans crave connection, and technology connects people to the broader world—but it also allows them to isolate much more easily. Technology allows us to expand our horizons and keep up with our relationships at the touch of a button, but it has also diluted the definition of the word *friend*. Now we can have hundreds of "friends" on Facebook whom we never see face to face, have never met, know little or nothing about, and might not even like! Technology also creates avenues for bullying that we could have never dreamed of even ten years ago.

We talked about "a screen in every room" in chapter 2, but what we actually have now is a screen in every pocket. Our cameras have become phones, our phones can send e-mail, and we can play games on our phones and online. Kristen calls tablets and smartphones "everything machines"—yet we hand them over to our kids like they were stuffed animals.

This chapter looks at the big cultural picture of how technology is shaping our society and our families, and reshaping our brains.

Bullies on the Screen

It has become appallingly obvious that our technology
has exceeded our humanity.

— ALBERT EINSTEIN

Today's kids spend more time online than on the playground. Facebook, Twitter, texting, and online role-playing games (RPGs) are all places our children socialize. Most children go online daily and spend much of their time on social networks and video-sharing sites such as YouTube.

Cyberbullying
Cyberbullying shares many of the same characteristics of traditional bullying, but with some major differences:

- Anonymity means it's often difficult to identify who is doing the bullying, and it removes inhibition—a child who normally wouldn't engage in bullying face to face feels free to do it online.

- Schoolyard bullies have always been trouble enough, but the school day ends around 3 p.m. Cyberbullying, which has increased in recent years, continues twenty-four hours a day, and can seem inescapable. Many children bullied in this manner may worry about threats if they report the harassing, or that their computer or phone privileges will be taken away. They feel more isolated and dehumanized than with playground bullying.

- Bystanders play a different role. In a traditional situation, there may be a small handful of bystanders. But in the world of cyberbullying, e-mails, texts, and Facebook posts are shared over and over, often by children who could be upstanders to stop traditional bullying.

- Girls are twice as likely to bully or be bullied online than boys.[2]

- Cyberbullying can ruin reputations and be more "permanent," because it is impossible to retract something that has been broadcast online.

Let's look at some ways online bullying can get out of hand.

E-mail

Computer users are bullied by spammers who send unwanted advertising and pornography that sucks their time and attention, and sometimes causes computer viruses. Increasingly, e-mail is used as a way for teens and adults to spread gossip—through hurtful jokes or embarrassing photos, for example—and do it all in secrecy over cell phones or on private accounts, which are difficult to police.

Facebook

If Facebook were a country, it would have three times the population of the United States. There are now over a billion active Facebook users in the world.

How does bullying happen on Facebook? One person says something personal about someone else. The "friends" in their network comment, either agreeing or disagreeing. Each comment is then visible to all (or many) of their friends. Another example: someone could post a photo and "tag" a bunch of people, who would then come and see the photo. Anyone can then "share" a comment or photo with any of his or her friends. As young friendships grow and fall apart, kids will "friend" and "unfriend" each other, adding to hurt feelings of being left out. And finally, people sometimes hack into other accounts to post mean things.

"Things are getting bad," says a middle-school physical education teacher. "There's always been drama with this age group. But now there is more stuff going on outside school that is for some reason so inflammatory. Kids bring their Facebook dramas to the yard. I can't turn my back for a second!" This coach advises parents not to let middle school kids get a Facebook account; they are not emotionally ready to handle the challenges and drama. Facebook does require children to be at least thirteen years old before they can create an account.

Texting and Sexting

Louise remembers the excitement when her family first got a telephone—one wall phone with a long coiled cord. When Kristen was a kid, it was a really big deal if a kid had a phone in his or her room. Today, 77 percent of teenagers own a mobile phone—a higher percentage than adults—and have their own personal, private phone number.[3]

Over the last decade, the annual number of text messages surged from 57 billion in 2005 to 1.8 trillion in 2010. Text messaging is the number one communication medium of today's youth.[4] There are many positive sides to texting, but it can also be a bullying tool. Cell phones are the most common medium for cyberbullying. The difference between using a cell phone to make a private call and using it to text is that, just like e-mails, texts can be stored, shown to others, forwarded, and broadcast to multiple addresses.

Many phones have cameras, and photographs can be sent via text message. When teens take and send sexually provocative photos of themselves to their boyfriend or girlfriend (sexting), these can become tools of revenge, bullying, and exploitation. Laws and school regulations are increasingly changing to deal with this problem, often tying it to bullying and even child pornography statutes. Most children do not have the judgment necessary to handle all of the decisions a cell phone requires. It's up to parents to educate themselves and their children, and to judge whether and/or when their child is ready for these responsibilities and risks.

Twitter

Twitter is a program that allows people to post short, topical messages that can be seen by the public. Tweets are directed toward topics or people and are organized using topical hashtags—a word or phrase preceded by the # symbol. Hashtags are often ironic, and can be very mean. Twitter actively censors hashtags that promote racism and pornography, but bullies practice free and creative speech that often cannot be censored. There are even Twitter communities formed around hate speech. Public figures are viciously and unscrupulously attacked on Twitter.

Researchers from the University of Wisconsin in Madison claim that over 15,000 bully-related tweets are sent every day, equaling more than 100,000 every week.[5]

Internet "trolls" also tweet terrible, hurtful things about people in the news who have suffered loss. A "troll" is someone who posts "inflammatory, extraneous, or off-topic messages in an online community—such as a forum, chat room, blog, or Twitter feed—with the primary intent of provoking readers into an emotional response or of otherwise disrupting normal on-topic discussion."[6] Trolling began as a game but has become, in this bullying culture, a destructive force.

Hackers

Another aspect of online bullying that is similar to trolling is hacking. Hacking is the unauthorized use of someone's account. Professional hackers write codes that can steal information, damage files, destroy hardware, or spy, causing untold social and financial damage. School-age bullies—even misguided friends—are eager to get passwords and cause mischief or damage. Four out of ten middle school students have had their password(s) stolen and changed by a bully who then locked them out of their own account or sent communications posing as the victim.[7]

Bullying can be in the form of harassment, derogatory statements or rumors, "flaming" (online arguments using vulgar or insulting language), impersonating another by using his or her passwords, tricking someone into sharing personal information or photos, and cyber-stalking, or using the Internet to stalk or harass someone. The emotional signs can be similar to traditional bullying, even if there's no outward sign of abuse, such as black eyes or torn clothing. Children who are bullied online may seem anxious, have mood swings, or withdraw from friends and social activities. They may avoid school or homework. Or they may seem upset after using their computer or cell phone.

It is important to discuss acceptable online behavior with your children, set limits, help them establish boundaries, and keep channels of communication open so that they will talk with you if they feel threatened or harassed online.

A Web of Support

Fortunately, not everything that happens online is evil. If you search for "bullying" on Google, thousands and thousands of sites appear in which people are educating others, sharing resources, and telling personal stories in chat rooms where help is available. People are tweeting about changing the bullying dynamic with hashtags like #bullying-stopshere, #gangupforgood, #stopbullying, and #nohate.

One teen in Minnesota who saw kids being bullied at school and online secretly started a Twitter account dedicated to sending positive and uplifting messages to kids at his high school. His idea caught on.[8] Millions of kids have committed to "Stomp Out Bullying" with an online pledge.[9]

The watchdog group Mean Stinks encourages girls to stick up for, and not bully, each other. They paint their pinky fingernails blue to show that they will be upstanders, not bystanders.[10]

Technology can be a powerful tool against bullying. Some students at a California high school invented a video game app called Bully Blaster in which students fight their way through cruel words and gather up positive messages. It helps children train their brains to notice negativity and automatically fight back.

One former principal we interviewed told of a student who said a teacher was being mean to him when no one was looking. "We wanted to take action, but it was the child's word against the teacher's." The child's parents placed a tape recorder in his backpack, and they were shocked to hear the teacher cutting their son down, telling him that he and his brother would never amount to anything. "I think recording devices would be an interesting use of technology as a bullying tool, whether secretly or openly. We don't like the idea that 'big brother is watching,' but the truth is, all children—maybe all people—behave better when they think someone might be watching."[11]

Some of today's kids have a horrible habit of pulling out their cell phones when a fight breaks out ("It's just like on *SmackDown*! That's so cool!"), but when authorities can get their hands on the video, events can be slowed down and analyzed, and used to identify the instigators of the fight and other bystanders. Hopefully, technology will become as good at stopping bullying as it is at creating it.

Bullies Behind the Screen

While parents busily try to set limits at home, marketing executives work day and night to undermine their efforts with irresistible messages.

— DR. SUSAN LINN, *CONSUMING KIDS*

Of course, technology-related bullying doesn't just occur online. In practically every form of technology children use, they are vulnerable to strangers who want to exploit them, control their brains and behavior, and win their allegiance. Do marketers have power and regularly attempt to control behavior? Yes, they do. Do they *intend* to do harm? Not necessarily. But they *do* harm children, in many ways.

Commercializing Kids

Ubiquitous, sophisticated, and portable screen technologies have arisen to allow marketers unprecedented direct access to children; because of this direct access, the effectiveness of key policies and agencies created to protect kids from harmful marketing has been weakened.

The average English-speaking child watches 20,000 TV commercials each year.[12] TV commercials are a powerful psychological phenomenon. They sell products, but they are also an important socializing instrument, promoting conformity and encouraging consumerism on a subconscious level. They do this in many ways, including combining entertainment with long-term product branding.

Most TV ads convey their message so effectively that the audience unknowingly captures the message and internalizes it within a few seconds. These effects are so subtle that consumers don't even realize what they've absorbed.

Many sophisticated psychological techniques are used to persuade, cajole, and seduce viewers in this vulnerable state:

- Embedding products in TV shows and movies inspires children to want to consume junk food, soft drinks, and alcohol because they see characters doing it.

- Bright colors and popular cartoon personalities encourage youngsters to request or demand certain foods and toys, especially "must have" items that are then purchased by parents.

- Emotional manipulation is a mind-control strategy; when people are afraid or angry, it's harder to be logical. TV commercials can persuade adults, for example, to buy an advertised item so their child will feel special, cool, or "in."

- Repetition of messages over and over implants jingles in the minds of viewers to cement brand awareness and loyalty.

- Association of a product with sex, wealth, and power is also emotional manipulation. Many advertisers believe "sex sells" and treat women and men (and sometimes children) as sex objects.

These subtle techniques manipulate, overwhelm, exploit—and have dire consequences for children. This is why parents must regulate their children's exposure to screens—what and how much they watch. Always keep in mind that marketers are concerned only with gain and profits. As previously stated, when children watch advertising, they are being shaped by forces that don't care what shape they are in.

Sexualizing Kids

"This generation has no resemblance to how you grew up!" says Rachel Simmons, author of *Odd Girl Out*. Starting with the "princess obsession" at age two, girls are bombarded by messages in clothing ads, TV, songs, music videos, and social media to believe that what matters most in life is looking grown-up and being "hot." High heels for four-year-olds, toy makeup kits, and thongs and padded bras for nine-year-olds are vivid examples of the exploitation of children's innocence. Movies for children and family audiences routinely contain tasteless sexual innuendo "for the parents." Kids today need to be protected from this onslaught.

"It's nothing short of corporate pedophilia and voyeuristic sleaze fouling up childhood, kids' socioemotional health, and our cultural compass as a whole," writes Amy Jussel, the executive director of Shaping Youth, a forum for exploring how advertising shapes our children's brains.[13]

The six-month "Letting Children Be Children" study by the U.K. Department of Education found that the pressure on children to grow up takes two different but related forms:

- The pressure to take part in a sexualized life before they are ready to do so.
- The commercial pressure to consume the vast range of goods and services that are available to children and young people of all ages.[14]

In this study, parents expressed frustration, irritation, worry, stress, and anxiety. They also expressed anger over the glamorization of alcohol use and aggressive behavior on TV, concern over "perfect" bodies for girls—and the resulting low self-esteem, along with damaged mental and physical health. They expressed frustration about the incessant nagging of their children, as well as the financial drain on family resources. Of even deeper concern was that children are learning values from the media that are in opposition to those of the family.

When put in front of a screen, our children's brains are programmed for arousal, addictions, aggression, isolation, and antisocial behaviors. By the time a boy reaches age twenty-one, he's played 10,000 hours of video games, mostly in isolation.[15]

Parents feel overwhelmed and helpless. They feel out of control of their lives and their families. The British study shows how popular culture is sabotaging harmony and unity, and creating division. The media has hypnotized children, molding their brains toward materialistic values and raising good "consumers" instead of good citizens. This report called on businesses and broadcasters to protect children from the increasingly sexualized and commercialized "wallpaper" that surrounds them.

Normalizing Violence

Normalization refers to the process by which an idea or behavior goes from being clearly problematic to becoming an accepted part of societal culture.

At one time, there were strict regulations about what could be shown on TV during "family time." Commercial TV programmers now think nothing of showing "mature" movies at any time of day, or playing commercials for R-rated movies and M-rated video games during family shows.

Now, before finishing elementary school, the average American child will watch 8,000 murders on TV. By age eighteen, the average American has seen 200,000 acts of violence on TV, including 40,000 murders. Producers argue that violent TV is an outlet for our dark emotions, and that if we work them out in our fantasies we won't work them out in real life. But the opposite has been shown: Out of 3,000 studies, 2,888 demonstrate that TV violence is a factor in real-life violence.[16]

Adding to the problem of "violence as entertainment" is the availability of guns. In 2009, guns killed over 31,000 American citizens. Eighty-five died each day, more than three every hour; of these, eight kids die each day from gunshot wounds.[17] Americans own more guns per capita than any other country by a long shot and kids "rehearse" using them with their video games. As a society, we are also inundated with images and messages that portray sexual exploitation and sexual violence as normal. These messages are everywhere, from TV shows and commercials, to movies and music, billboards and bus shelters—even products designed for and marketed to kids.

The Screen as the Bully

Not only are there problems *on* the screen but also screens *themselves* can cause our children harm. Our brains are wired to notice movement. When screens are on, we want to look at them—and the bigger the screen, the better! Kids are especially mesmerized by screens.

A phenomenon called "supernormal stimuli" describes the brain's attraction to anything that is newer, bigger, or faster. Part of our evolution involved instincts such as choosing the largest piece of fruit, the tallest mate, or the fastest horse. We continue to do this, automatically, even when it's not good for us. In a time when the word *temperance* has all but disappeared from modern conversation, we "follow our instincts"—even when we know, for example, that supersized drinks are not good for us. The stimulation of the screen is so alluring—the light, the reliable user-friendly interface designed to attract and hold our attention, the fascinating content—that we want to repeatedly turn it on and live in a virtual reality.

The Bully Box

Americans love TV: there is so much to learn, to see, to think about, and to feel, and TV brings us these things easily and in the comfort of our homes. Unfortunately, we consequently suffer a host of TV-related health problems, including eating disorders and obesity. The American Psychological Association is also raising concerns about the impact of television on the mental health and well-being of children. When kids watch more than two hours of TV a day, their risk for both obesity and behavior problems increases. "Sustained TV watching has a negative effect on behavior and social skills," says Carla Weidman, a psychologist in the child development unit at Children's Hospital of Pittsburgh.[18]

Common Sense Media reports that the average child today spends forty-five hours a week with some form of media, compared with just thirty hours in school. Media exposure can contribute to childhood obesity, tobacco use, drug use, alcohol use, poor school achievement, sexual behavior, and attention problems.[19]

Consider what we know about the plasticity of the brain. Exposure to environmental influences—and the flow of thoughts—can change the structure of the brain. The media habitually shapes, alters, forms, morphs, and distorts reality. Entertainment culture is rewiring our brains to be broader and less deep.

Yet 53 percent of parents of eight- to eighteen-year-olds have no rules about TV use.[20] Children of permissive parents are especially in danger; unprotected and unguided, they learn violence and narcissism, and they are programmed for materialism. They think that's what life is all about.

Let's look at an example of how the media subtly hijacks self-restraint. In the past—and even in the present—board games ended, and were put away. Now, with computers and digital games, there is always another level to play. It becomes a three-way battle of wills between the game, the child, and the parent who is trying to get the child to switch gears and go set the table.

Years ago, kids came home from school, and then went outside to play until their parents called them in for dinner. These days, grandparents give iPads to their six-year-old grandkids and parents readily buy digital toys for children. These cool, captivating, engaging toys, given with the best of intentions, can hijack and derail a child's healthy development.

Although a world of "good stuff" is available on the screen, every hour in front of one is an hour not going to accomplish the important work of childhood. We have to ask ourselves: *What are today's technologies displacing in human development and quality of life?* More and more, kids are missing out on essential real-life experiences that help them learn about life in a healthy way.

The Neuroscience of Internet Addiction

Addiction is good for business! Ask the tobacco industry. Internet companies and advertisers hire psychologists to use brain science techniques to create ever more compelling obsessions in the virtual world. They exploit emotions in order to sell their products. In the Internet Age, more and more companies live by the mantra "create an obsession, then exploit it." [21]

Video game developers create what is called a "compulsion loop." The player plays the game, achieves the goal, and is rewarded with new content, which makes the player want to continue playing and re-enter the loop to explore the new content. During this process, the pleasure center of the brain is activated, releasing dopamine. It feels good—it's fun! At lower levels, rewards are easy. Higher levels require more work, yet the player has difficulty stopping.

About 10 percent of Internet users have become obsessed with the Internet, which undermines their relationships and family life, as well as their effectiveness at work. While it isn't recognized as an official diagnosis, the American Psychiatric Association includes "Internet Use Disorder" in the new *DSM* (*Diagnostic and Statistical Manual of Mental Disorders,* viewed as the authority on mental illnesses) as a condition recommending further study, signifying the seriousness of the problem.

A study suggests that more than 5 million American kids ages eight to eighteen meet the definition of video game addiction. All children are susceptible, but especially those with poor self-restraint and poor impulse control:

- Even the healthiest kids are susceptible when their parents allow them to play without limits.

- Kids with attention deficit are more vulnerable; the stimulating effect helps them focus, like medication would, and matches their strongest mental processes.

- Bored kids who depend on external stimulation delight in video games; playing interactive games is more exciting than passive TV viewing and they can quickly become dependent on them.

- Video gaming with multiple online users can give lonely children the illusion of having friends—even best friends.

- Children with low self-esteem can find relief from discomfort in video games, as can those who are abused or neglected, those who suffer from ADD or Asperger's syndrome, and those suffering from unhappiness and depression.[22]

Addiction is good for business because users keep coming back. The classic kids' games of checkers, chess, and board games had a clear finish: game over! With video games, there is not an ending—only a pause that entices players to keep playing.

Roots of Self-Regulation

Early on in life, during the peak learning period when the brain is fresh and the most malleable, young American kids are learning to identify brand logos and be consumers. Meanwhile, kids in other countries are learning five languages and memorizing their ancestry—family histories and stories. Futurist John Naisbitt predicts, "The most exciting breakthrough of the 21st century will occur not because of technology, but because of an expanding concept of what it means to be human."

Everything kids experience in the first six years of their lives is downloaded into the brain. TV programs and commercials can fill children's ready-and-eager-to-learn brains with the wrong stuff, especially if they watch shows inappropriate for their age level. As a consequence, children are showing up in kindergarten with greater disrespect, incivility, and violence than before. Technological and commercial pressures are hampering healthy development, obstructing the learning of important life skills, and changing the architecture of the brain.

Some of the things that have been swept away in our high-tech society are things that help children learn self-regulation: freewheeling imaginative play, nature, chores, and touch.

Freewheeling Imaginative Play

Bullying and other problems have repeatedly been linked to diminished self-regulation, self-control, self-discipline, and ability to resist impulses. When the upstairs (thinking) brain is working well, youngsters can regulate emotions, consider consequences, think before acting, and consider how others feel. Those who are able to manage their feelings and pay attention are better able to learn. Remember, however, that the cognitive brain is slow to develop and does not mature until one is in his or her mid-twenties.

Traditionally, children enjoyed freewheeling imaginative play out of doors, more or less supervised, focused more on activities than on objects. They came up with their own rules; they self-regulated by talking things over, either internally or to each other. This self-regulating language—which is at its most creative during make-believe play—is predictive of good executive functioning of the thinking brain later in life.

The concept of play changed radically in the second half of the last century. Parents now purchase specific toys with predetermined scripts from movies, such as a toy light saber to play Star Wars or Disney princess dresses with matching shoes and wigs, instead of dress-up clothes that could be imagined to be anything. As freewheeling imaginative play has declined, self-regulation has been weakened.

Less than 4 percent of the world's children are American, yet they consume more than 40 percent of the world's toys.[23] But Geek Dad, a blogger for *Wired* magazine, lists the five best toys of all time: a box, a stick, string, cardboard tubes, and dirt. They're fun, and they're free![24]

This "commercialization and co-optation of child's play," as cultural historian Howard Chudacoff calls it,[25] began to shrink and narrow children's imaginative possibilities, and diminish their cognitive and emotional development. Ads for toys bombard children every day of the year, especially during the winter holiday season. Seeing bad news on TV every day worried some working parents to the point that, concerned for their children's safety, they decided children were safer at home watching television than they were playing outside. Schools removed slides, swings, and merry-go-rounds from play equipment—all of which teach balance, perception, and motor skills—thinking them too dangerous. And because of the current heavy emphasis on passing tests, play is viewed as an unnecessary waste of time.

Nature

According to the National Wildlife Federation, the average kid spends only four to seven minutes in unstructured outdoor play each day, and more than seven hours each day in front of an electronic screen. This shift inside severely impacts their wellness and well-being.

"Childhood obesity rates have more than doubled the last 20 years," the site reports. "The United States has become the largest consumer of ADHD medications in the world; and pediatric prescriptions for antidepressants have risen precipitously. Our kids are out of shape, tuned out and stressed out, because they're missing something essential to their health and development: connection to the natural world."[26]

Playing outdoors gives children a safe and captivating outlet for pent-up stress, agitation, and aggressive energy. Creative, unstructured free play is a remedy for overscheduled, overprogrammed, stressful lives. Exercise and exploration in nature is an antidote to negative influences, and can have enormous benefits—including plain old-fashioned fun.

Chores

When she was a child, Kristen longed for an Easy-Bake Oven. The commercial was so enticing: girls worked together to mix a real cake from a real box and cook it in their own real oven. But as with so many toys, it was only fun to play with a few times. Louise thought, "If I have to supervise her anyway, why not use a real oven and bake some real food?" Cooking from a recipe with Mom is a great brain-building skill as well.

Making applesauce became another fun family activity. After Louise cooked up the apples, the kids gathered around the table and took turns cranking the food mill—and eating the results. All of the neighbor kids enjoyed being part of the annual ritual.

Little kids like to "play house" with great earnestness. They assign each other roles (mom, dad, baby, dog) and attend to all the mundane tasks that grown-ups do, such as sweeping, cooking, and shopping. Doing chores has traditionally been something children do willingly, participating in the activities of their family in order to belong to a family group.

You will recall from chapter 17 that in order for children to become resilient, three fundamental needs must be met: (1) they must have caring relationships; (2) these relationships must convey positive and high expectations; and (3) children must be given opportunities for meaningful participation—which includes helping out with chores. When children work alongside their parents and siblings, they learn skills and values, and feel a sense of belonging. Also, as they develop and demonstrate competence, they are valued and their self-esteem and self-efficacy improve.

Touch

Kids who are punished become angry and may want to get even. They may hit, slap, or victimize classmates who also want to get even, creating more bullies and victims. Punitive touch is readily available, but good, nurturing touch is absent in the lives of many children.

The United States has much higher rates of violence than the rest of the world. Thirty-one states have banned corporal punishment in schools, but many American parents and teachers still use force and physical punishment to discipline children. In some schools, teachers are not allowed to touch children at all—even for connection and calming—because touch has been so misused.

Twenty-five years ago, John Naisbitt, the world's foremost social forecaster, predicted this technological tsunami that is now saturating our lives. He forecast increased isolation and disrupted interpersonal relationships and also prescribed the antidote for these "high tech" troubles: "high touch." The more technology influences our lives, the more indispensable warm human contact and interaction become.

Our children are growing up in a high-tech/low-touch culture. Yet they need positive nurturing touch in order to feel loved and secure.

Boys are touched less often than girls. More boys are referred to special education than girls, and boys are more likely to be expelled from school—even from preschool. More boys than girls are involved in pushing, pinching, shoving, and tripping behaviors.

Professor Sid Simon coined the phrase "skin hunger" to explain the prevalence of hitting, punching, and tripping in middle school. For some people, violence is an indirect way of being touched.

Cultures high in positive human touch tend to be low in violence; conversely, cultures that are high in negative touch tend to be high in violence. Touch calms the nervous system, and children who are reared without nurturing touch are more "touchy" than others—inclined to be on edge and anxious.

Power on the Screen

For all of the damage screens do and might do, there is no turning back the tide of technology. It's not all bad news—the wonders of technology allowed us to write this book, after all! Parents need to learn skills (such as technology skills) that are new to humanity, and to use their personal power to protect and guide their kids. Positive parenting can be their guide. Recall some of the characteristics of positive parenting:

- a warm family climate
- an optimistic mindset
- self-care and self-responsibility
- family connections
- social and emotional skills
- assertive communication
- a democratic power structure

Building High-Tech Zorgos

Kids who are not developmentally ready for what the mainstream media has to offer are the ones who are most at risk. It is therefore the parent's job to decide what and how much a child can watch or play.

Consider the following age-appropriate suggestions:

All ages

- No TV or Internet in children's bedrooms.

- Treat media as a special, occasional activity, not a daily event or a right.

- Make face-to-face people time the highest priority.

- Prioritize family time—playing, listening, eating together.

- Shut off gadgets and put them out of reach in another room.

- Be strict about ratings on video games and movies, making only rare exceptions when you know the material and your child.

- Be clear with your children and their friends about your house rules. Talk to parents of their friends about their own rules.

- Choose or encourage video games that permit free play and problem solving, rather than competition and violence.

- Steer kids away from video games that increase antisocial behaviors; steer them instead toward "pro-social" games that feature characters helping each other—and actually help make kids friendlier.

- Keep *your* screen time to a minimum when children are around.

- Watch what your children watch, and talk to them about what they see. Your relationship will help to prevent harm.

- Have a "Screen-Free Week" every so often. It's like a reset button for childhood. Consider having regular "Screen-Free Sundays," when you give your family and all tech toys a day of rest and enjoy old-fashioned free time.

- Be aware of eye-to-eye vs. eye-to-screen time.

- Set a time every night when screens go off for the whole family so there is time to "be human" before bedtime.

- Model good media skills at home, monitor screen time for all family members, and be sure you spend more time as a family away from screens than with.

0–3 years

- Avoid TV, movies, or video games.
- Listen to musical recordings with your children.
- Avoid electronic toys.

4–8 years

- Limit combined screen time to no more than two hours per day. Less is better. Set timers and give warnings.
- Teach and practice the eye-contact rule: When someone says your name, you pause and look up from the screen.
- Teach children to ask permission before they use media.

9–12 years

- Be very strict about age limits online. No Facebook or other social media accounts until at least age thirteen. Companies often try to enforce age limits, but they rely on you to supervise your child.
- Beware of this phrase: "Can I just finish this level?" Be consistent about the limits you set.
- Watch less commercial and more public broadcasting. If programs have been recorded, fast-forward through the commercials, and teach and encourage your children how to do so. Have children count the advertisements they see in an hour; help them become aware of advertising tricks and messages.

13–17 years

- "Friend" your teenagers on Facebook, and keep an eye on what they post. Speak to them offline or in a private message— firmly and gently—when they post something that could hurt others or their own reputation.

- Remind teens that employers and college administrators might see what they post. Kids often repost things from offensive pages without realizing the damage it can cause.

- Have a "no apps" rule on Facebook until age eighteen, including games such as FarmVille. This reduces the risk of privacy violations.

- Discuss all online purchases. Read the fine print of every game—many are designed to automatically debit your credit card.

- Follow your teens on Twitter and talk to them about the things they tweet.

- Talk about the difference between real face-to-face friends and Facebook "friends" whom they may have never met and don't really know. Encourage them to be friendly—but also to be choosy with whom they share intimate information.

- Emphasize the influence your teenagers have in setting a tone in all social media.

- Teach them not to use expletives or hurtful language. Remind them that younger people may be reading and viewing what they post, and that their words represent their character. Talk about and emphasize nonviolent speech.

- Teach kids how to block followers (Twitter), unfriend bullies (Facebook), and change their settings so that not everyone sees everything.

- Don't get your teens a cell phone until they absolutely need it. When and if you do, get a service that allows you to turn phones off at night and during school, and block numbers. Do not let them sleep with their phone.

- Keep a list of passwords in a place where you can access it in case of emergency.

- Watch what your teenagers are watching; observe their games and online activities. Know what they play. Play with them.

- Have conversations with them using their tools (text on a cell phone, for example); keep lines of communication open with teenagers and ask how they feel about issues you hear them talking about.

- Monitor their communications periodically and openly, without judgment, while at the same time respecting their growing need for privacy.

18–25 years

As children become adults and pursue relationships and careers, "netiquette" (Internet + etiquette = netiquette) becomes more important than ever. For example:

- When in the company of others, always excuse yourself before using a cell phone.

- Don't e-mail when you are angry.

- Keep a balance between online and off-line life. Too much time spent online results in social isolation, which can be both mentally and physically harmful.

- Don't use social media to announce big news (deaths, births, marriages, breakups) without first letting loved ones know by phone or in person.

The Off-Switch

Without resorting to throwing out our TVs, how do we raise our kids to counter a force as strong as the tides of technology?

There is one simple tool that all parents need to use daily and confidently: the off-switch. At large family gatherings, one mother we know of passes a basket around and collects all cell phones and gadgets for a portion of the day.

A nonprofit arts group, Reboot, has created a National Day of Unplugging once a year as a modern observance of the Jewish day of rest. You can take the pledge at www.sabbathmanifesto.org.

We encourage every parent to instate a day of rest from technology, whether it's a "Screen-Free Sunday" or a weekly "blackout," to allow for more family time.

Parent Power

To change the world we need to combine ancient wisdom with new technology.

— PAULO COELHO

In the face of the new media environment, parents need to maintain or regain control of their households. Use the off-switch with authority. You pay the bills, and you have the fully developed brain. You have power over the seduction of technology that hijacks healthy child development. Make sure your children are firmly grounded in the "real world," aware of their identity outside the commercial and media culture. Use your voice to create better off-switches in your community. Here are some more technology-related suggestions:

• Teach children they must be upstanders and talk to an adult if they are being cyberbullied or know of someone who is. Ninety percent of cyberbullying victims will not inform a parent or trusted adult of their abuse. [27]

• Talk to other parents about the impact of video games and make pacts to support each other's rules. Currently, only a small percentage of parents actually prohibit children from playing video games with improper ratings.

• Call local TV stations and cable providers when they play commercials for violent, R-rated movies or M-rated video games during times when children may be watching. Encourage them to stop showing these ads during family viewing hours.

• Talk to your school board and teachers association about following MPAA (Motion Picture Association of America) ratings when they show classroom movies.

• Go outside and meet your neighbors!

We worry a lot about children being "flummoxed" by technology. *Flummoxing* is a wonderful word that means "confusing, bewildering, and greatly perplexing." At a time when our young children are most vulnerable and impressionable, advertising and entertainment flummox their brains by appearing to be all good while actually being quite bad for them. Positive parents must be watchdogs for their children's natural, inborn developmental trajectory.

. . .

19
. . . .

Superpowering Our Kids

No man is a failure who has friends.

— CLARENCE, THE ANGEL IN THE FILM *IT'S A WONDERFUL LIFE*

Imagine yourself in the hallway of an American high school where a group of bullies are picking on a kid. As if out of nowhere (although they were there all along), six other kids step in.

- The first one *silences* the cruel words with a powerful glance.
- The second one *chills* the action, creating an aura of calm.
- The third one *sends secret strength* to the kid's legs, so they continue to stand.
- The fourth *says just the right thing,* creating awareness with well-spoken words.
- The fifth one *un-links* the powerful peer pressure that has encouraged the bullying.
- The sixth creates a sense of *engagement,* and suddenly everyone understands that they are all in this together; they are all part of the solution.

They smile and stand with the child who had been under attack, thus invisibly bestowing their victimized classmate with a seventh superpower: un-bullyable *awesomeness.* The bullies get it and stop making trouble; they apologize and make amends. The victim stands tall. All is forgiven.

Silencing meanness, chilling anger, creating calm, lending "leg strength," saying the right thing, personal power, unlinking peer pressure, creating engagement, and bestowing awesomeness . . . these are all superpowers against bullying imagined by children and potentials every child has, cool costumes or not, when they are supported by parents and schools in developing positivity. Imagine this scene coming to life over and over, in schools all over the country, all over the world. This is what the end of bullying could look like, starting now.

The Opposite of Bullying

While writing *The Bullying Antidote*, we thought long and hard about what we wanted to convey to parents who were struggling with the bullying dynamic. We did not want to use the word *bully-proof*, because it sounds too much like "bullet-proof," and weapons are not the answer. Also, there's no way to completely guarantee your children will never face bullying in their lives. Besides, "bullet-proof" suggests the image of a shield, and being truly immune to bullying is not about keeping one's guard up; it's about being fully engaged and developing empathy and resilience that permeate the world around us.

So we approached the problem by brainstorming answers to the question that has been on our minds for years: *What is the opposite of bullying?* We came up with many answers:

- kindness
- connection
- love
- respect
- empathy
- pro-social skills
- friendship
- alliance
- buddies
- democracy
- safety
- self-esteem
- attachment
- cooperation
- good communication
- uplifting
- boundaries
- laws
- assertiveness
- prevention
- coolness
- gentleness
- upstanding
- peacemaking
- compassion
- relationships
- wholeness

Late in the writing process, the word *mercy* arrived. We rarely hear this word these days, outside of church services and clichés. But we see it beautifully modeled in every really good movie with a hero fighting a bully. In these types of movies, the hero never kills the bully; he or she shows mercy, following his or her own guiding principles. Mercy involves caring, compassion, forgiveness, kindness, and discipline. Mercy also means fairness, justice, and a long-term view. Showing mercy can make us stronger and better people.

Mercy is a virtue common to many major world religions—just like the Golden Rule:

- In Catholicism, it is one of the Beatitudes: *Blessed are the merciful, for they shall have mercy.* St. Augustine called mercy "ever ancient, ever new."

- In Judaism, mercy is one of God's outstanding attributes: *The Lord is a merciful and gracious God, slow to anger, abounding in steadfast love and faithfulness.*

- In Islam, the "Most Merciful" (al-Rahman) is a name for Allah; mercy is one of the requirements of the faithful.

- Kwan Yin is the goddess of mercy and compassion, and one of the best-known and most venerated bodhisattvas in Buddhism.

Mercy, whether it is the opposite of bullying or an antidote for it, is certainly bigger than bullying. Mercy comes from a greater and deeper place inside of us.

Bullying and Human Rights

Mercy certainly is a cure or remedy that can help counteract the poison of bullying and violence—but it's not the only antidote. As wonderful a word as mercy is, it still implies the dynamic of the powerful and the powerless. And as much as we like the idea of an antidote to bullying, what we *really* love is the idea of building *immunity*. We really love the idea of a superpower: *Zorgos!* Our secret word represents all the antidotes we've mentioned rolled into one. To be called forth, it must be nurtured from the inside *and* the outside.

347

A school with a bullying problem is more likely to stop bullies in their tracks if the school has a vigorous anti-bullying program in place (refer to chapter 6 for a list of some of these programs). Bullying prevention programs are powerful tools for raising awareness and creating a cultural shift. But they only work as long as there are dedicated people—teachers, parents, student leaders, staff—who are committed to working and upholding the program in class, on the streets, and at home. Without a total commitment to the program, bullying tends to resurface after a few years.

Studies have shown there are really only two ways to transform a bullying culture:

1. Start from scratch: Raise children with positive parenting, as we've described in detail in this book. This is true positive prevention.

2. See bullying as a human rights issue.[1]

For thousands of years, the idea of human rights has been a guiding force for the nations of the world. It is the core idea behind democracy and carries within it the core of all spiritual disciplines: that each of us is a worthy being. Human rights are the foundation of many of our laws.

Although no federal law directly addresses bullying, in some cases bullying overlaps with civil rights issues; it can be seen as discriminatory harassment when it is based on race, national origin, color, sex, age, disability, or religion. Seeing bullying as a human rights issue, however, is a higher level of thinking than "breaking the law."

Being safe in relationships is a fundamental human right. All children have the right to be safe and free from bullying—in their homes, at school, and in their communities. The Robert F. Kennedy Center for Justice and Human Rights provides a curriculum entitled *Speak Truth to Power*. The curriculum urges students to become personally involved in the protection of human rights. When students are taught about human rights in school, they tend to treat one another and themselves better.

The Rights of the Child

The United Nations Convention on the Rights of the Child, Article 29 (d), specifies that countries must take responsibility for

> The preparation of the child for responsible life in a free society, in the spirit of understanding, peace, tolerance, equality of the sexes, and friendship among all peoples, ethnic, national and religious groups and persons of indigenous origin.

In other words, children must be educated to ensure they develop positive attitudes and behaviors, and avoid using their power to bully or harass others.

Article 19 (1) states the following:

> Parties shall take all appropriate legislative, administrative, social and educational measures to protect the child from all forms of physical or mental violence, injury or abuse, neglect or negligent treatment, maltreatment or exploitation, including sexual abuse, while in the care of parent(s), legal guardian(s) or any other person who has the care of the child.[2]

Under this global vision of children's rights, a child has the right to not be bullied.

The Convention on the Rights of the Child has been ratified (agreed to) by all members of the United Nations, except for three: the United States, South Sudan (the newest nation), and Somalia, which has declared its intent to do so. We are the only country in the world that seems to want to do it "our own way."

Not all perpetrators of child abuse are adults. Children also experience the troubles listed in the UN article above—*physical or mental violence, injury or abuse, neglect or negligent treatment, maltreatment or exploitation, including sexual abuse*—at the hands of their peers. One study shows that for every one child concerned about being sexually abused by adults, there are three children concerned about being beaten up by peers.[3]

All children require support to promote healthy development and positive relationships, and to protect their welfare. All adults can help prevent bullying by supporting youth in the positive development of social skills, respect, responsibility, and citizenship. These attributes are the foundation for a cohesive, productive, and peaceful society.

Whenever she gets the chance, Kristen likes to point out that *human rights are something we give one another.* We need to protect our own rights, while also respecting and protecting the rights of others.

By Bullies, for Bullies

There is only so much parents can do, however, or that one school or one program or one writer (or even two) can do in a culture and a society that sometimes seems as if it were built by bullies, for bullies. Cultural norms are upheld by written and unwritten rules.

Let's take another look at the definitions of bullying:

- A bully is a person who uses strength or power to harm or intimidate those who are weaker.

- Bullying is the activity of repeated aggressive behaviors intended to hurt another person physically or mentally.

- Bullying involves three things:

  1. The repeated mistreatment of targets by one or more perpetrators

  2. An imbalance of power

  3. The use of superior strength or influence to intimidate someone, typically to force him or her to do something he or she doesn't want to do

As we discussed in previous chapters, corporate marketers, drug companies, and banks target our innocent children—in many instances without care or regulation.

We see bullying in many subcultures in the United States:

- in professional sports, where bullying and domination are celebrated on the playing field

- in fraternities and sororities with hazing rituals

- on AM radio, from coast to coast, where highly paid, controversial radio personalities demonize public leaders and public figures
- in video games
- in political debates

We have to look at bullying and see the truth: Our society supports and admires aggression in many ways.

Even Fox News commentator Bill O'Reilly, in a display of humility, admitted to Jon Stewart that capitalism drives hate speech. "The problem with the discourse in America is capitalism. You can make a lot of money being an assassin—right wing or left wing. If you're a hater—radio, cable, print, whatever—you get paid. There are people who go in, they don't even believe half the stuff they say—and they just rip it up—and they get paid a lot of money. That has coarsened everything. They're phonies."[4]

Fix from the Bottom Up

Finding ourselves at the bottom of a list is hard for America, since we like to be "number one." If, as the UNICEF report from chapter 1 puts it, "The true measure of a nation's standing is how well it attends to its children—their health and safety, their material security, their education and socialization, and their sense of being loved, valued, and included in the families and societies into which they are born,"[5] then our nation needs to do some work. How devastating for hardworking parents in the "richest country in the world" to discover that the United States is one of the worst countries in which to be a child! *What is the purpose of our wealth, if not to take care of our families?*

The UNICEF study measured all of the above factors and averaged them out. The number one nations in each of these dimensions were:

1. Health and Safety—*Sweden* (U.S. was 21st)

2. Material Security—*Sweden* (U.S. was 17th)

3. Educational Well-being—*Belgium* (U.S. was 12th)

4. Family and Peer Relationships—*Italy* (U.S. was 20th)

5. Behaviors and Risks—*Sweden* (U.S. was 20th)

6. Subjective Well-being—*Netherlands* (U.S. provided insufficient data)[6]

What does the United States need to do to get off the bottom of the UNICEF list? What can we learn from Sweden?

Every so often you hear a story about a Swedish mother who gets arrested in the United States for leaving her sleeping baby parked outside a store in a stroller. She is viewed as a terrible mother, but then the rest of the story comes out: all mothers do this safely in Sweden. What an inconceivable idea to American parents! Don't these people know that the world is full of crazy people who can harm their kids? But in Swedish society, everyone is expected to care for babies together. In Sweden, mothers with babies board buses first, and strangers help them load their strollers. The Swedish government supports the vital parent-child attachment process that promotes healthy development, allowing couples to enjoy thirteen months of paid leave. Most of that time is available to be split between the two parents, so families can decide which parent should stay at home. Meanwhile, the United States is the *only* country in the developed world without a mandatory paid maternity leave.[7] Even in Afghanistan, the worst country in the world in terms of mothering support, mothers get ninety days of paid leave.

Here are a few more facts about Sweden:

• Its murder rate is among the lowest in the world.[8]

• It has raised a successful generation without spanking its children.[9]

• It has been at peace for one hundred years.[10]

• It provides universal day care.[11]

• 85 percent of Swedish fathers take a paid paternity leave.[12]

It's the Economy, Stupid!

As we have mentioned over and over throughout this book, to prevent bullying, children need caring adults around them. They need adults to comfort them, teach them, and play with them, to give them attention and to build connection. They need adults to supervise them and to provide opportunities for them to socialize and grow. It has become very clear that parents who raise children with positive parenting do not raise bullies—or victims.

But there are many obstacles to parents being able to do this. Parents who live under the stress of poverty and hardship, for example, are less likely to be able to build solid connections that help avoid behavior issues. A 2010 British study showed that poor children are twice as likely to start school with behavior problems, compared with their more privileged peers.[13]

This brings up a troubling question we encountered while writing this book: does building *Zorgos* cost money?

Unfortunately—although low-income parents are perfectly capable of superpowering their children with kindness, confidence, and empathy—the answer on a larger scale is undeniably *yes*. Why? Because it costs money to keep adults around children, be they teachers, child-care providers, or parents who must otherwise work. It costs money to keep teacher-student ratios low. It costs money to provide enrichment programs like sports and music. And many of these things are being cut from our schools nationwide.

Another explanation for the troubling amount of bullying in the United States is the sharp rise in income inequality in the past twenty years; the rich have grown richer and the poor have grown poorer. Countries with high income inequality have more school bullying among preadolescents than countries with low income inequality.[14] And the United States has one of the highest levels of income inequality of any nation.

For our children to survive and thrive, we need caring economic systems that do not exploit and damage them, but instead promote their healthy development, well-being, and happiness.

The United States and the United Kingdom, clumped together at the bottom of the UNICEF child well-being list, have economic systems that fall short in many areas, including caring for their citizens and the environment. With rapid technological changes, a new type of economy is more urgent than ever.

The countries at the top of the UNICEF list have "caring economies" that transcend traditional categories like "capitalism" and "socialism." The definition of a caring economy is "an economic system in which genuine caring for people and nature is the top priority."[15]

Making Bullying Illegal

*Corporal punishment does for childhood what
wife beating does for marriage.*

— JORDAN RIAK, DIRECTOR OF PARENTS AND TEACHERS AGAINST VIOLENCE IN EDUCATION

Sweden has not always been such a supportive place for children. Fifty years ago, it had one of the highest rates of child abuse in the world.[16] In the early 1970s, Swedish psychologist Dan Olweus initiated the first systematic research study in the world on aggression and the bullying dynamic. In 1979, Sweden was the first country in the world to prohibit corporal punishment of children. Since then, thirty-two countries have taken the same step, with many more stating that they will. Since physical punishment and child abuse are so closely linked, all of these countries are making significant strides toward reducing child abuse as a whole.

A Parent's Right to Bully

The main argument *against* a no-spanking law, and against ratifying the Convention on the Rights of the Child, is that parents have a right to punish their children according to their own conscience. In America, it is often a religious freedom issue. But we are not clear enough on what constitutes right and wrong in this country. We have very slippery codes that say sometimes abuse is okay and sometimes it isn't; but even if parents who spank love their children, children who are spanked can feel victimized and engage in bullying dynamics down the road.

Remember, all bullying involves a power dynamic. Even when a parent's intention is to "get their attention" or "teach them a lesson," physical punishment of children does not promote pro-social development, but instead is associated with higher rates of aggression toward peers.[17] This is true for verbal domination as well.

Many families simply grow apart as kids grow up, and there can be a code of silence about naming the reasons for growing apart. It is difficult for people of any age to tell their parents, "Hey, you kind of bullied me." But identifying those issues today can make a huge difference tomorrow. Similarly, it is difficult for a parent to acknowledge the pain he or she may have caused. But only with acknowledgment can there be forgiveness and a future together.

If there is the slightest chance you might be putting your children in this same position, let them know that you are aware of your behaviors. Tell them you want to change, and that it will require some time and some soul searching. Then take heart, because now that you've read this book, you are equipped with tools you can use to replace unintentional bullying behaviors with positive ones.

Anti-Bullying Laws

The Swedish parliament went against popular opinion when it changed Sweden's laws regarding physical punishment. Governments typically prefer to wait until popular opinion is favorable before creating new laws. But American philosopher William James suggested the opposite back in the 1870s: we can use our behavior to control our attitudes and beliefs, he said, and in fact, behavior is *easier* to control than attitudes and beliefs. In other words, sometimes it takes some external support to initiate a mindshift.

Sweden adopted its unpopular no-spanking law believing that child abuse cases would diminish only when *every form of force* used against kids could be covered by normal criminal law. By changing the country's legal structure, forward-thinking Swedish officials promoted better parenting, encouraging parents to depart from harmful family patterns.

Building on this success, the government started looking at school safety as a fundamental human right. Olweus's proposals for legislation against bullying in schools were enacted by both the Swedish and the Norwegian parliaments in the mid-1990s. The revolution continues. As of this writing, forty-nine states in the United States have passed anti-bullying laws, giving teachers the authority to discipline bullies and those engaged in cyberbullying. Unfortunately, many of these laws are mandates without adequate funding for meaningful change. New Jersey has framed bullying as a rights issue with its (fully funded) Anti-Bullying Bill of Rights, which explicitly requires all employees to be upstanders.

Zorgos: The New Normal

Families need families. Parents need to be parented.
Grandparents, aunts, and uncles
are back in fashion because they are necessary.

— T. BERRY BRAZELTON, ACCLAIMED PEDIATRICIAN AND AUTHOR

Michele Mason, a beloved educator of new mothers who inspired UNICEF's Child Friendly Cities initiative with her work, once had an unforgettable conversation with Kristen. They discussed recent articles in the media about how humans are hardwired for war. Michele had seen a story of a dog in Africa that had rescued an abandoned newborn baby: she saw how animals (including humans) are hardwired for nurturing.[18] "The force of nurturing is so strong that it crosses the boundaries of species. Without this force, humanity would not have survived, and it certainly would not have thrived. Nurturing is stronger than war, and we shouldn't be so afraid to rely on it in ourselves."[19]

Nurturing is certainly the opposite of bullying. Bullying is cold, short-term, and destructive. Nurturing is warm, long-term, and constructive. To end bullying we must live up to Article 29—*the preparation of the child for responsible life in a free society*—and prepare our children with *Zorgos!*

It is in the American character to build *Zorgos* into our kids. Having freedom has always meant having a conscience. It means standing up for oneself with confidence. It means looking for solutions to problems. It means hard work, caring for oneself, looking out for others, and protecting the weak until they find their own strength. It means grit.

Expand Your Supports

Personal power starts from within, but as in the high school hallway story that began this chapter, it becomes a superpower when it is supported by others.

Think about the lives of your grandparents. For hundreds of generations, built-in safety nets of extended family and close-knit community members helped people survive. Yet enormous changes to basic structures of the culture that we detailed in chapter 2 have caused considerable destruction during the last sixty years. Our traditional safety nets of nurturing are frayed, and, in many cases, broken or gone.

When fishers mend their nets, they find the holes and reconnect the broken threads. We need to repair the safety nets for our families by reinforcing the natural social bonds, connecting with real friends, and developing supports, one by one. Reweaving safety nets brings meaning, satisfaction, support, and great pleasure back into people's lives.

The hardest part in changing family patterns is not the horrible realization that begins the process, nor is it the difficult mustering of the guts to put one's intention into words. The hardest part is the growth and stabilization of that vision. No one can do this alone! Author Pam Leo reminds us, "Parenting never used to be—and was never intended to be—a one or two person job." Adults, just like children, are influenced by peers. The conversations we have, the news we watch and listen to, the interactions with other adults—all of these things influence us. It is essential that you find a buddy who shares your vision of positive parenting. Or better yet, a community. It's fine to start with a counselor or a class, but don't stop there—make *real* friends. *The choice to get support makes all the difference.*

Kristen and her husband didn't have many friends in common when they married, but having a child opened up new social connections for them. When their son was two, they joined a cooperative preschool where parents were the teachers. United by a common philosophy they learned from the director, the moms and dads of the school trusted one another to parent each other's children positively.

No one ever had to hire a babysitter, since there was always a play date available. Over the years, a small group of families from the school kept in touch, having monthly—and later, semi-annual—dinners and outings. Kristen's career as "Mama K" allowed her to co-create cooperative summer camps and various adventures and outings with the other mothers and dads. All of the parents and youngsters have remained friends into high school and beyond.

Parents must make an effort to build bonds that will sustain them over the years. It takes time to nurture connections. Adults who have ongoing significant contact with a child—grandparents, aunts and uncles, child-care providers, neighbors—are part of that child's extended family and safety net. We can reweave the web that connects us, so we have a safety net for when we slip, or when our kids slip. We need many caring people in our lives. And when we extend our families, we expand our lives.

Instead of nurturing bullying, let's get to work with our voices and our vote to nurture *Zorgos*! Call, write, and talk to elected officials, entertainment companies, insurance companies, corporations, and schools to build communities everywhere that nurture the following:

- tolerance—curtailing hatred, bullying, and bigotry while boosting respect, kindness, and understanding
- human rights awareness
- resilience training
- assertive communication training
- positive psychology and optimism
- positive parenting
- social and emotional skills development

What we nurture is what we get. Instead of nurturing bullying, we need to invest in superpowering our kids. Remember, *Zorgos* means "I will care."

. . .

NOTES

• • • •

Introduction: Connecting the Dots: From Bullying to Breakthrough

1. National Institutes of Health, SAFE, Tony Bartoli, as quoted on "Risk(Within) Reason" by Alissa Sklar, http://www.risk-within-reason.com/2012/03/page/2/.

Chapter 1: "And How Are the Children?"

1. UNICEF, *Child Poverty in Perspective: An Overview of Child Well-Being in Rich Countries,* Innocenti Report Card (Florence: UNICEF Innocenti Research Centre, 2007).

2. International Centre for Prison Studies, "Entire World: Prison Population Rates per 100,000 of the National Population," http://www.prisonstudies.org/info /worldbrief/wpb_stats.php?area=all&category=wb_poprate.

3. Jennifer Warren, Adam Gelb, Jake Horowitz, and Jessica Riordan, *One in 100: Behind Bars in America 2008* (Washington, DC: Pew Charitable Trusts, Pew Center on the States, 2008), http://www.pewstates.org/uploadedFiles/PCS _Assets/2008/one%20in%20100.pdf.

4. "Stanford Prison Experiment," http://www.prisonexp.org/.

5. "Maine Project Against Bullying," page last updated February 2004, http://lincoln .midcoast.com/~wps/against/bullying.html.

6. Michael Petit, "America's Child Death Shame," *BBC News US & Canada,* October 17, 2011, http://www.bbc.co.uk/go/em/fr/-/news/magazine-15193530.

7. National Association for Children of Alcoholics, "Children of Alcoholics: Important Facts," http://www.nacoa.net/impfacts.htm.

8. National Association for Children of Alcoholics, "Children of Addicted Parents: Important Facts," http://www.nacoa.net/pdfs/addicted.pdf.

9. Jessie Klein, *The Bully Society: School Shootings and the Crisis of Bullying in America's Schools* (New York: New York University Press, 2012).

10. Rape, Abuse, and Incest National Network, "Statistics," http://www.rainn.org /statistics; Rape, Abuse, and Incest National Network, "97 of Every 100 Rapists Receive No Punishment, RAINN Analysis Shows," http://www.rainn.org /news-room/97-of-every-100-rapists-receive-no-punishment.

11. National Institute of Justice, "Most Victims Know Their Attacker," October 1, 2008, http://www.nij.gov/topics/crime/rape-sexual-violence/campus/know-attacker.htm.

12. United States Census Bureau, "Poverty: Highlights," www.census.gov/hhes/www /poverty/about/overview/. The data presented on this web page are from the Current Population Survey (CPS), 2012 Annual Social and Economic Supplement (ASEC), the source of official poverty estimates.

13. Madeline Levine, *The Price of Privilege: How Parental Pressure and Material Advantage Are Creating a Generation of Disconnected and Unhappy Kids* (New York: HarperCollins, 2006).

14. Campaign for a Commercial-Free Childhood, "Marketing to Children (Overview)," http://commercialfreechildhood.org/issue/marketing-children-overview.

15. David Walsh, foreword to *How Much Is Enough? Everything You Need to Know to Steer Clear of Overindulgence and Raise Likeable, Responsible and Respectful Children,* by Jean Illsley Clarke, Connie Dawson, and David Bredehoft (New York: Marlowe & Company, 2004), xii.

16. Michele Borba, "Nurturing Tolerance to Reduce Bullying," *Reality Check* (blog), March 17, 2011, http://www.micheleborba.com/blog/2011/03/17/teaching -children-tolerance/.

17. Centers for Disease Control and Prevention, "Attention-Deficit / Hyperactivity Disorder (ADHD)," last updated December 12, 2011, http://www.cdc.gov/ncbddd /adhd/data.html.

18. U.S. Department of Health and Human Services, "Children and Adolescents Age 9-17 with Mental or Addictive Disorders," in *Mental Health: A Report of the Surgeon General* (Rockville, MD: U.S. Department of Health and Human Services, Substance Abuse and Mental Health Services Administration, Center for Mental Health Services, National Institutes of Health, National Institute of Mental Health, 1999), http://www.surgeongeneral.gov/library/mentalhealth/chapter3/sec1.html.

19. Barbara Dafoe Whitehead, quoted in Ellen Goodman, "Battling Our Culture Is Parents' Task," *Chicago Tribune,* August 18, 1993. Whitehead's current studies can be found at nationalmarriageproject.org.

Chapter 2: Enormous Changes in Society

1. Robert B. Textor, ed., "Cultural Confrontation in the Philippines," in *Cultural Frontiers of the Peace Corps* (Cambridge, MA: MIT Press, 1965).

2. Alvin Toffler, *Future Shock* (New York: Bantam, 1984).

3. Norman Herr, "Television and Health," Internet Resources to Accompany *The Sourcebook for Teaching Science,* 2007, http://www.csun.edu/science/health/docs /tv&health.html.

4. American Academy of Child and Adolescent Psychiatry, "Children and TV Violence," *Facts for Families,* no. 13 (March 2011), http://www.aacap.org/galleries /FactsForFamilies/13_children_and_tv_violence.pdf.

5. Tara Parker-Pope, "A One-Eyed Invader in the Bedroom," *New York Times,* March 4, 2008.

6. L. Rowell Huesmann, Jessica Moise-Titus, Cheryl-Lynn Podolski, Leonard D. Eron, "Longitudinal Relations between Children's Exposure to TV Violence and Their Aggressive and Violent Behavior in Young Adulthood: 1977–1992," *Developmental Psychology* 39, no. 2 (March 2003): 201–221.

7. Claudia Wallis, "The New Science of Happiness," *Time,* January 17, 2005.

Chapter 3: Problematic Childrearing Practices

1. Rick Hanson, *Buddha's Brain* (Oakland, CA: New Harbinger Publications, 2009).

2. Gabor Maté, *When the Body Says No: The Cost of Hidden Stress* (Toronto: Random House of Canada Limited, 2004).

3. Vincent J. Felitti, Robert F. Anda, Dale Nordenberg, David F. Williamson, Alison M. Spitz, Valerie Edwards, Mary P. Koss, and James S. Marks, "Relationship of Childhood Abuse and Household Dysfunction to Many of the Leading Causes of Death in Adults," *American Journal of Preventive Medicine* 14, no. 4 (May 1998): 245–258, http://www.ajpmonline.org/article/PIIS0749379798000178/abstract; Vincent J. Felitti, "The Relationship of Adverse Childhood Experiences to Adult Health: Turning Gold into Lead," http://www.acestudy.org/files/Gold_into _Lead-_Germany1-02_c_Graphs.pdf.

4. Charles Whitfield, "Adverse Childhood Experiences and Trauma," *American Journal of Preventive Medicine* 14, no. 4 (May 1998): 361–64.

5. Lance Morrow, *Heart: A Memoir* (New York: Warner Books, 1995).

6. American Psychological Association, "Corporal Punishment," policy statement, http://www.apa.org/about/policy/corporal-punishment.aspx.

7. Ibid.

8. Murray A. Strauss, quoted in Bernadette J. Saunders and Chris Goddard, *Physical Punishment in Childhood: The Rights of the Child* (New York: John Wiley and Sons, 2010). Also read Strauss's book *Beating the Devil Out of Them: Corporal Punishment in American Families and its Effects on Children* (New Brunswick, NJ: Transaction, 2001).

9. Robin Kittrelle, review of *For Your Own Good: Hidden Cruelty in Child-Rearing and the Roots of Violence*, 3rd ed., by Alice Miller, *The Permanente Journal* 6, no. 1 (Winter 2002): 94–95, http://xnet.kp.org/permanentejournal/winter02/owngood .html.

10. Joan E. Durrant, Ron Ensom, and the Coalition on Physical Punishment of Children and Youth, *Joint Statement on Physical Punishment of Children and Youth* (Ottawa: Coalition on Physical Punishment of Children and Youth, 2004).

11. Personal conversation with Kristen Caven.

12. Pam Leo, *Connection Parenting: Parenting through Connection instead of Coercion, through Love instead of Fear*, 2nd ed. (Deadwood, OR: Wyatt-MacKenzie Publishing, 2007).

13. Adapted from Jane Nelsen, Lynn Lott, and H. Stephen Glenn, *Positive Discipline A-Z: 1001 Solutions to Everyday Parenting Problems*, rev. ed. (New York: Three Rivers Press, 2007), 1–2.

14. Charles L. Whitfield, "Adverse Childhood Experiences and Trauma."

Part 2: Focus on Bullying

1. Corinne Gregory, author of *The Polite Child*, and founder of the SocialSmarts® program in Bellevue, WA, http://www.socialsmarts.com/about_corinne_new.cfm.

Chapter 4: Understanding Bullying

1. Coalition for Children, "Take A Stand Prevention of Bullying," http://www .safechild.org/new/educators-2/bully-prevention/.

2. Pat Palmer, *The Mouse, the Monster and Me,* 3rd ed. (Weaverville, CA: Boulden Publishing, 2011).

3. Michael F. Shaughnessy, "An Interview with Rick Phillips: About Columbine Ten Years Later," Education News, May 12, 2009, http://www.educationnews.org /articles/an-interview-with-rick-phillips-about-columbine-ten-years-later.html. Rick Phillips is the executive director of Community Matters (www.community -matters.org) and author of several notable books about violence prevention.

4. Rosalind Wiseman, *Queen Bees and Wannabes: Helping Your Daughter Survive Cliques, Gossip, Boyfriends, and the New Realities of Girl World,* revised and updated ed. (New York: Three Rivers Press, 2009).

5. Jessie Klein, "Gender Is Key to the Bullying Culture," Women's Media Center, March 27, 2012, http://www.womensmediacenter.com/feature/entry/gender-is -key-to-the-bullying-culture.

6. Adele Faber and Elaine Mazlish, *Siblings Without Rivalry: How to Help Your Children Live Together So You Can Live Too* (New York: W.W. Norton, 2012).

7. Bullying expert Jonathan Cohen, president of the National School Climate Center, in personal e-mail communication with Louise Hart, February 10, 2013.

8. Liz Urbanski Farrell, "Workplace Bullying's High Cost: $180M in Lost Time, Productivity," *Orlando Business Journal,* March 18, 2002, http://www.bizjournals .com/orlando/stories/2002/03/18/focus1.html?page=all referencing.

9. American Academy of Pediatrics Committee on Public Education, "Media Violence," *Pediatrics* 108, no. 5 (November 1, 2001): 1222–26, http://pediatrics .aappublications.org/content/108/5/1222.full.

10. Henry J. Kaiser Family Foundation, "Daily Media Use among Children and Teens up Dramatically from Five Years Ago," news release, January 20, 2010, http://www .kff.org/entmedia/entmedia012010nr.cfm.

11. National Television Violence Study, 1995, 1996, adapted from Amy Aidman, "Television Violence: Content, Context, and Consequences," Early Childhood and Parenting Collaborative, http://ecap.crc.illinois.edu/pubs/ivpaguide/appendix/ aidman-tv.pdf.

12. American Academy of Pediatrics Committee on Public Education, "Media Violence."

13. Dr. James Gilligan is a professor and author of seven books about violence. This quote is from "Shame, Guilt and Violence," *Social Research: An International Quarterly* 70, no. 4 (Winter 2003): 1149–80.

14. Bruce Perry, "Why Does Violence Happen?," Scholastic, http://teacher.scholastic .com/professional/bruceperry/why_violence.htm.

15. Victoria J. Rideout, Ulla G. Foehr, and Donald F. Roberts, *Generation M²: Media in the Lives of 8- to 18-Year-Olds* (Menlo Park, CA: Henry J. Kaiser Family Foundation, 2010).

16. A. C. Huston et al., *Big World, Small Screen: The Role of Television in American Society* (Lincoln: University of Nebraska Press, 1992).

17. American Academy of Pediatrics, "Where We Stand: TV Viewing Time," Healthy Children.org, last updated November 30, 2012, http://www.healthychildren.org /English/family-life/Media/Pages/Where-We-Stand-TV-Viewing-Time .aspx?nfstatus=401.

18. Law Center to Prevent Gun Violence, "Gun Violence Statistics," http://smartgun laws.org/category/gun-studies-statistics/gun-violence-statistics/.

19. Dan Olweus, *Bullying at School* (Malden, MA: Blackwell Publishing, 2006).

20. Teresa Watanabe, "Thousands of LAUSD Students Gather to Discuss Bullying," *Los Angeles Times*, April 18, 2012, http://articles.latimes.com/2012/apr/18/local/ la-me-bully-20120418.

21. Valerie Jarrett, "Empowering Young People to Build a Kinder, Braver World," *The OPE Blog*, August 8, 2012, http://www.whitehouse.gov/blog/2012/08/08 /building-kinder-braver-world.

Chapter 5: How Parents Can Interrupt and Prevent Bullying

1. Adapted from "The Truth About Bullying," *Psychotherapy Networker,* last modified November 7, 2012, http://www.psychotherapynetworker.org/magazine/current issue/item/1800-in-consultation.

2. Adapted from "Support the Kids Involved," StopBullying.gov, U.S. Department of Health and Human Services, http://www.stopbullying.gov/respond/support-kids-involved/index.html.

3. Stan Davis, "The Truth About Bullying," *Psychotherapy Networker,* last modified November 7, 2012, http://www.psychotherapynetworker.org/magazine/currentissue /item/1800-in-consultation.

4. Amy Milsom and Laura L. Gallo, "Bullying in Middle Schools: Prevention and Intervention," *Middle School Journal* 37, no. 3 (January 2006): 12–19, http://www .amle.org/publications/middleschooljournal/articles/january2006/article2/ tabid/693/default.aspx.

5. Julian Guthrie, "Minnesota Teens, Jane Lynch Honored at NCLR Event," *SF Gate,* May 7, 2012, http://www.sfgate.com/cgi-bin/article.cgi?f=%2Fc%2Fa%2F2012%2F 05%2F07%2FBAF41OD568.DTL.

6. Barbara L. Fredrickson, *Positivity: Top-Notch Research Reveals the 3 to 1 Ratio That Will Change Your Life* (New York: Three Rivers Press, 2009).

7. Ibid.

Chapter 6: Toward a Bully-Free Culture

1. Jenifer Goodwin, "Nurturing Moms May Help Their Child's Brain Develop," Philly.com, January 30, 2012, http://www.philly.com/philly/health/topics /138359599.html?c=r#ixzz1stmO213r (page no longer available).

2. Dan Olweus, Susan P. Limber, Vicki Crocker Flerx, Nancy Mullin, Jane Riese, and Marlene Snyder, *Olweus Bullying Prevention Program: Schoolwide Guide* (Center City, MN: Hazelden), 52–53.

3. *New York Times,* quoted in Harlem Children's Zone, "The HCZ Project," http://www.hcz.org/index.php/about-us/the-hcz-project.

4. Harlem Children's Zone, "The HCZ Project," http://www.hcz.org/index.php/about-us/the-hcz-project.

5. Richard Warren (superintendent, 18 years in Franklin Public Schools, Franklin, MA), quoted in "Safe and Caring Schools Program," Safe and Caring Schools, http://safeandcaringschools.com/programs.asp.

6. Jennifer R. Loyd, "Johnson High Athletes Tackle Bullying," April 11, 2012, http://www.mysanantonio.com/news/education/article/Football-players-step-up-as-a-defense-against-3472442.php.

7. "Safe School Ambassadors Program (SSA)," Community Matters, http://community-matters.org/programs-and-services/safe-school-ambassadors.

8. For those interested in the underlying model that guides Turner's teaching, it's the ARC model developed at the Trauma Center at Justice Resource Institute (http://www.traumacenter.org/research/ascot.php). Turner and her coworkers were also influenced by the trauma-sensitive classroom movement, for which more information can be found in *Helping Traumatized Children Learn* (also known as the purple book), published by Massachusetts Advocates for Children.

9. "Massachusetts, Washington State Lead U.S. Trauma-Sensitive School Movement," *ACEs Too High News* (blog), May 31, 2012, http://acestoohigh.com/2012/05/31/massachusetts-washington-state-lead-u-s-trauma-sensitive-school-movement/.

Part 3: Positive Parenting for a Bully-Free World

1. Tina Daniels, "Promoting Resilience Among Youth Through Families," updated January 20, 2010, http://www.schools-for-all.org/page/Resilience+through+family+programs+(EE).

Chapter 7: A New Psychology

1. Martin E. P. Seligman and Mihaly Csikszentmihalyi, "Positive Psychology: An Introduction," *American Psychologist* 55, no. 1 (January 2000): 5–14.

2. Ibid.

3. Martin E. P. Seligman, *Authentic Happiness: Using the New Positive Psychology to Realize Your Potential for Lasting Fulfillment* (New York: Free Press, 2002), 9–10.

4. Martin E. P. Seligman, *Learned Optimism: How to Change Your Mind and Your Life* (New York: Simon and Schuster, 1998).

5. Principles are adapted from Martin E. P. Seligman, *The Optimistic Child: A Proven Program to Safeguard Children Against Depression and Build Lifelong Resilience* (Boston: Mariner Books, 2007).

Chapter 8: Parenting for a Positive Present . . . and Future

1. Becky Eanes, "Skeptical About Positive Parenting?," *Positive Parenting* (blog), January 31, 2012, http://www.positive-parents.org/2012/01/skeptical-about-positive-parenting.html.

2. Glennon Melton, *Momastery* (blog), Momastery.com.

3. Naomi Aldort, *Raising Our Children, Raising Ourselves* (Bothell, WA: Book Publishers Network, 2005).

4. Julianne Idleman, "Parent-Child Connectedness Takes Us Beyond Emotional Intelligence," *Theparentscientist* (blog), November 28, 2011, http://theparent scientist.wordpress.com/2011/11/28/parent-child-connectedness-takes-us -beyond-emotional-intelligence/.

5. In September 2012, Invest in Kids transferred ownership of "The Parenting Partnership" to the Phoenix Centre for Children and Families (http://phoenix pembroke.com/node/93).

6. Kenneth R. Ginsburg, the Committee on Communications, and the Committee on Psychosocial Aspects of Child and Family Health, "The Importance of Play in Promoting Healthy Child Development and Maintaining Strong Parent-Child Bonds," *Pediatrics* 119, no. 1 (Jan. 1, 2007): 182–91, http://pediatrics.aappublications .org/content/119/1/182.full.

7. Daniel Siegel and Mary Hartzell, *Parenting from the Inside Out* (New York: Tarcher/Penguin, 2004).

8. David Kerr, quoted in National Science Foundation, "Positive Parenting Can Have Lasting Impact for Generations," *U.S. News and World Report,* September 4, 2009, http://www.usnews.com/science/articles/2009/09/04/positive-parenting-can -have-lasting-impact-for-generations.

Chapter 9: A Warm Family Climate

1. Lisa S., quoted in Hilary Flower, *Adventures in Gentle Discipline: A Parent-to-Parent Guide* (Schaumburg, IL: La Leche League International, 2005).

2. Adapted from Rebecca Thompson, *Consciously Parenting: What it Really Takes to Raise Emotionally Healthy Families* (Crystal Beach, FL: Consciously Parenting Project, 2012), e-book.

3. Lisa S., in Flower, *Adventures in Gentle Discipline: A Parent-to-Parent Guide.*

4. "Power of Playtime: Single Mothers Can Reduce Stress by Playing, Engaging With Children," *Science Daily,* June 19, 2012, http://www.sciencedaily.com/releases /2012/06/120619103622.htm.

5. Daniel Siegel and Mary Hartzell, *Parenting from the Inside Out* (New York: Tarcher/Penguin, 2004).

6. The Axelsons Institute in Stockholm, "Peaceful Touch," http://www.axelsons.com /peaceful-touch.php.

7. John Naisbitt, *Megatrends: Ten New Directions Transforming Our Lives* (New York: Grand Central Publishing, 1988).

8. David Elkind, *The Power of Play* (Cambridge: Da Capo Press, 2007).

Chapter 10: Your Most Important Relationship

1. Melinda Beck, "Helping Kids Beat Depression . . . by Treating Mom," *Wall Street Journal,* online ed., May 17, 2011, http://online.wsj.com/article/SB10001424052748 703421204576327192431250306.html.

2. Brené Brown, *The Gifts of Imperfection* (Center City, MN: Hazelden, 2010).

3. James Baraz and Shoshana Alexander, *Awakening Joy: 10 Steps That Will Put You on the Road to Real Happiness* (New York: Bantam Books, 2010).

4. Kisha M. Haye, Susan M. Swearer, Kelly Brey Love, and Rhonda K. Turner, "Reexamining Locus of Control and Aggression along the Bully/Victim Continuum" (research presented at the American Psychological Association, Toronto, Canada, 2003).

5. Thanks to Dr. Kristin Roush for sharing her wisdom and insights, http://www .movedandshaken.com/.

6. Society for Prevention Research, "Girls Who Are Bullied Are at Risk for Substance Use Through Depression," *ScienceDaily,* January 19, 2011, http://www.sciencedaily .com/releases/2011/01/110119120539.htm.

7. National Association for Children of Alcoholics, "Children of Alcoholics: Important Facts," http://www.nacoa.net/impfacts.htm.

Chapter 11: Connection: The "Super-Protective" Factor

1. Attachment Parenting International, "What Is Attachment Parenting?"

2. Christine Kearney, "A Parent's Nurturing Results in Larger Hippocampus in Children," *Medical News Today,* January 31, 2012, http://www.medicalnewstoday .com/articles/240992.php.

3. Attachment Parenting International, "What Is Attachment Parenting?"

4. Melinda Smith, Joanna Saisan, and Jeanne Segal, "Attachment and Reactive Attachment Disorders: Warning Signs, Symptoms, Treatment and Hope for Children with Insecure Attachment," Helpguide.org, last updated January 2013, http://www.helpguide.org/mental/parenting_bonding_reactive_attachment _disorder.htm.

5. Gabor Maté, "Wooing the Child," in *Scattered: How Attention Deficit Disorder Originates and What You Can Do About It* (New York: Plume/Penguin Putnam, 1999).

Chapter 12: Social and Emotional Learning

1. Collaborative for Academic, Social, and Emotional Learning, National Center for Mental Health Promotion and Youth Violence Prevention, Education Development Center, "Social and Emotional Learning and Bullying Prevention," November 2009, http://casel.org/publications/sel-and-bullying-prevention/.

2. Adapted from Collaborative for Academic, Social, and Emotional Learning, National Center for Mental Health Promotion and Youth Violence Prevention, Education Development Center, "Social and Emotional Learning and Bullying Prevention," November 2009, http://casel.org/publications/sel-and-bullying -prevention/.

3. Adapted from Daniel J. Siegel and Tina Payne Bryson, *The Whole Brain Child* (New York: Delacorte Press, 2011).

4. *Wikipedia*, s.v. "Stanford Marshmallow Experiment," last updated March 29, 2013, http://en.wikipedia.org/wiki/Stanford_marshmallow_experiment#Follow-up _studies.

5. Personal conversation with Laurie Grossman, cofounder of Mindful Schools, Oakland, CA, http://www.mindfulschools.org/.

6. Jon Kabat-Zinn, *Wherever You Go, There You Are* (New York: Hyperion, 2005), 22.

7. Shadra Bruce, "Mindfulness Training Improves Well Being in Teen Boys," *Mental Health News*, September 7, 2010.

8. Louise Hart, *The Winning Family: Increasing Self-Esteem in Your Children and Yourself* (Berkeley, CA: Celestial Arts, 1995).

9. David Servan-Schreiber, *The Instinct to Heal* (Emmaus, PA: Rodale, 2004).

10. Pat Palmer, *Liking Myself* (Weaverville, CA: Boulden Publishing, 2011).

11. Adapted from Gwen Dewar, "How to Be Your Kid's 'Emotion Coach,'" *BabyCenter Blog*, April 13, 2012, http://blogs.babycenter.com/mom_stories/how-to-be-your-kid's-"emotion-coach". We also recommend parents read what Dewar has to say about bullying and baboons on her website, www.parentingscience.com.

12. Tammy Hughes, quoted in Katia Hetter, "Bully-Proofing Your Kids," CNN.com, October 11, 2011, http://www.cnn.com/2011/10/11/living/bully-proof-kids-hetter.

Chapter 13: Good Communication = Good Relationships

1. Center for Nonviolent Communication, "Foundations of NVC," http://www.cnvc .org/learn/nvc-foundations.

2. From a hallway poster at Bentley Elementary, Oakland, CA, developed by Bentley School Committee, http://www.bentleyschool.net.

3. Usha Sutliff, "Nutrition Key to Aggressive Behavior," USC News, November 16, 2004, http://www.usc.edu/uscnews/stories/10773.html. The authors of this USC study were Jianghong Liu, Adrian Raine, Sarnoff A. Mednick, and Peter H. Venables.

4. National Center on Addiction and Substance Abuse at Columbia University, "The Importance of Family Dinners VIII," A CASAColumbia White Paper, September 2012, http://www.casacolumbia.org/templates/NewsRoom.aspx?articleid =695&zoneid=51.

Chapter 14: Assertive Communication = Effective Communication

1. Pat Palmer, *The Mouse, the Monster and Me,* 3rd ed. (Weaverville, CA: Boulden Publishing, 2011).

2. The University of Chicago Crime Lab, "Becoming a Man (BAM)—Sports Edition Findings," July 2012, http://crimelab.uchicago.edu/page/becoming-man-bam-sports -edition-findings.

3. Jack Canfield and Mark Victor Hanson, *The Aladdin Factor* (New York: Berkley Books, 1995).

4. Adapted from Jean Illsley Clarke and Connie Dawson, *Growing Up Again,* 2nd ed. (Center City, MN: Hazelden, 1998).

Chapter 15: Restructuring Family Power

1. Gordon Neufeld and Gabor Maté, *Hold Onto Your Kids: Why Parents Need to Matter More Than Peers,* rev. ed. (New York: Ballantine Books, 2006).

2. Linda Harrison, "Counterwill: Why Did I Never See It This Way Before?," *Linda's Daily Living Skills* (blog), March 1, 2012, http://www.lindasdailylivingskills .com/2012/03/counterwill-why-did-i-never-see-it-this.html.

3. Cameron French, "Spanking Kids Can Cause Long-Term Harm—Canada Study," *Reuters U.S. Edition,* February 7, 2012, http://www.reuters.com/article/2012/02 /07/canada-spanking-idUSL2E8D1F1C20120207.

4. Bonnie Rochman, "Hitting Your Kids Increases Their Risk of Mental Illness," Time.com, July 2, 2012, http://healthland.time.com/2012/07/02/physical -punishment-increases-your-kids-risk-of-mental-illness/.

5. Jane Nelsen, quoted in "Parenting Without Punishment Campaign," http:// parentingwithoutpunishment.org/?page_id=2.

6. Constantinos M. Kokkinos and Georgia Panayioto, "Parental Discipline Practices and Locus of Control: Relationship to Bullying and Victimization Experiences of Elementary School Students," *Social Psychology of Education* 10, no. 3 (September 2007): 281–301.

7. Kim John Payne, "Soul of Discipline: In the First Nine Years," Simplicity Parenting, http://www.simplicityparenting.com/soul-of-discipline/.

8. Steve Andreas, *Transforming Your Self: Becoming Who You Want to Be* (Moab, UT: Real People Press, 2002).

Chapter 16: Brain Science: Cultivate the Positive

1. Wonderful charts and diagrams are available at http://thebrain.mcgill.ca.

2. B. D. Perry, "Traumatized Children: How Childhood Trauma Influences Brain Development," *Journal of the California Alliance for the Mentally Ill* 11, no. 1 (2000): 48–51.

3. Daniel Siegel and Mary Hartzell, *Parenting from the Inside Out* (New York: Tarcher/Penguin, 2004).

4. Daniel J. Siegel and Tina Payne Bryson, *The Whole Brain Child* (New York: Delacorte Press, 2011).

5. John Medina, *Brain Rules,* quoted in "Lincoln High School in Walla Walla Tries a New Approach to School Discipline," April 23, 2012, http://acestoohigh.com /2012/04/23/lincoln-high-school-in-walla-walla-wa-tries-new-approach-to -school-discipline-expulsions-drop-85.

6. G. di Pellegrino, L. Fadiga, L. Fogassi, V. Gallese, and G. Rizzolatti, "Understanding Motor Events: A Neurophysiological Study," *Experimental Brain Research* 91 (1992): 176–80.

7. Inspired by Parenting Beyond Punishment at www.facebook.com/pages /Parenting-Beyond-Punishment.

8. Ibid.

9. Anna Wong (psychologist and clinical manager of Child and Family Psychiatry, Kaiser Permanente Oakland), in discussion with Kristen Caven, 2012.

10. Download the free printable "25 Things to Love about Attention Deficit Disorder" from http://www.additudemag.com/resources/printables.html. A few examples are spontaneity, ingenuity, and a sparkling personality!

11. I. J. Baguley, J. Cooper, and K. Felmingham, "Aggressive Behavior Following Traumatic Brain Injury: How Common Is Common?" *The Journal of Head Trauma Rehabilitation* 21, no. 1 (January–February 2006): 45–56; Rick Nauert, "Head Injuries Linked to Violent Behavior," PsychCentral, June 3, 2011, http://psychcentral.com /news/2011/06/03/head-injuries-linked-to-violent-behavior/26656.html.

Chapter 17: Hardwired for Resilience

1. YouthARTS, "Glossary," 2003, http://www.americansforthearts.org/youtharts /glossary.asp.

2. City of Mukilteo, Washington, "At Risk Youth–Definition," http://user.govoutreach .com/mukilteo/faq.php?cid=5948.

3. UN-HABITAT, "UrbanYouth-At-Risk in Latin America and the Caribbean and the Key Role of Local Authorities in Addressing Youth and Crime and Promoting Citizenship Among Youth," 2003, http://ww2.unhabitat.org/programmes /safercities/uyr.asp.

4. This concept is from Jane Middelton-Moz, *Will to Survive* (Deerfield Beach, FL: HCI Books, 1992).

5. Staff Writers, "15 Famous and Successful People Who Were Bullied in School," Online Colleges, November 2, 2011, http://www.onlinecolleges.net/2011/11/02 /15-famous-successful-people-bullied-school/.

6. Gabor Maté, *Scattered,* interview by Tracy Frisch, "What Ails Us," *Sun Magazine,* August 2012.

7. Ishmael Beah, *A Long Way Gone: Memoirs of a Boy Soldier* (New York: Sarah Crichton Books, 2007).

8. Workplace Bullying Institute, "The WBI 3-Step Action Plan," http://www .workplacebullying.org/individuals/solutions/wbi-action-plan/.

9. Ending Violence Association of British Colombia, "End Violence Together Fact Sheet: Acquaintance Rape," http://www.endingviolence.org/files/uploads /Aquaintance_Rape_Fact_Sheet-1.pdf.

10. Rape, Abuse, and Incest National Network, "How Often Does Sexual Assault Occur?," 2009, http://www.rainn.org/get-information/statistics/frequency-of -sexual-assault.

11. United States Army, "Comprehensive Soldier and Family Fitness," http://csf2.army .mil/index.html.

12. Jane Gilham and Karen Reivich, "Description of PRP Lessons," Penn Resiliency Project, Penn Positive Psychology Center, www.ppc.sas.upenn.edu/prplessons.pdf.

13. K. Dodge, "A Social Information Processing Model of Social Competence in Children," in *Cognitive Perspectives on Children's Social and Behavioral Development*, ed. M. Perlmutter (Hillsdale, NJ: Lawrence Erlbaum, 1986); K. A. Dodge, and C. L. Frame, "Social Cognitive Biases and Deficits in Aggressive Boys," *Child Development* 53, no. 3 (1982): 620–35.

14. Bonnie Benard, *Resiliency* (San Francisco: WestEd, 2004).

15. Jonathan Cohen, quoted in Sam Goldstein and Robert B. Brooks, eds., *Handbook of Resilience in Children*, 2nd ed. (New York: Springer Publisher, 2013).

Chapter 18: Swept Away by Technology

1. PBS, "The Amish," *American Experience*, directed by David Belton, aired February 28, 2012.

2. "11 Facts About Cyber Bullying," DoSomething.org, http://www.dosomething.org /tipsandtools/11-facts-about-cyber-bullying.

3. Amanda Lenhart, "Teens, Smartphones and Texting," Pew Research Center, March 19, 2012, http://pewinternet.org/Reports/2012/Teens-and-smartphones.aspx.

4. Ibid.

5. Jun-Ming Xu, Kwang-Sung Jun, Xiajin Zhu, and Amy Bellmore, "Learning from Bullying Traces in Social Media," 2012, http://aclweb.org/anthology-new/N/N12 /N12-1084.pdf.

6. *Wikipedia*, s.v. "Troll (Internet)," last modified March 11, 2013, http://en.wikipedia .org/wiki/Troll_(Internet).

7. "11 Facts About Cyber Bullying," DoSomething.org.

8. HLNtv.com Staff, "Take Th@t! His Tweets Uplift Bullied Classmates," updated August 17, 2012, http://www.hlntv.com/video/2012/08/16/online-bullying-stopped -high-school-football-captain.

9. Stomp Out Bullying homepage, http://www.stompoutbullying.org/.

10. Secret Mean Stinks Facebook Group, https://www.facebook.com/meanstinks.

11. Private conversation with retired school principal, Oakland, CA.

12. Norman Herr, "Television and Health," Internet Resources to Accompany *The Sourcebook for Teaching Science*, 2007, http://www.csun.edu/science/health/docs /tv&health.html.

13. Amy Jussel, review of *Sext Up Kids: How Children are Becoming Hypersexualized*, directed by Maureen Palmer and produced by Rick LeGuerrier and Timothy M. Hogan of Dream Street Pictures in association with CBC, http://www.mediaed .org/cgi-bin/commerce.cgi?preadd=action&key=248.

14. Reg Bailey and UK Department for Education, *Letting Children be Children: Report of an Independent Review of the Commercialisation and Sexualisation of Childhood* (The Stationery Office, 2011).

15. Luis von Ahn, quoted in Josh Seftel, "Games With a Purpose," NOVA science-NOW, April 1, 2009, http://www.pbs.org/wgbh/nova/tech/von-ahn-games.html.

16. Barbara Dafoe Whitehead, quoted in Ellen Goodman, "Battling Our Culture Is Parents' Task," *Chicago Tribune*, August 18, 1993. Whitehead's current studies can be found at nationalmarriageproject.org.

17. Violence Policy Center, "Gun Violence," 2013, http://www.vpc.org/gunviolence .htm.

18. Serena Gordon, "TV Time May Not Be Benign," *HealthDay News*, April 3, 2009, http://www.summitmedicalgroup.com/healthday/article/622021/.

19. Common Sense Media, "Media + Child and Adolescent Health: A Systematic Review," November 2008, http://ipsdweb.ipsd.org/uploads/IPPC/CSM%20 Media%20Health%20Report.pdf; Harvard School of Public Health, "Television Watching and 'Sit Time,'" The Obesity Prevention Source, http://www.hsph .harvard.edu/obesity-prevention-source/obesity-causes/television-and-sedentary -behavior-and-obesity/.

20. Truth on Earth Band, "Take Action: Effects of Media Exposure," http:// truthonearthband.com/action_mediaexposure.html.

21. Bill Davidow, "Exploiting the Neuroscience of Internet Addiction," *Atlantic*, July 18, 2012.

22. Hilarie Cash and Kim McDaniel, *Video Games and Your Kids: How Parents Stay in Control* (Enumclaw, WA: Issues Press/Idyll Arbor, 2008).

23. Anthony Doerr, "Garbage Night," *Morning News*, February 26, 2007, http://www .themorningnews.org/article/garbage-night.

24. Jonathan H. Liu, "The 5 Best Toys of All Time," *Wired*, January 31, 2011, http:// www.wired.com/geekdad/2011/01/the-5-best-toys-of-all-time/all/.

25. Howard Chudacoff, quoted in Alix Spiegel, "Old-Fashioned Play Builds Serious Skills," *NPR*, February 21, 2008, http://www.npr.org/templates/story/story .php?storyId=19212514.

26. National Wildlife Federation, "Health Benefits," http://www.nwf.org/Get-Outside /Be-Out-There/Why-Be-Out-There/Benefits.aspx.

27. "11 Facts About Cyber Bullying," DoSomething.org.

Chapter 19: Superpowering Our Kids

1. M. B. Greene, "Bullying in Schools: A Plea for Measure of Human Rights," *Journal of Social Issues* 62 (2006): 63–79, doi: 10.1111/j.1540-4560.2006.00439.x.

2. United Nations, Office of the High Commissioner for Human Rights, "Convention on the Rights of the Child," September 2, 1990, www.ohchr.org/EN/Professional Interest/Pages/CRC.aspx.

3. N. L. Asdigian, J. Dziuba-Leatherman, and D. Finkelhor, "The Effectiveness of Victimization Prevention Instruction: An Evaluation of Children's Responses to Actual Threats and Assaults," *Child Abuse and Neglect* 19, no. 2 (1995): 141–53.

4. Gregory Wallace, "O'Reilly, Stewart 'Rumble' No Average Debate," *Political Ticker* (blog), CNN.com, October 6, 2012, http://politicalticker.blogs.cnn.com/2012/10/06/oreilly-stewart-rumble-no-average-debate/.

5. UNICEF, *Child Poverty in Perspective: An Overview of Child Well-Being in Rich Countries,* Innocenti Report Card (Florence: UNICEF Innocenti Research Centre, 2007).

6. Ibid.

7. "United States Only First-World Country Without Mandatory Paid Maternity Leave: 'A Human Rights Issue' (VIDEO)," Huff Post Parents, *Huffington Post,* updated December 15, 2012, http://www.huffingtonpost.com/2012/10/15/united-states-only-first_n_1968193.html.

8. *Wikipedia,* s.v. "List of Countries by Intentional Homicide Rate," last modified March 18, 2013, http://en.wikipedia.org/wiki/List_of_countries_by_intentional_homicide_rate.

9. Jamie Gumbrecht, "In Sweden, a Generation of Kids Who've Never Been Spanked," CNN.com, November 9, 2011, http://www.cnn.com/2011/11/09/world/sweden-punishment-ban.

10. Swedish Institute, "Sweden and Swedes," Sweden.se, 2006, http://www.sweden.se/upload/Sweden_se/english/slides/Flash/Sweden_Swedes_20_Speakers_notes.pdf.

11. Clearinghouse on International Developments in Child, Youth and Family Policies at Columbia University, "Sweden," http://www.childpolicyintl.org/countries/sweden.html.

12. Katrin Bennhold, "In Sweden, Men Can Have It All," *New York Times,* June 9, 2010, http://www.nytimes.com/2010/06/10/world/europe/10iht-sweden.html?pagewanted=all&_r=0.

13. Jane Waldfogel and Elizabeth Washbrook, "Low Income and Early Cognitive Development in the U.K.: A Report for the Sutton Trust," February 1, 2010, http://www.suttontrust.com/research/low-income-and-early-cognitive-development-in-the-uk/.

14. Frank J. Elgar, Wendy Craig, William Boyce, Antony Morgan, and Rachel Vella-Zarb, "Income Inequality and School Bullying: Multilevel Study of Adolescents in 37 Countries," *Journal of Adolescent Health* 45, no. 4 (October 2009): 351–59, doi: 10.1016/j.jadohealth.2009.04.004.

15. "Caring Economy," BusinessDictionary.com, http://www.businessdictionary.com /definition/caring-economy.html#ixzz28Uv5IHyC. For more information, read *The Real Wealth of Nations* by Riane Eisler.

16. For more information on Sweden's legal evolution on corporal punishment, see http://www.nospank.net/durrant.htm.

17. Zvi Strassberg, Kenneth A. Dodge, Gregory S. Pettit, and John E. Bates, "Spanking in the Home and Children's Subsequent Aggression toward Kindergarten Peers," *Development and Psychopathology* 6 (1994): 445–61, http://journals.cambridge .org/action/displayAbstract?fromPage=online&aid=2540224.

18. DogHeirs, "Mkombozi the Stray Dog Saved the Life of a Newborn Baby," February 13, 2012, http://www.dogheirs.com/tamara/posts/533-mkombozi-the-stray-dog -saved-the-life-of-a-newborn-baby.

19. Michele Mason, phone conversation with Kristen Caven, 2005.

ABOUT THE AUTHORS

After teaching school for four years and being an at-home mom to her three children for thirteen years, **Louise Hart** attended graduate school for a doctorate in the prevention-based field of community psychology. She wrote *The Winning Family* and became a thought leader in positive parenting, speaking to thousands nationwide for more than twenty-five years. The U.S. Army Family Advocacy Program hired her to teach at installations from Alaska to Alabama and West Point, and from Germany to Japan and Okinawa. During that time she completed her second book, *On the Wings of Self-Esteem.*

Dr. Hart retired from speaking and moved 1,500 miles from Boulder, Colorado, to Oakland, California, to be close to her three young grandchildren. Yet she was inspired to continue teaching pro-social skills by publishing assertiveness books for children. You can find her videos and articles at www.drlouisehart.com.

While trying to get her break as a cartoonist, **Kristen Caven** worked as an illustrator, graphic designer, editor, and assistant to her mother, Louise Hart. She helped develop *On the Wings of Self-Esteem* and rewrite *The Winning Family* for its second edition before becoming coauthor of *The Bullying Antidote.* As a work-at-home mother, she provides creative and marketing assistance to small businesses, writers, and artists in the Oakland area and takes leadership in the school communities where her son attends and her husband teaches. The author of two memoirs about cartooning, a novella, an enhanced e-book, and a musical trilogy, Kristen writes a blog called *Life in the Fast Brain* for ADDitudemag.com. Learn more at www.kristencaven.com.

Hazelden, a national nonprofit organization founded in 1949, helps people reclaim their lives from the disease of addiction. Built on decades of knowledge and experience, Hazelden offers a comprehensive approach to addiction that addresses the full range of patient, family, and professional needs, including treatment and continuing care for youth and adults, research, higher learning, public education and advocacy, and publishing.

A life of recovery is lived "one day at a time." Hazelden publications, both educational and inspirational, support and strengthen lifelong recovery. In 1954, Hazelden published *Twenty-Four Hours a Day,* the first daily meditation book for recovering alcoholics, and Hazelden continues to publish works to inspire and guide individuals in treatment and recovery, and their loved ones. Professionals who work to prevent and treat addiction also turn to Hazelden for evidence-based curricula, informational materials, and videos for use in schools, treatment programs, and correctional programs.

Through published works, Hazelden extends the reach of hope, encouragement, help, and support to individuals, families, and communities affected by addiction and related issues.

For questions about Hazelden publications,
please call **800-328-9000**
or visit us online at **hazelden.org/bookstore.**